Controlling Reproduction

Controlling Reproduction

Women, Society, and State Power

Nancy E. Riley
Nilanjana Chatterjee

polity

First published in 2023 by Polity Press

Polity Press
65 Bridge Street
Cambridge CB2 1UR, UK

Polity Press
111 River Street
Hoboken, NJ 07030, USA

ISBN-13: 978-1-5095-3991-8
ISBN-13: 978-1-5095-3992-5(pb)

A catalogue record for this book is available from the British Library.

Library of Congress Control Number: 2022935233

Typeset in 10.5 on 12.5pt Sabon
by Fakenham Prepress Solutions, Fakenham, Norfolk NR21 8NL
Printed and bound in Great Britain by CPI Group (UK) Ltd, Croydon

For further information on Polity, visit our website:
politybooks.com

Contents

Figures

Acknowledgments

This book is rooted in an intensely intellectual comradeship and treasured friendship spanning three decades. We salute each other's effort across time, space, political and social upheaval, and quotidian distraction to imagine the project and write it into reality together.

Nila acknowledges a debt of gratitude to the memory of her parents Ranji and Manju, and to her sister Radha who made her a reader. She thanks her husband Wil and son Nikhil for heated dinner table discussions which remind her that thinking critically is a life skill and an art form. Nancy thanks Bob for his tolerance of her wild ideas and Maggie, whose fierce commitment to social justice inspires Nancy daily.

We thank all those who helped on this book. Jonathan Skerrett has been a wonderful editor throughout this project – giving us free rein for much of our work, but pushing and questioning when he needs to. Others at Polity have also helped the book along: thanks to Karina Jákupsdóttir, Neil de Cort and the production team, and Sarah Dancy for her great copyediting. Many thanks to Bob Gardner for constructing the index. We also thank the outside reviewers for their care and suggestions as they read the manuscript.

We also thank colleagues Sara Dickey, Deb DeGraff, and Jan Brunson; our conversations and work with them have allowed us to think better about many issues related to reproduction. Belinda Kong's insights and advice strengthened the last chapter. Mary Jane Riley contributed to our thinking about cover images. Thanks to Lori Brackett for all her help on so many things and to the wonderful Bowdoin College library staff for just the kind of support we needed.

Students have also taught us about different ways to think about and work for reproductive justice. A special shout-out to the students in Nancy's Reproductive Health and Politics class over the years, and to individual students – Theo Hurley, Brooke Bullington, Amanda Burrage, Meghan Bellerose, and Joy Lee among them – for knowing the importance of these issues and, especially, for their willingness to work toward a just world.

The heart of our book is about a woman's control of reproduction and we dedicate it to women fighting for dignity and empowerment in the process. Their struggles against enormous odds, challenges won and lost, are a testament to resilience and resolve and fundamentally about human rights. These are the stories we want to share in the classroom and with a wider readership – to stir imagination and, perhaps, action.

Prologue

The ongoing struggles in the United States around reproductive justice, access to abortion, and other reproductive services underscore the central issues of this volume. In June 2022, the US Supreme Court overturned the 1973 Roe *v.* Wade decision, removing the constitutional protection for abortion that had existed for fifty years. That ruling, and individual states' responses to the ruling, makes clear just how powerful the state remains in controlling reproduction, even as other entities (religion, family, corporations, NGOs) play a role. In the US, religion, politics, state power, and resistance are all involved in what kind of access and control individuals will have over their own reproductive decisions. While many have seen spring 2022 as a time of acute crisis for reproductive control in the US, in fact, assaults on access to reproductive services have been ongoing for years. Because of local laws, many people have long lived in areas with little or no access to abortion. But the removal of federal protection for abortion has highlighted just how deeply threatened is women's control of their reproduction and their right to bodily autonomy. More than two-thirds of the US population were born after 1973 and have always lived with abortion as a constitutional right. The overturning of Roe will likely result in abortion being banned in half of all individual US states. Such bans will change lives and assumptions in fundamental ways that have been unimaginable by many.

Although abortion in other countries is regulated, the US's increasingly restrictive laws make it an outlier in the world today. Only three other countries have moved in that direction since 1994, while fifty-nine countries have expanded abortion access (Miller and Sanger-Katz 2022). As we discuss in this book, the outsized role the US plays in reproductive politics, access, services, and information across the world means that what happens there impacts people well outside the country's borders – in the health services funded or provided by the US and in the ways that the actions there may encourage other countries to act in similar disregard of women's human rights. The international attention garnered by the US Supreme Court ruling on abortion is testament to the large US influence on reproductive politics across the globe.

The politics of reproduction in the US and elsewhere is fluid and constantly shifting, again pointing to just how important the control of reproduction is to the state, to local governments, families, and individuals. Struggles around these issues will continue, with those in power grabbing control when possible, and those with less power – in marginalized communities, or among ordinary citizens – refusing to surrender the right to control their own reproduction. The changing landscape in the US has spurred many – individuals, organizations, and states – to action. Their efforts to find ways to shore up abortion access to as many as possible is another example of the resistance that arises when reproductive control is threatened. We know most readers – like we ourselves – will be watching as these struggles play out in the US and across the world.

Nancy Riley and Nila Chatterjee
July 2022

1

Introduction: Controlling Women, Controlling Reproduction

In 1984, in the revised *(New) Our Bodies Ourselves*, the Boston Women's Health Book Collective argued that reproduction and its control were central to women's lives as social citizens. The authors wrote, "Unless we can decide whether and when to have children, it is difficult for us to control our lives or participate fully in society" (p. 291). Ten years later, the Beijing Declaration at the 1995 United Nations Conference on Women similarly argued that "the explicit recognition and reaffirmation of the right of all women to control all aspects of their health, in particular their own fertility, is basic to their empowerment" (UN Women 1995). In this book, we examine the power of reproduction and the importance of the struggle to control it.

Like other feminists over the past many decades and throughout the world, we see reproduction as central to how women and gender are constructed and to the role of women in social life. In societies across the world, the continuing struggles over control of reproduction have involved many people, organizations, and institutions: churches and mosques, schools, health institutions, businesses, government agencies, families, NGOs, as well as individual women themselves. We argue that early feminists were right in seeing reproduction as central to women's place in their societies. But while we recognize the importance of reproduction to individual women, in this book we go beyond the level of individuals and focus on ways that broader social forces and institutions have been involved in reproduction and its control. At the same time, we examine how these larger social processes are linked to and influence the most intimate and individual levels of social life. We keep in mind that the direction of influence goes in both directions: reproduction is both shaped by and shapes all social institutions.

If we accept the premise that reproduction is central to women's lives and to their ability to live as engaged social citizens, we can then widen our lens and change its focus and ask: if you control the reproduction of a population or a group of people, what is it you control? We argue that reproduction is so powerful and so intertwined with other social processes and institutions that control of reproduction means control of women, who sit at the center of nearly all reproductive processes. But the importance of reproduction and its control means that these processes also shape most corners of social, economic, and political life, thus the social world well beyond reproduction itself. As another feminist scholar working in this field has argued: "How societies handle human reproduction ... shapes hierarchy and subordination on the basis of class, gender, age, race, and a host of other social orderings, and is a core concern of the social policies of states" (Sen 1994: 5).

The stakes are high for women, families, communities, and nations in this process; in her investigation of reproductive control in Romania, Gail Kligman wrote, "In view of the multiple interests and values attached to reproduction it is understandable that ... individual, familial, and political interests in reproduction differ so dramatically ... [Reproductive] issues constitute a focus for contestation within societies as well as between them" (1998: 5). Further, because it is women who are most involved in all aspects of reproduction, the imperative of reproductive control means that all aspects of women's lives are under scrutiny, regulation, and control as well. Early American feminists who argued that "the personal is political" were right to point to how individual lives are also entwined with processes at the levels of family, community, nation, and globe.

At the center of control of reproduction – and of our own inquiry and analysis – is the modern state (Foucault 1978, 1991; Gal and Kligman 2000), long a principal player in reproductive politics and outcomes. While there are many forces that influence reproduction in any society, including family and religion – and we address those forces too – most of those forces find their way into, through, or out of state practices and regulations. The state has a vital interest in reproduction for many reasons: reproduction is often linked to economic structures, policies, and goals; how the state envisions the nation and who is and is not included in that vision usually revolves around reproduction; and the way that state control of population – size, growth, and composition – is often deemed the purview of the modern state and acted on through policies, regulations (or their absence) that directly or indirectly affect reproduction. In our focus on state involvement, we see the state not as a monolith or universal across time and place, but, rather, as a set of processes that are "evolving, dialectic, and dynamic" (Waylen 1998: 7), intertwined with the surrounding society; state practices and outcomes do not arise independently but are integrally connected to and arise from the norms, values, practices, and ideologies of the social institutions and communities among which the state resides.

Throughout this volume, we trace and analyze how states are involved in processes shaping reproduction and show how states influence gender, reproduction, and their connections both directly and indirectly. State involvement in reproduction has changed in recent decades; with the spread of neoliberal capitalism, we see a decline in direct state involvement in this and many other aspects of social life. Nevertheless, even as the state's role in society has undergone change, efforts to control reproduction have not disappeared, but have taken on new, or related, forms (Foucault 1978, 1991; Harvey 2005; Scott 1999).

We draw examples from across the globe and, in doing so, highlight how "reproductive governance," as it is sometimes called (Morgan and Roberts 2012), comes in many shapes and forms. Reproductive control has both a structural and an ideological aspect to it, and we examine how those pieces are related and supported. We address coercive efforts to control population (because the state believes fertility is too low or too high, we discuss examples of both), but also the less coercive means (and programs) that control population/fertility, which have been much more common in recent decades. These latter programs include those that run through the state, such as economic interventions (e.g., tax breaks for those who have kids) and programs or the lack of them (maternity leave, child care). But with the decline in states' power under neoliberal capitalism, nonstate forces, such as NGOs, corporations, and other private sector institutions, have become especially important.

We do not see the state as always opposite to or antagonistic toward women. But at the same time, it is nearly always women who are most affected by reproductive governance policies, practices, and outcomes. While men are also involved in reproduction, and reproductive politics affect men as well – especially through how reproduction is connected to the ways masculinity is constructed – it is the physicality of reproduction that is specific to women's place in reproductive politics; it is women who get pregnant or do not, who carry babies to term, who bear children. It has nearly always been women and their bodies that have been targeted in family planning and fertility control programs, and we will make that case through our examples. We will be exploring the reasons why women have been the focus not only for some of the obvious physiological reasons but also because they are often seen as the keepers of culture; their role in reproduction is thus explicitly connected to the goals of state and nation. "Women are often the ones who are given the social role of intergenerational transmitters of cultural traditions, customs, songs, cuisine and, of course, the *mother* tongue (*sic*!)" (Yuval-Davis 1993: 627; emphasis in original). The patriarchal[1] organization and ideology that structure societies are also key: although in most societies men have power that women do not, especially in the public spheres, there is also power in reproduction; thus, controlling that reproductive power is important in maintaining gender hierarchy. Within a neoliberal framework, with its focus on individuals (and the importance of individuals making good choices), women continue to be the targets of population and reproductive governance today. Even some of the more "feminist" turns in population control (e.g. the Cairo [1994] and Beijing [1995] UN Conferences on Population and Women, respectively) use this neoliberal framework – promoting women's "empowerment" (a focus on individual efforts) rather than efforts to dismantle the larger systems of inequality.

Throughout the book, we will be applying a "sociological imagination" (Mills 2000 [1959]): connecting individuals and larger social processes and institutions. Thus, while the state or the global economy might be involved in state policies, they also influence the daily lives of individuals, women, and families. We will also be drawing on Foucault's (1978, 1991, 2004) arguments about population, particularly issues of biopolitics and governmentality. "Biopolitics allows for conceiving power as not merely top down but as diffuse, such as when individuals become subject to norms of behavior and may internalize those norms yet also modify them as they do so" (Krause and De Zordo 2012: 139). We analyze how reproduction and its control move across the many levels of society: in the geopolitical sphere; at the state level, involving social institutions such as family and religion; at the individual level – these various levels of society interact with and respond to one another. In the next pages, we outline the major frameworks that we use throughout the volume.

Defining Gender and Reproduction

Simone de Beauvoir famously wrote "One is not born but rather becomes a woman" (Beauvoir 1979: 301). Her statement makes the argument for understanding gender as a social construction that is shaped by society. In that way, "gender is not a set of traits, not a variable, or a role, but the product of social doings of some sort ... gender itself is constituted through interaction ... gender [is] exhibited or portrayed through interaction, and thus [is] seen as 'natural,' while it is being produced as a socially organized achievement" (West and Zimmerman 1987). As a social construction, what constitutes male or female, what is expected of women and men, and how behavior is interpreted as gendered will all depend on the social and historical context. Though women and men have different bodies, gender is shaped beyond those bodies and is not simply tied to biological traits. The feminist historian Joan Scott put it this way: gender is "a social category imposed on a sexed body" (1988: 32). And as Scott continues her argument, "gender is a constitutive element of social relationships based on perceived differences between the sexes" (1988: 42). In later writing, she expanded on this, arguing that we need to think "critically about how the meanings of sexed bodies are produced in relation to one another, how these meanings are deployed and changed" (2010: 10).

A key aspect of gender is power; gender can be seen as "a primary way of signifying relations of power" (Scott 1988: 42). Gender orders social relationships in such a way that some individuals have greater power than others. "Power to" allows individuals access to things, opportunities, and events. Compared to men, women often have less "power to" – to go to school, to get training, or to move freely in public areas. Another kind of power might be described as "power over" – the ability to influence others in particular ways. Thus, in most societies, men occupy positions of power and decision in government, in religious organizations, and in the economic sector. That positioning gives males more power than women to direct courses of action, policies, and individual lives (Riley and DeGraff 2018).

Although we recognize the role that gender plays in the lives of individuals, we also must recognize that gender's larger influence lies beyond the individual. At the individual level, we can note the differences between women and men – that men are more likely to do some jobs than others, or that women face discrimination in schooling or the job market. But gender is a social institution, a set of social and cultural practices that shape all aspects of society, including its economic, political, and social arenas. That points to how the very structure of society is gendered. For example, men's role in the labor market has important ramifications for men, for women, for their families. But the larger influence of gender in the labor market may be the way that the economy is structured around gender so that it mirrors the expected ways that men live and work, and is unable to accommodate other versions of work and family, ones that reflect women's lives. Workers are expected to work long hours or be at their employers' beck and call because employers assume these workers are supported by women who care for the home and children. When women move into the labor market, they often continue to carry the responsibility of child care and housework. That makes it particularly difficult for them to balance the expectations of good worker and good mother/wife. In this volume, we pay particular attention to the social institution of gender, and how gender and reproduction are constructed together.

Even as gender emphasizes the social aspects of individuals' gendered lives, it is also true that reproduction – also a biological process – is central to gender across the world. Reproduction and gender are so interwoven, it is almost impossible to think about what it means to be a woman without thinking in terms of reproduction (Flavin 2009: 3). Even as norms and expectations around reproduction vary greatly across space, time, community, and era, reproduction has served to help define and shape women's lives, acting to constrain or expand their roles in all societies. In the nineteenth century, American women who were married were not allowed to practice law or take the bar exam that would give them licensure to do so. In Bradwell *v.* Illinois, the US Supreme Court denied Myra Bradwell the right to practice law, arguing that women's rightful place was in the home, taking care of children, and that participating in the law would interfere that that duty (Vogel 1993: 11ff.). In some societies today, education of young women is still seen as potentially interfering with their more important roles as mothers and wives (Lewis 2019).

In this volume, we are most focused on biological reproduction – events and actions surrounding pregnancy and birth. But social reproduction – defined as the processes necessary for the continuance and maintenance of any society – is also important. We address aspects of these processes throughout the book, with particular attention to those involving reproductive labor: among them, the raising and caring of infants and children; feeding and housing of community members; care of ill and elderly community members; and the construction and maintaining of community ties. The ways these processes are vital to community and individual survival reinforces the overall importance of reproduction more generally.

Of course, reproduction does not involve only women; men participate in reproductive processes and their lives are also shaped by reproduction, often in key ways. But, again, when we talk about control of reproduction, women remain the central players. As Almeling (2015: 426) argues, "responsibility for reproduction is lodged within women's physical bodies." Thus, even as there are others involved in reproduction, and even as it is the social aspects of reproduction that concern us in this volume, it is how reproduction, with its obvious and necessary biological components, is a process particularly located in women's bodies that remains key. It is these social and biological interactions and connections that make clear that controlling reproduction and controlling women move in parallel fashion in any society. We thus focus on women and reproduction as we work to understand how these bodily processes and their connections and meanings are also shaped and interpreted by the social world.

Just as gender operates at different levels of any society, so too does reproduction operate at multiple levels and sites. And these levels and sites are interlinked.

> At the level of bodies ... biological and social processes [are] associated with genes, cells, organs, and entire organisms. At the level of the individual [are] the biological and social processes associated with identities and experiences. [or] ... the interactions ... between family, friends, educators, employers, clinicians, and any others relevant to the biological and social process of reproduction. Finally, [reflecting reproduction's role in] historical, structural, and cultural processes ... biological and social processes [are] associated with states, markets,

> medicine, media, religions, social movements, and cultural norms ... Biological and social processes come together at the level of the individual, the family, the clinic, the market, and the state. (Almeling 2015: 431)

Reproduction organizes institutions from the family to the economy to the state, and tracing the importance of reproduction and its control necessitates attention to different institutions and levels of societal organization. Using multiple lenses allows us to investigate how "seemingly distant power relations ... shape local reproductive experiences" (Ginsburg and Rapp 1995: 2; see also Murphy 2017).

Importance of Reproduction

Because of the centrality of reproduction to the organization and future of all social and economic institutions, the stakes are high around reproduction at all levels of society and across the world. Its importance underscores how reproduction is both a private and a public issue. It operates in some of the most individual and protected areas of social life, and is at the same time part of any society's organization and its economy, and part of global politics as well. Because women's bodies are at the center of these politics, control of those bodies is sometimes seen to be the purview of the state or community and not the woman herself (Denbow 2015: 59). In these ways, "state policy and ideological control are experienced in everyday life" (Kligman 1998: 3, quoted in Gal and Kligman 2000: 17; see also Riley and McCarthy 2003).

Sometimes, it is at the individual level that it is most easy to see the importance of reproduction. It is a key piece of identity for any person (particularly a woman) in any society and often determines what roles she plays or is allowed to play; being a mother is often central to how women are defined *as* women (Inhorn 1996) or how they see their own value in the community (Edin and Kefalas 2007). But women have to navigate sometimes conflicting norms and expectations around motherhood. In Egypt, motherhood is so central to a definition of gender that women who are unable to bear a child violate the very definition of woman. As Inhorn explains, "a woman's adult gender identity can only be completed through motherhood, since what makes a woman a woman is ultimately her ability to *khallafa*, to produce offspring for herself and husband, and to demonstrate her ability to mother these progeny appropriately" (1996: 60). Or, as one Egyptian woman explained: "We are created into this sex just to be mothers" (1996: 60). The way that gender identity and place is tied to reproduction helps to explain why some see infertile women as pseudo-males, closer to men than women (1996: 59). Even if motherhood is not as defining a status as in Egypt, in most societies, motherhood and womanhood are tightly linked. Sojourner Truth's famous speech "Ain't I a woman?"[2] was partly about claiming the womanhood she shared with other, non-enslaved women. She used her own experience as a mother to emphasize the evils of slavery, declaring, "I have borne thirteen children, and seen most sold off to slavery, and when I cried out with my mother's grief, none but Jesus heard me! And ain't I a woman?" She addressed just how dehumanizing slavery was: she was a woman, but slavery meant she was not allowed to be a proper mother to her children.

At the family level too, reproduction is key. How many and when children are born are often vital to a family's position in society, and sometimes to its future. In places like China, where the family line is traced through males (a patrilineal family structure), bearing sons for their husband's family has been seen as women's most important role in the family. A woman who was unable to produce a son could be divorced or sent back to her parents' home for her inability to carry out her responsibility. But well beyond patrilineal societies like China, fertility has been seen as a central element of family organization, relations, and power. The Value of Children study, a large, multi-country study of six Asian and Pacific societies done in the 1970s, was part of widespread efforts to bring down national fertility rates, particularly in poorer countries (Arnold 1975). This study recognized that the goal of national fertility reduction was not always compatible with the needs and desires of families, who often wanted children for their own purposes. As one of the researchers involved in the project explained, policymakers had to find a way to balance parents' desire for children, "while minimizing the number of children because of additional burdens they place on society, its institutions, and support systems" (Bulatao 1975: 204).

We can also see how women's power in families is connected to their ability to control reproduction. While not bearing children – particularly sons – in China can result in women's lesser power, in many societies (including China) being able to bear and raise children can be the basis of women's power, especially where the family plays a strong role in organizing society and social life. In Indonesia, where interdependence on and with others, rather than autonomy, is most valued, women derive social power through their family roles, most importantly as mothers. Men may be more involved in political life outside the family, but Blackwood (2000) argues that women have outsized influence because of their central roles in the family. It is women who organize family activities around what they themselves see as most important, and they gain power through bearing and raising children, teaching them how to act and, through that work, reinforcing certain norms and not others (see also Riley and DeGraff 2018). Being able to control their own reproduction options gives women a stronger place in the family and community.

The importance of reproduction, or the number and timing of children, can be expected to shift as a society undergoes change. Demographer John Caldwell (1976) has shown that, as societies move from family-based economies to market-based economies, the need for many children often decreases. In economies based on the family, those in power – usually elder males – want as many children as possible. More children bring more help in working the family farm or business, more profit for the family, and thus more power for the eldest male. Wealth flows upward to the older generation. But under a market economy, individuals are hired, evaluated, and compensated as *individuals*, not as family members. In that case, having a lot of children will not benefit the family, nor will it benefit the older generation. Indeed, Caldwell argues, wealth flows toward children, who need education and training to be competitive in the new market economy. Under such conditions, even as children and reproduction remain important, having fewer children is often better for the family.

Reproduction is also important to any society. Reproduction is necessary to any community's very future. Population numbers can influence the strength and stability of a society; when a population is too large or too small, growing too slowly or too quickly can threaten its stability or strength. As we will see in later chapters, some communities that feel vulnerable to outside forces – whether those are cultural, economic, or political – see high fertility as vital to their very survival. While in the past, the focus of leaders might have been on how much land they controlled, over the past century or more, states are more focused on population – its size, shape, productivity, and, in many places, its composition (Foucault 1978; Gal and Kligman 2000). Population became an entity that could be measured, known, and the subject of control (Foucault 1991; Murphy 2017; Hacking 2015 [1983]). The size and quality of that population are regularly seen as connected to modernist goals and a country's place on the world stage. In Morocco, for example, "the control of reproduction continues to be seen as a foundation for development in Morocco – if population growth is not controlled, there will not be enough academic and professional opportunities for children as they become older; this would hinder the country's role in global politics and economics" (Hughes Rinker 2015: 233).

In addition to concern about numbers is a concern about "population quality." Sometimes referring to level of education or type of job, quality can also be used in ways that signal concerns about racial or religious composition of a population. These issues might arise over immigration policy. Germany, for example, has debated whether to allow more refugees and immigrants from Syria and Iraq. While some of the discussion is about the effects of the newcomers on the economy, much of it – explicitly or implicitly – is about race and religion and about who Germany is willing to accept as a citizen. Organizations such as Pergida (Patriotic Europeans Against the Islamisation of the Occident) have argued that Germany will be harmed if it allows itself to become more heterogeneous; Pergida regularly protests against the admission of Muslim refugees into Germany (Eckner 2018). In this volume, we look at several societies, including the United States, Palestine, Singapore, and India, to examine the rhetoric that focuses on who is bearing children and who is not, addressing how control of reproduction is linked to questions of "population quality," citizenship (both legal and social), and the imagining of what and who constitutes the "nation." Gal and Kligman (2000: 25) elaborate: "In this process, some forms of reproduction are defined as the sole legitimate, genuine, authentic means of national reproduction."

Population, births, and reproduction have also all played an important role in global politics throughout recent centuries. Colonial powers were always interested in the numbers of people, births, and deaths in their colonies, and worked to keep those numbers in line with their own needs and expectations. But long after the colonial era ended, western powers remained interested in demographic issues in the Global South,[3] perhaps even more so than previously, especially after birth rates in their own countries had begun to decline. After World War II, concerns and worries arose about how population size and growth in countries in the Global South might lead to an imbalance in world political power (Davis 1944). Such anxieties led to a massive population control effort, led and funded by powerful western countries, and mostly focused on the world's poorest countries. For example, we will see how the development of India's family planning program over the past several decades reflects these global actors, forces, and concerns. Partly because of those concerns, India's population program – the first national program in the world – was originally funded by US sources, and the US retained an important role throughout many decades. Even as India worked to assert itself and its independence in this area, the program continued to be shaped by global forces. US involvement in population size and family-planning programs in countries like India was partly about helping to reduce population growth rates in the hope that that would help the country develop economically. But it also came from a concern that a growing population in the Global South could mean a change in the balance of world power. As one demographer wrote, these demographic changes would mean that, "to the extent that numbers are a factor in the distribution of economic and political power, there will be some redistribution of power from old to new centers" (Kirk 2000 [1943]: 595; see also Connelly 2009). Even as many of these programs provided local women with more access to contraception that then allowed them to take more control over their own reproduction, because many family planning programs were introduced and often run by western powers, they brought with them new norms and expectations that sometimes aligned with and sometimes clashed with local norms, values, and expectations.

Geopolitics continues to play a role in reproduction, as we discuss in detail in Chapter 7. We examine the "global gag rule," a US injunction that prohibits discussion of abortion with clients by any organization that gets US funding. Because so many poorer countries rely on US funding for development and health programs, this move has had huge impacts on women's lives (Filipovic 2017). It is one of many examples of how the US is able to export its own values around reproduction and abortion to places far from its own shores. In Chapter 7, we also discuss other ways that reproductive processes have been spread across the world and shaped the lives of women and others. Stratified reproduction draws our attention to the ways that different practices – including new reproductive technologies, surrogacy, adoption, and other practices – means that reproduction sometimes involves more than one (or two) people. The buying and selling of gametes, the hiring of surrogates and the adoption of children across national borders reflects the increasing commercialization of reproduction and its many elements, often in ways that reflect social and economic inequalities. The global care chain (Hochschild 2000) is also a reflection of how global capitalism has organized reproductive labor – here the care of children, the ill, and the elderly – so that those with means can purchase the labor of others, usually women.

Today, reproduction continues to be multileveled in its importance. Individuals seek fertility goals in the context of social norms around reproduction, have more or less access to the means to control pregnancies, and experience pressures from family, community, state, and others. Even as families take on new forms in many societies, reproduction remains at the center of how families are defined, monitored, or ignored. And at country and global levels, reproduction is as important as ever. Where once the emphasis among demographers and policymakers was on "too-high" fertility, we are as likely today to hear about fertility being "too low," or to hear concerns about which people are having too many or not enough children. Marginalized groups, particularly immigrants, have been targets of concern in many locations, where their reproduction is seen to threaten the status and health of a society in some of the same ways that reproduction in the Global South was of concern in previous decades.

Controlling Reproduction

Given the importance of reproduction to constructions of gender, to the organization of family, state, and society, it is not surprising that many entities have worked and continue to work to control reproduction. Contestations around control of reproduction occur because of sometimes contradictory goals or visions of reproduction or population on the part of states, other social institutions such as religion or family, and individuals as well.

Forms of control, levels of control

Control (of reproduction and women) takes on both structural and ideological forms. For example, tax laws might act as a way to encourage or discourage parents from having more or fewer children, with some governments offering tax bonuses for large families and others punishing large families with high taxes. But equally influential might be social norms that discourage behavior or family size or something else, beyond a prescribed model. In some villages in Sicily in the early 1900s, a smaller family began to be seen as a modern family (Schneider and Schneider 1996). In this new era, those parents with many children were often socially sanctioned by their neighbors. But with no reliable contraception available, husbands and wives might have to rely on refraining from sex to limit their family size. If they ended up with many children, it was suggested they had not been able to "control themselves" sexually, bringing disapproval from those around them. That social pressure was a key factor in reducing fertility in these areas.

Control and its attempts can be systematic, explicit, and visible, and can be coercive and even violent. Perhaps the most extreme example of violent control over women, their bodies, and their reproduction is when rape is used as an act of war. Raping women and girls in such situations is considered an attack not only on the individual women, but on the group itself. If women are seen as the keepers of culture, and their children seen as the future of the community, rape is, then, an attack on that culture and community as a whole, and impregnation by the dominant group acts as a form of ethnic cleansing. The use of rape "as an instrument of terror" received heightened international attention and opprobrium after Serbian forces systematically used rape as a strategy during the Bosnian War (1992–5); in that conflict, it is estimated that between 12,000 and 50,000 women were raped as part of Serbian forces' attempt to erase the Bosnian Muslim (Bosniak) population (Salzman 1998). After international tribunals investigating these acts indicted some of those involved in the Bosnian War, in 2008, the United Nations Security Council went on to declare Resolution 1820, classifying rape and other sexual violence as war crimes and crimes against humanity.

Most control of reproduction is not as violent as that of rape, but some state measures are explicit and coercive. We will see how state control of reproduction was strong in both Romania – where state measures required women to produce more babies – and China – where the state restricted women from having children beyond the one or two that were allowed. In recent decades, most states and organizations have moved away from direct control of population, and the rhetoric connected to it. But that does not mean that these states and organizations have discontinued efforts to control population – and women's bodies – but rather that control comes in new forms or language. Control can come through the less direct and less obvious paths of legislation, economics, shaping of social norms, rhetoric, and moral injunctions (Morgan and Roberts 2012), which can also be powerful in shaping reproduction. We see that less direct – but still powerful – form in several Nordic countries. There, the state has stepped in in various ways to support parents' struggles to balance family and work lives. In all of these (Denmark, Norway, Sweden, Finland, Iceland), state provision of child care and parental leave is extensive, especially compared to what is found in other countries (Lammi-Taskula 2006). Many in these countries hope that such injunctions might have a positive effect in boosting the low fertility rates seen across the region, and encourage more couples to have children, and to have more children. But in some, like Denmark, the state hoped their policies could do more; to promote more fathers' involvement in child care, they offered specific "daddy leaves" – parental leave only offered to fathers – to encourage fathers to stay home longer after their child is born, and therefore take a more active role in parenting (Borchorst 2006). Whether state provision of such measures as child care and parental leave can encourage more births, or a change in how parenting is done, remains under debate (Lammi-Taskula 2006).

The state's interest in controlling reproduction sometimes supports and sometimes contests individual women's efforts to control their own reproduction. With the development and introduction of reliable contraceptive methods and safe abortions, women in most societies have been able to wrench control over reproduction away from other institutions and employ these methods to reach their own reproductive goals. Reliable contraception, combined with a desire for fewer children, has resulted in the plummeting of total fertility rates (TFR)[4] across the world over the past two centuries. Where the TFR was nearly 6 in 1800 – i.e., women had close to six children on average in 1800 – the TFR is now about 2.4. While different places experienced these declines earlier or later, or more quickly or more slowly, this vast change in reproduction signals fundamental change – in every aspect of social, political, and economic life. Where women once spent most of their lives in childbearing and childrearing, with fewer children, they have more time and energy to pursue other endeavors.

Such reproductive shifts do not lessen the importance of reproduction to all social institutions and individuals, and often bring with them further contestations about reproduction. Tracing the multiple reasons for fertility decline, we can see the likely players. We can assume that in some cases and places, fertility declines took place because states and other governing structures wanted birth rates and population growth to be lower. But it is also true – and often at the same time – that those fertility declines reflect the increasing access that women had to controlling their own reproduction. Reliable contraception meant that they could decide whether and when to get pregnant, whether to carry a fetus to term, and whether to stop childbearing altogether. Contraception freed women from the burden of repeated and often dangerous pregnancies, and has allowed the separation of sexual activity and pregnancy: a woman could enjoy sexual relations without fearing the consequence of pregnancy. That newfound freedom has been celebrated in society after society, as access to birth control became increasingly commonplace. But we point out that even as reliable and accessible contraception has given women newfound control of reproduction, that process has also resulted in less attention to the ways that forces beyond individuals are involved and can be a major factor in women's control of reproduction. We elaborate on this in our discussion of "choice," below.

Multiple Influencers: The Role of the State and Other Actors

Although in this book we highlight state involvement in reproduction, we will underscore throughout the volume the ways that influence on and control of reproduction comes from multiple sites, sometimes working together and sometimes in opposition to one another. As we have explained, there are many reasons that the state seeks to control reproduction and women's bodies. At the same time, it is also important to keep in mind that, while the state has been powerful in the area of reproduction in most places and times, it rarely operates alone. Communities, social institutions such as the economy, education, families, and religion, as well as corporations and NGOs all play a role. This process involves a complex interweaving, with resistance and complicity from many sides. Norms, values, and expectations are connected to social structures and institutions and so these different levels of any society often work together to influence both reproduction and women's lives more generally. Thus, family control of reproduction is usually linked – positively or negatively or both – to how the state regulates reproduction.

In our selection of examples, we make the case that, while the state plays a role in all modern societies, time and place are crucial to the kinds of reproductive control that are in play and to the outcome of those efforts. Different histories, government structures and forms, and different cultural values, norms, and beliefs all play a role, as do events, such as wars, colonial experience, mortality (epidemics, or general mortality levels), and geopolitical inequalities.

Religion and family are two social institutions that have often been involved in reproductive control. The Catholic Church, Islamic institutions such as mosques or Muslim clergy, ecumenical councils in Protestant sects, shamans, priests and local spiritual leaders, and other religious entities have regularly weighed in on reproduction – on what kind of intervention (birth control methods, abortion) are or are not acceptable according to their interpretation of religious dogma. These institutions have been just as powerful in encouraging or even dictating social forms around reproduction. Do women have to be married to have sexual intercourse? How is childbirth outside marriage considered? What are the expectations around same-sex relationships? Religion has played a central role in these and many other questions about reproduction and its context in most societies and in most eras of human history.

Families – both extended family or kin networks or nuclear families where husbands and wives might be the decision-makers – are also key social institutions in reproduction, especially given the way reproductive processes are shaped by and themselves shape family size, extent, members, and even power structures. Families can be bulwarks against state action, mitigating some of the force of the state or community. But it is as often the case that families make it difficult for women – as individuals – to achieve their own reproductive goals. Many women live within structures of patriarchy, in which men have, take, and are given more say in reproductive and other family outcomes. Here again, families – their shape and structure, what is accepted or denounced, and the roles that family members play – are shaped and shape the society around them.

The role that society plays in families is related to another influence on reproductive outcomes: social norms – the role of moral injunctions on reproduction is clear in how the media, the government, or others talk about the fertility or reproduction of particular groups of people. In some places, attention might be on those who are "too young" or "too old" to be having children; in other places, we hear questions about whether "poor women have the right to bear children" (Jencks and Edin 1985) with some arguing that motherhood in the US is sometimes considered a class privilege (Solinger 2001: 183). Norms, values, and sanctions are nearly always connected to more formal routes of enforcement such as policies, restrictions, and rules. Thus, for example, in the US, attitudes about which women should and which women should not have more children are reinforced by policies that make family planning available and low cost for women who receive government funding ("welfare"), but at the same time restrict government funding for treatment of infertility (Briggs 2017: 126ff.). In some Nordic countries, access to assisted reproductive technology is only allowed for heterosexual couples, making pregnancy or family-making difficult or impossible for others, such as lesbian couples or single women.

Values play a role in other population-focused programs too. Control of reproduction has become part of the rhetoric of the environmental movement. While attention to environmental crisis is necessary and important, some of the rhetoric of those in the field relies on a kind of "populationism" (Bhatia et al. 2020), a belief that population size is at the heart of environmental degradation. Notably missing in such an approach is attention to the way that how we abuse environmental resources plays a much larger role in the destruction of the environment. While it may not necessarily be deliberate, a discourse that focuses on population growth and fertility rates relies on old notions of "population bomb," "overpopulation," and the need for population control. That again puts a focus on controlling fertility – and women and their bodies – and diverts attention from the other sides of the environment–population equation, those that address how people use and abuse the earth's resources, how the use of those resources is distributed unequally, and the ways our systems encourage such environmental destruction.

While control of reproduction and debates around it are present in most societies, the historical, cultural, and geographic settings matter in how reproduction is viewed, and what kind of intervention it invites. A good example about the importance of historical and geographical context is the varying and changing concern about teenage pregnancy. In many time periods, and in many places, women married while still in their teens. But worries about teen pregnancy can be found in many regions. Sometimes, the issue is how an early pregnancy can derail a young woman's chance of getting an education, or – for very young teens – how the physical danger of pregnancy carries risks at such an age. But often, teenage pregnancy brings with it stigma, arising from a belief that teens, and particularly unmarried teens, should not be having children. These concerns have been shared by parents and governments. In the US in earlier times, especially before the introduction of reliable methods of birth control in the 1960s and 1970s, parents worried about the challenges they and the family would face should their unmarried daughter get pregnant. The US government also wanted a reduction in teenage pregnancies, convinced that these were an added burden not only on the young mother but on social institutions such as schools, state-supported income and food programs, and even the economy. Social norms – and the stigmas attached – often shaped how young women acted and how they reacted if they found themselves pregnant when they did not want to be. Young women might avoid having sexual relations, or even a boyfriend, if they were not sure they could prevent a pregnancy. If they did get pregnant, white and Black single teenage women usually found themselves in very different circumstances (Solinger 1992). During earlier eras, there were institutions (homes for single pregnant girls) that allowed white girls to find a way to conceal the pregnancy, place the baby for adoption, and avoid stigma, eventually resuming their lives. Black girls who became pregnant unintentionally often had no access to such institutions, and were more likely to bear and raise a child with their family's help. Teenage pregnancy no longer has the same menacing qualities it once had. In most places, birth control is more accessible and reliable, and in places like the US and many other societies, there is more acceptance of family forms beyond the two-parent, married, heterosexually based nuclear family, and births outside that model are more easily part of any community. But in some other societies, pregnancy outside marriage is still considered shameful, potentially disruptive to the community, and can bring shame to the young woman and her family.

An increasingly powerful influence on reproduction is the market; connections between state and market allow for powerful influence on most aspects of society. For example, one important role of governments today is to create environments for profitable businesses, with the expectation that investment will benefit the community and nation and help to build and sustain a strong national economy. These connections – and those goals – are also traceable in the arena of reproduction. Michelle Murphy, in her book *The Economization of Life* (2017), argues that in the past several decades, as neoliberalist ideologies have taken a deeper and wider hold across the world, economy and population have become increasingly linked. We will explore neoliberal effects on reproduction in Chapter 6, but here, we introduce neoliberalism because of its current pervasiveness and power. Arising in the 1970s, this ideology, which is centered around a reliance on competition and markets to structure societies, supports a global capitalist system. It sees citizens as consumers, in charge of their own success or failure, with government support for social programs reduced or absent altogether. It first took root in the US and the UK, but soon spread throughout the world, as countries in the Global South were drawn into a global capitalist system and its rules and hierarchies, and have been constrained in their efforts toward economic development by neoliberalism's forces.

Murphy and others (Rao and Sexton 2010; Janes and Chuluundorj 2004) have explored the effects of the spread of neoliberalist thinking on health, welfare, and reproduction. In a neoliberal framework, life is reduced to its market value. The phrase "economization of life" points to how life is "differentially value[d] and govern[ed]" according to how a life is perceived as contributing to the economy, now or in the future. For example, "for the sake of the economy," Murphy (2017: 7) argues, some births are more valued than others – those that contribute more fully to economic growth. And in some cases, such calculations are taken further: it is better for the economy to prevent some births, for some individuals not to be born (2017: 47). Here, we see just how interconnected are state, economy, and reproduction, as state leaders have come to believe that "a national macroeconomy ... could be fostered, directed, and triggered by rearranging reproduction en masse" (2017: 51). That kind of conviction was behind the massive population programs of the 1950s and 1960s, when governments and intergovernmental and global organizations focused their attention on population – its size and growth. Central to that focus was the way that, to grow the economy and to become a modern nation, population and those that produce need to be controlled, convinced to use contraception, to not bear the children who would not contribute adequately to the economy. Neoliberalism has had powerful effects on reproduction and its "history puts questions of reproduction at the center of how capitalism summons the world" (Murphy 2017: 7).

Control of women and their bodies continues to be part of neoliberalism's processes. Reflecting the increasing recognition of the central role of women, multilateral organizations have recently turned their attention to addressing gender inequality, and have begun to speak about the importance of moving toward a more gender-equal world. While gender equality seems a just and good cause, it is in the reasons for their interest in equality that we can see the links between women, bodies, and neoliberalism. Arguing that gender equality is "smart economics," the goal of many of these programs is instrumental. Thus, rather than working toward gender equality as a good in itself, they hope their efforts will bring women more fully into the consumerist economy. The World Bank (2007), for example, argues that "greater gender equality in access to opportunities, rights, and voice can lead to more efficient economic functioning and better institutions, with dynamic benefits for investment and growth. The business case for investing in [gender equality] is strong – it is nothing more than smart economics." In this way, smart economics is solidly based in neoliberalism, and the role of consumption and consumers in the global economy. It involves "a new, and more invasive, range of biopolitical interventions that aim to … transform women into consumers, investors and producers for global markets; [this process] legitimiz[es] a range of techniques to transform women's bodies, subjectivities and lives accordingly" (Calkin 2015: 625). As we will discuss more fully in Chapter 6, women's reproduction is a central piece of any attempt to incorporate women's bodies into this capitalist system.

While much of this critique of the connections between gender, reproduction, and the economy is focused on the neoliberal era, similar connections existed long before this era. Gayle Rubin, in her 1975 essay, "The traffic in women," argued that the control of women (and reproduction) has been central to societies for a long time and in many places, and long before capitalism came to be such a powerful force throughout the world. She draws on the work of social theorists Claude Lévi-Strauss and Marcel Mauss. Mauss makes clear how important exchange is to a society because of the connections and alliances that are formed around any exchange. Lévi-Strauss's theory focused on the way in which gendered kinship is at the center of societal organization. Rubin brings these perspectives together, and highlights the central role of women and how their exchange and control, particularly in kin networks, are central processes to that organization. Key to our work here is that it is men who exchange and women who are exchanged; "women are given in marriage, taken in battle, exchanged for tribute, traded, bought, and sold" (Rubin 1975: 175). Women are valuable for political and economic reasons, as their exchange helps to strengthen and build families and alliances. But central to women's importance is their biological role in producing children. Reproduction is a way to change the shape of a community, a family, a nation. It means production of the next generation. Because of its importance, those in power – who are nearly always men – work hard to control reproduction.[5]

These insights on societal organization of earlier communities and the ways that women and reproduction have always been valuable helps to explain the continuing and fluid ways of control of women and reproduction by those in power, whether that is men in families, leaders (usually male) of communities, or states. Thus, as Rubin argues, we can see the forerunners of today's world: "far from being confined to the 'primitive' world, these practices seem only to become more pronounced and commercialized in more 'civilized' societies" (1975: 175). Evidence from earlier societies and from communities throughout the world today makes clear that reproduction is so important that it is central to any exchange or political economic system. Its importance helps to explain why women, who have always been closest to all reproductive processes, are also subject to control. It is partly because she saw biological reproduction as the reason for women's subordination that Shulamith Firestone, a 1970s radical feminist, argued that the way to gender equality was to make reproduction no longer connected to women's bodies. She asserted that technology, in the form of artificial wombs, would free women from reproduction and allow them to escape the subordination they experienced under patriarchy. As we will explore in Chapter 8, where we discuss several feminist utopias and dystopias, other feminists have come to similar conclusions: that reproduction is at the core of gender inequality.

Contest over Reproduction and the Problem of Choice

With reproduction so important to so many social institutions and players, it is easy to see why contestation over reproduction and its associated processes and structures is common and pervasive. Again, because of the intimate connections between gender and reproduction, women are at the center of these processes of and disagreements about reproductive control. The reasons for that include physiological reasons – bodies are important; it is women who get pregnant and it is women who do most reproductive labor in any society or community. But because gender operates on reproduction at other levels too, other players get involved, and often feel that they have as much at stake in decisions about reproduction as do individual women. In most places, women are seen as keepers of culture, as bearers of the nation; women, therefore, are often seen as having a responsibility to do the right thing for the public, for the nation. Women's bodies become public terrain (Denbow 2015). "The control of women thus becomes a logical project of nationalism. A classic means of such control is the regulation of women's reproductive capacity, whether by forcing unwanted births or restricting wanted ones" (Gal and Kligman 2000: 26). In addition, in societies where men have and seek to retain their power over most social, political, and economic processes, preventing women from having complete control over their reproduction can help to mitigate any power women derive from their reproductive roles. A village woman in India explains how it is women's reproductive power that is behind men's efforts to control them, describing this conflict in a way that resonates with the power that motherhood gives to some Indonesian women, as mentioned above: "[We have] the power of giving birth, of creating new life. Men do not have this kind of power. Only women have it. So men are afraid we may rise above them because of this power. To control it ... they impose all these restrictions on women to control our power, and use it for their own benefit" (SLaW 1993).

Indeed, as reliable birth control has given individual women increasing control over their own reproduction, it has often brought a new set of contestations, when a woman's own reproductive desires and goals have clashed with those around her. If she does not want another pregnancy and child, but her husband does, who has the last word? If she wants three children, or no children, but those desires clash with the state, whose goal is met? Should women be the ones to decide whether to have an abortion, or does the state have a say in abortion access? Also significant is how a nonprocreative stance – opting out of reproduction through voluntary sterilization or abortion, for example – can be seen as a challenge to other entities like the state or the family, especially in ways that can disrupt assumptions that connect womanhood to motherhood (Denbow 2015: 182). Reproduction, it is clear, is both a very private matter and something that is also public. That tension between private and public is readily apparent in recent clashes around abortion and other birth control in the US over the last several decades, as we discuss in Chapters 3 and 4.

These clashes around abortion in the US also underscore the importance of the framing of arguments about control of reproduction. In 1973, in the Roe *v.* Wade decision, the US Supreme Court ruled against a challenge by the state of Texas and declared that women have a fundamental right to choose to have an abortion, without "excessive" government restriction. The language around this decision – that from the Supreme Court and from the activists pushing to make abortion legal – often centered on "choice," a strategy some believed as most effective at the time. But as feminist scholars and activists have since argued, granting women "choice" actually narrows their reproductive control. A choice framework brings with it many problems; perhaps most importantly, it mixes choice and rights. "Right [is] a privilege to which one is justly entitled and choice [is the] privilege to exercise discrimination in the marketplace among several options, *if* one has the wherewithal to enter the marketplace to begin with" (Solinger 2001: 7). Some women – with resources like abortion access and the money to pay for an abortion – have the choice, but others do not have the resources to make that choice. In addition, activists supporting legal abortion have often raised the dangers of illegal "back-alley" abortions – and the danger that these pose to women. While it is true that abortion, especially if self-administered, can harm women, the back-alley "butcher" image suggested that women needed protection – not rights. In this way, as some argued, Roe *v.* Wade became a "consumer protection ruling" (Flavin 2009: 22). Thus, abortion took on the elements of other consumer choices. It leads to discussions and assumptions about women who make "good" choices and those who make "bad" choices, and may even invite outside intervention into the lives of those who seem "unable" to make correct choices (Denbow 2015: 178). "The contemporary language of choice promises dignity and reproductive autonomy to women with resources. But for women without such resources, the language of choice is a taunt and a threat … women who cannot afford to make choices are not fit to be mothers" (Solinger 2001: 223).

Perhaps most problematic is the way that choice is relentlessly focused at the level of the individual, and omits, makes invisible, and can even erase the context around those choices. At the time of the 1973 Supreme Court ruling, choice seemed an easier sell than an argument about reproductive rights. But choice is unstable and is not likely to allow women access to bodily autonomy or a guarantee of reproductive rights. As Dorothy Roberts argues, this choice framework limits our vision and we begin to think that "the right to choose is contained entirely within the individual and not circumscribed by the material conditions of the individual's life" (1998b: 147). As disagreements about abortion continue to take place in the US and in many other places – in the streets, in homes, and in the courts – the framing of abortion as a choice continues today; women's right to bodily and reproductive autonomy is not guaranteed through choice, but in fact lies further out of reach. As one scholar makes clear: "When we rely on choice as our main framework for understanding women's reproductive and sexual experiences, reproductive health matters become configured from a commodity perspective … the social, political, and economic factors that surround how choices are made become hidden" (Bakhru 2019: 7). Here, we see the power of hegemonic thinking and discourse, when a particular framing of an issue or problem dominates and permeates a society and its institutions. It is because of how individualism has become hegemonic – now reinforced by neoliberalist ideologies – that the language of choice and the narrow focus on individuals is so prevalent.

These discussions about the framing of reproductive rights around choice also remind us about how individual decisions are not always in accord with the desires and plans of other social entities, such as communities, religious groups, or the state. When there is disagreement, whose desires and goals are prioritized? That question is at the heart of much controversy around abortion legality and access. These and many other potential disagreements make clear how reproduction and its control continue – and will continue – to be something that is debated, discussed, and struggled over.

Resistance

Throughout these contestations and debates, even in some of the most difficult of circumstances, women have been active in working to gain more control over their own bodies and reproduction; they resist and accommodate expectations and explicit rules in many different ways. Sometimes, individual women resist quietly, as have women in China who found ways to avoid the very strict birth planning policies. Sometimes, that resistance is public and done as a group – as in demonstrations in Poland in 2021 against the government's increasing restrictions on abortion. Such groups might be made up of women from across many ethnic or racial groups – as in marches aimed to protect legal abortion in the United States. Or women of a marginalized community might push back against restrictions and constraints. Sistersong, a group working for reproductive justice in the US, focuses on the abuses and discrimination faced by women of color, and especially African American women. Part of their work addresses the problematic framing of choice, as discussed above. In Latin America, indigenous women have been active in organizing and pushing for their needs as women – at times working against both the majority culture and fighting for a place within the indigenous movements as well (Hernandez Castillo 2010).

As is true for most resistance, in many times and places women assert (and even construct) their reproductive intentions "within existing power structures" (Hughes Rinker 2015, citing Rachel Newcomb; Kandiyoti 1988). For example, in the classic Chinese patriarchal family, a woman was expected to bear sons for her husband's family; sons would mean the continuance of his family line and a stronger role for the family in the community. But women had their own reasons to bear children: children gave them status in the family, but it also gave them their own "uterine" family (Wolf 1972), children who would love them and support them. In this way, women's reproductive goals aligned with those of her husband's family, even as the reasons for wanting children differed for each. Recognizing and tracing the influence of those existing power structures – and the sometimes quiet resistances of women – is key to understanding women's efforts to control reproduction, in their many iterations. We will see this resistance – in its myriad forms, targets, and outcomes – throughout the world. Sometimes that resistance is overt, public, and collective, but even more often, it is quiet and sometimes hidden (Scott 1987, 1990).

Outline of Chapters

In the following chapters, we address these various topics through discussion of specific examples and cases. In many instances, there were other, similar examples and we chose those that best illuminate a larger issue in the control of reproduction. Nearly all have occurred since World War II, and most much more recently.

In Chapter 2, we examine some representative cases of state control of reproduction that is direct and explicit. Our analyses here focus on programs and laws in Romania, China, and India. In Chapters 3 and 4, we focus on two social institutions that are most often also involved in control of reproduction: religion (Chapter 3) and the family (Chapter 4). We demonstrate that, as powerful as the state is, it rarely acts alone to influence reproductive processes. To illustrate how family, religion, and state work together (and sometimes against one another) to influence reproduction, we rely on examples from a number of places, including Poland, Brazil, Egypt, China, Uganda, Japan, and the United States.

In Chapter 5, we argue that reproduction often operates to make or unmake communities. We draw examples from an indigenous community in Mexico, from Palestine, and from African American and Native American communities to illustrate how reproduction is part of community construction or destruction, seen as both a threat and a source of power. Immigration is also a major influence on communities, and we discuss how immigration and links to reproduction and reproduction policies have played a role in communities and their futures, looking at examples from several societies, including the US, Italy, and Japan. As we will discuss, in all these situations, women are regularly caught in the contests around community formation/marginalization. Chapter 6 focuses on how control of reproduction has shifted in recent decades. We look at how neoliberal capitalism and globalization have affected reproduction in countries like the Philippines and Egypt. By looking closely at programs such as The Girl Effect and the UN International Conference on Population and Development (ICPD) in Cairo in 1994, we demonstrate how neoliberal notions of reproduction are central to the shape and reach of these programs, and the ways that nonstate actors, often in conjunction with the state, are involved in reproduction in today's neoliberal world.

Chapter 7 explicitly links the many sites involved in reproductive control across our increasingly transnational world. We look at how discourses and practices of reproduction and its control circulate globally, often built on longstanding structures and ideologies of inequality such as gender, race, and colonialization. In addition to discussing the global gag rule, we discuss how the bodies of women are linked across the globe through stratified reproduction and through the global care chain.

In Chapter 8, we discuss several utopian and dystopian novels that have addressed the issues of reproduction and gender. "Speculative fiction" can be seen as a critique of current societies and practices, and an imagining of what might be under different circumstances. These novelists help us explore the central place of reproduction to a society, what happens when reproduction goes awry, and the connections between reproduction and gender in social organization and processes.

The examples we draw from throughout this volume illustrate several key themes and echoes. Contestation over reproduction is found everywhere, at the level of the state, in communities, in families, and among individuals. Reproductive processes, like all social processes, are shaped by inequalities around race, ethnicity, religion, class, and gender. And while many social entities – from religion to indigenous community leaders – have a part in shaping reproduction, it will become clear how central are the state and the market in these processes. The ways in which reproduction is shaped by large social issues and institutions spotlight how we must look beyond the individual to understand the forces that shape reproduction. Individual women are at the center of reproductive processes, but they must also navigate influences from family, economy, community, state, and nation. Controlling reproduction nearly always involves controlling women. Identifying and tracing the players in the "disciplining of reproduction" (Morgan and Roberts 2012) is key to recognizing the cross-cutting influences on women's lives. Even as we will see variety, change, and discord across the world on these issues, these themes will echo throughout, reminding us again about just how important reproduction is to all social entities and how intertwined it is with other social processes.

2
Direct State Control of Reproduction

Even while reproduction is a private process, about the desires and behaviors of individuals, it is also always public; reproduction is important to the entire society and to all facets of society, from the economy to politics to education and family structure and function. It is shaped by cultural and social expectations, and by "biopolitics" (Foucault 1978) or state management of population. State involvement in these processes takes different forms and directions: coercive (even violent, as when states have used rape as a weapon of war), less coercive, strong or weak, focused on particular groups, or for a particular time period. But in most situations, state efforts – whatever form they take – are directed at and through women's bodies. In this chapter, we examine three examples of explicit state control over reproduction: in China, Romania, and India. The programs differ in each country. But we will see that while the motivations and even goals of the state differ from place to place, the outcomes for women are often similar.

To be sure, there are many other times and places where state control is as explicit and direct as some of the actions we describe and analyze here. But while there are many instances of state control of a particular group or community – and we discuss such incidences in other places in this volume – what distinguishes the three countries we focus on in this chapter is that control is over the entire population, and that control is both pervasive and deep. In both China and Romania, which ran two of the most coercive population control programs in the world, state control over the population was part of the totalitarian regime, allowing for little place or opportunity for citizens to hide from or resist state directives. "In a neo-Stalinist state, the legitimate spaces in which citizens could seek refuge or resist the penetrating gaze of state surveillance were greatly reduced. The state's presence was maximal" (Kligman 1998: 7). In India, on the other hand, control of population did not arise out of a totalitarian state's directives; India's government – a parliamentary democracy – had embraced a postcolonial agenda of national development. Nevertheless, Indian state involvement in population control has been permeating, intrusive, and even coercive at times. If control of reproduction pits the desires of individuals against the needs of the society or community, in these three countries, with their very different state forms, state goals have taken precedence over individual desires and needs.

In spite of the strong role of these states in reproduction, in every setting we see resistance. Places and means of resistance have probably been more available in India than in Romania or China; women might be able to find the money available to pay for an otherwise illegal and unavailable abortion, have the ability to travel outside state lines to access reproductive technology, or find or avoid contraceptives. But we will see that even in China and Romania, where the reach of the state was long and near-total, women and their families found ways to resist and to exercise agency over reproductive decisions. By looking at these three countries, we are able to observe several key things: the struggle between state and individual control of reproduction; the importance of reproduction to the state and the reasons states seek ways – directly or indirectly – to shape their population; and the ways that even in the most restrictive of circumstances, individuals find ways to resist.

China's "One-Child Policy"

When we think about state control of population, China is one of the first countries to come to mind. Indeed, the Chinese state has explicitly, and sometimes harshly, sought to control the country's population, seeing fertility control as important to the country's successful future as is state control of the economy.

Concern for population grew out of the tumult faced by China in the first half of the twentieth century. The end of the dynasties in 1911 brought with it enormous social and political unrest. Between 1911 and the founding of the People's Republic of China (PRC) in 1949, China experienced initial civil war, the establishment of the Republic of China, entanglement in World War II, and a continued civil war as the Guomindeng (Nationalists) and the Chinese Communist Party vied for control of the country. For ordinary Chinese, these decades were filled with uncertainty and political turmoil that had huge impacts on family structure and processes (Stacey 1983). Families faced a crisis, unable to support their members because of severe poverty; young people did not marry because the future was so uncertain; death rates, particularly for infants and children, were very high. Story after story told of the disasters that families faced. To survive, people sold land, their labor, and even family members. One woman recalled the past and how difficult it was, telling a common story of being so unable to meet the basic needs of her family that she had to resort to infanticide. She recounts, "I even had to kill my own baby" (Hinton 1984).

By the time the Communist Party won the Civil War and declared the founding of the PRC, the country faced huge problems of poverty and social disorganization; the new leaders set to work quickly and often effectively dealing with the worst of them, focusing on bringing stability to hard-hit rural areas: they put workers to the task of flood control; they reorganized land ownership and use to provide for food for everyone in the country; they began to address issues of disease and sanitation. In fact, the early decades of the PRC saw remarkable progress in many areas of social and economic life. Even as some peasants might have been opposed to the Communist take-over, they nevertheless appreciated the newfound relief from war and civil strife, and the ways in which the state was helping to make their lives livable.

But as a Communist state, the new government also changed the organization of social, village, and family life in unprecedented ways. Individuals could no longer own property, businesses, or land. Land was now worked by collectives; peasants worked with other villagers to raise and harvest crops not as members of families or clans, as had been the case for centuries, but now as part of brigades, collectives, and communes. The state put into place a health system that focused on basic health care for all, and brought about rapid reduction in basic diseases and in deaths from them. In many areas, infant mortality plunged during the early years of the PRC, making clear what a difference basic, universal health care could make (Riley

2017b). Nevertheless, China continued to face challenges: as a very poor country, it struggled to feed and care for the whole population. The PRC's first national census, conducted in 1953, allowed the state to "know" the population (Foucault 1991; Scott 1999). Newly available data on population size, where people were living, and differences and inequalities across the country prompted the state to change course about its population and to focus on its control and develop a strategy of limitation.

Leaders believed that only by giving the same attention and planning to population as was given to the economy would China be able to achieve modernity and status on the world stage. Even the terminology used underscored how reproduction was central to national progress and development. Whereas in many other societies, the term "family planning" is focused on families' and individuals' needs and interests in shaping fertility around family goals, the proper term in China is "birth planning." That term indicates how state leaders – and most Chinese citizens in fact – believe that reproduction is the purview of the state, that the state needed such oversight in order for it to do its job to move China from a poor country into one that provided security and opportunities for its citizens. In 1970, Premier Zhou Enlai made clear the connections between population and the future when he argued: "Birth planning isn't a health question, it's a planning question; if you can't even plan the rate of natural increase, how can you have a national plan?" (White 2006: 59). Soon after the new government was founded, the state began to put into place a series of increasingly strict rules regarding birth planning.

The earliest measures, instituted in the late 1960s and the 1970s, were local in scope, and often were focused on convincing parents to limit the number of children they had. The "Later, Longer, Fewer Policy" (Wan, Xi, Shao), begun in 1971, worked to educate citizens about the importance of postponing childbearing until a later age, having longer intervals between births, and having fewer births overall. While there were areas in China where couples were actively prevented from having the number of children they wanted, in most areas the Wan, Xi, Shao policy focused on voluntary fertility reduction. But that changed around 1980, when the Chinese state put into place its strictest population policy, what is often called the "one-child policy": in urban areas, no couple was allowed to have more than one child. In rural areas, most couples were allowed to have two children. Marriage was also a focus of the state's birth planning program; the minimum age of marriage for both women and men was raised, to 18 for women and 20 for men in 1950, and then to 20 and 22, respectively, in 1980; many locations prohibited marriages until even later ages. Delaying marriage can act as a very effective brake on population growth in a society like China, where there are few births outside marriage. Such a delay results in the lengthening of "generation time," the number of years between one generation and the next.[6] These birth planning laws were interpreted and enforced differently in different parts of China, but these were national laws, and all couples were required to obey the strictures.

Enforcement of the birth planning policy took many forms, some focused on education and many others much more coercive. In every locality, one person (usually a woman) was the local birth planning official, and it was her responsibility to give permission for couples of the right age to marry and, most importantly, to guarantee that the women in her jurisdiction did not have children "out of plan." Each locality (village or urban area) was given a quota of births for a particular calendar year, and every birth was to be planned for (White 2006). Individuals applied for permission to have a child and local officials were responsible for ensuring that only the allowed number of births occurred in their jurisdiction by carefully monitoring the women in their area. In the cities, women's menstrual cycles were closely tracked, and birth planning officials made sure that women were preventing unauthorized births through contraceptive use. In cities, then, it was pregnancies that were controlled. In rural areas, such control was harder, and there, it was unauthorized births that were the focus. All women were required to use contraception, usually an IUD, and in many areas, any woman who had a second child was required to undergo sterilization. The program relied heavily on the "four operations" – female sterilization, vasectomy, abortion, and IUD insertions. How rigorously rules and restrictions were enforced depended on the year and the locality, but women, their reproduction, and thus their bodies, remained under constant surveillance. Women who were trying to evade state regulations would try to hide their pregnancy from authorities, and might even move to another location for the later months of pregnancy. If caught, however, they would be subject to state rules and punishment, which might include a late-term abortion, fines, or even loss of a job or house; "extra" children were sometimes denied educational opportunities (Greenhalgh 1994).

While coercion was part of birth planning, the program also needs to be contextualized in order to understand why there were not more incidents of overt or organized resistance to the regulations from within China. At the time, most aspects of an individual's life were highly regulated by the state. Where one went to school, and for how long, were the state's decision. At the end of a young person's education, it was the state that decided where she or he would work, and individuals were sometimes forced to move far away from family and friends to a job that the state deemed necessary. Even distribution of food and other goods was highly regulated, with many purchases being rationed and requiring coupons to precure. Births, then, were seen in a similar light. Decisions about reproduction were not considered the right of individuals but, rather, a process that needed state control, and most people acquiesced to state population regulations.

The involvement of outsiders in the lives of individuals was, in many ways, not new in China. For centuries, the needs of the collective were believed to supersede the needs of the individual (Fei 1992). We can see this by noting how, across history, individuals sacrificed their own interests for the good of the family. The Communist government built its own system on that sense of collective responsibility. The changes it made were not to the collective spirit per se, but how that collective was defined – the commune instead of the family (see Figure 2.1). Indeed, many in China agreed that the state was right to try to bring population in line with production; they agreed even when they themselves would have preferred to have more children. Even in the 1980s, during the height of birth planning enforcement, women acknowledged the benefits of one-child families; a study that examined attitudes about the birth planning policy found that while most women said they would have liked to have had more than one child, nearly all (88.2 percent) believed that "the individual must voluntarily submit to the policy of the nation" (Milwertz 1997, quoted in Riley 2017b: 46). Some, however, see the state's long and often brutal policies and restrictions as implicated in shaping these responses; under such a regime, it may well be that "what was demographically thinkable bore the firm imprint of state desires for fertility limitation" (Greenhalgh 1994: 12).

Even as most Chinese acknowledged the necessity of state control of population, however, many wanted more children than the regulations allowed, and did what they could to evade the rules.

Figure 2.1. Posters promoting family planning from the early 1970s: "Practice birth control for the revolution" and "It is a revolutionary requirement to marry late"
Source: https://chineseposters.net

They did not resist in organized ways, but rather resisted quietly, mostly as solitary individuals. We can see that resistance in the many instances when China's fertility exceeded its targets; data at the community, provincial, and state levels provide the cumulative evidence of thousands of cases of individual resistance. Nearly every one of those "unexpected" or "unplanned" births happened because a woman resisted the restrictions and gave birth without state permission. In each case, a woman, and perhaps those around her, was quietly risking a great deal to have more control over her own reproduction than the state would allow. Local officials also evaded state control. They were often sympathetic to the desires of their neighbors to have another child and they regularly misreported births, thereby avoiding sanctions themselves (White 2006: 83ff.). Consequently, birth statistics at this time were notoriously unreliable (Bloomberg 2021). In addition to these kinds of resistance, undertaken to find ways to bear more children than the government allowed, some families raised children, often girls, who had been abandoned, often by parents forced by the birth planning policies to give up their children (Johnson 2017). Parents who took such children in were also evading state strictures, as domestic adoption was generally not permitted in China; these families struggled to raise these "hidden children" out of sight of the state, providing a family for the children and giving the parents children they so desperately wanted.

It is important to recognize the role of gender in all of these processes. The Chinese government targeted women in its birth planning policies: it was women's bodies on which the state's program depended; it was women to whom contraceptives were taught or pushed; when the government decided that sterilization was necessary, and undertook sterilization campaigns, it was women who underwent sterilization, even though vasectomies would have been less risky and easier. Gender played out in larger ways as well. In 1984, the Chinese government loosened the policies in rural areas; recognizing the importance of sons to rural families, the state decided that families who had had "only a daughter" were now allowed to have a second child, giving them another chance to have a boy. As Greenhalgh and Li (1995) have argued, state leaders changed the policy not to give families more reproductive control, but rather because they acknowledged the strength of rural resistance to the policies; in these changes, the government actually incorporated and institutionalized gender discrimination into its birth planning policy, formalizing the lesser value of daughters.

It was also women who bore the brunt of any resistance, whether that was hiding a pregnancy, leaving a village with a child born out of plan, illegally removing a contraceptive device, or being subjected to a late-term abortion of an un-allowed pregnancy. Any resistance "brought with it potential for corporeal harm. The more women contested the policies, the greater the risk to their bodies" (Greenhalgh 1994: 25) from these procedures and practices. And by nearly all accounts, the state's birth planning policy, coupled with a long-held preference for sons, led to the disaster of the "missing girls." Parents depended on sons to continue the family line, and because daughters married into their husbands' families, it was sons who provided support for parents in their old age. Because the state allowed only one child, parents knew they had only one chance to have a son and many made desperate attempts to have that one child be a son (Riley 2017b). Many millions of girls were either killed or allowed to die after birth, or were prevented from being born, through sex-selective abortion, as parents sought a way to have a son. It was girls – those missing, hidden, killed, or aborted – who came to bodily harm through the combination of strong son preference and very restrictive birth planning policies. And it was women who were caught between state and family pressures, with one side forbidding any more children, and the other insisting that more children – and a son – were necessary to future survival.

Thus, while sacrificing to the collective was widely seen as necessary for most of Chinese history, including the modern era, it is important to recognize that women were more likely to do the sacrificing than men. They have always had low status in Chinese families, which are patriarchal, with elder men having the most power, and young women at the bottom of both age and gender hierarchies (Wolf 1972). Those family inequalities remained after the Communist Revolution, when women were pushed into the labor force by the state but retained near-total responsibility for child care and housework (Stacey 1983). Today, gender inequality in China is as pervasive as it is in most societies. Thus, in China, longstanding gender inequalities have been compounded by state intervention in population control and women have borne the brunt of these state directives.

China no longer has a national program restricting births. Indeed, the state is now concerned that not enough babies are being born, and it currently encourages women to have two or three children. But China's fertility rate remains very low (in 2019, the TFR stood at 1.7 in 2019), well below replacement level of 2.1, and China's leaders are now worried that these low rates will hurt the country's economic goals.[7] As happens in low-fertility countries, the population is aging rapidly and there are fears that there will not be enough laborers to maintain production in China's growing economy. Couples and women are not eager to have many children, with some expressing a plan to avoid having any at all. They feel unable to afford children, and see the absence of state support for family and work as an impediment to having many – or any – children (Yip 2021). The many decades of missing girls also has longstanding implications: in a country where marriage is nearly universal, many men are unable to marry because they cannot find a wife. China may have loosened its restrictions on births, but its earlier policies continue to reverberate today. It is not clear what lessons the state has learned after decades of state intervention in birth planning. Today, it remains committed to involvement in reproduction; for example, in order to increase fertility, in some places in China, women are prevented from undergoing abortion (Yeung and Gan 2021). Women's reproductive activities are again (or still) under state scrutiny as the state continues to see reproduction as central to its political and economic goals.

Romania: Coercive Pronatalism

Romania might be one of the clearest examples of how "demographic concerns and nationalistic politics [can] turn ... women's bodies into instruments to be used in the service of the state" (Kligman 1995: 234). Romania's population program in the 1960s through 1980s bore the heavy hand of the state, as has been true in China. But in Romania, the state was pro-natalist, and women were forced to bear more – not fewer – children than they wanted. Nicolae Ceausescu, the Communist dictator who ruled from 1965 to 1989, wanted a stronger Romania, a country that could act independently, and he sought independence from the Warsaw Pact in foreign relations and domestic policy. He believed a large population size and fast growth were key to building a strong nation. "As elsewhere, 'the population' served as a strategic element to be disciplined and manipulated, ostensibly for purposes of maximizing development potential" (Kligman 1998: 10). In his efforts to make Romania strong and powerful, Ceausescu put into place a series of restrictions and laws that severely curtailed women's reproduction options and made Romania a reproductive nightmare.

The fertility rate had been falling for years in Romania and, by 1966, the TFR had reached 1.9, below the 2.1 level needed to replace the population. To Ceausescu, this was not only a demographic disaster but a political one as well (Soare 2013); he saw this fertility decline as an indication of national decline and suggestive that the state would be unable to meet its economic and political goals. Determined to change the direction of fertility decline, he enacted a series of laws and regulations designed to increase fertility and population growth. The goal of his regime was to grow the population from 22.6 million in 1984 to 25 million by 1990; to reach that goal, women were expected to produce as many babies as possible (Kligman 1995). Because Ceausescu believed that restricting access to contraception and abortion was the fastest and least expensive way to reach his demographic goals (Soare 2013), one of his first actions, in 1966, was to outlaw abortion. Those restrictions had an immediate and major effect on women's ability to control their reproduction because, at that time, contraception was not widely available and abortion was the way that most women prevented unwanted births. By some estimates, women, on average, underwent five to seven abortions over the course of their reproductive years (Kligman 1998: 47ff.). Ceausescu did not stop with restricting abortion but soon made it a criminal act, with anyone found receiving or providing abortion services subject to criminal punishment, including jail time. Under his rule, contraception also became very expensive and increasingly hard to precure; it was soon nearly completely unavailable, and, by 1985, became formally banned. In addition, women's bodies came under increasing surveillance. The government put into place a program of required monthly gynecological exams of women between the ages of 16 and 45. These exams allowed women to be closely monitored for pregnancy, and, if a pregnancy was detected, measures were put in place to ensure that it was carried to term. In 1986, Ceausescu proclaimed that "the fetus is the socialist property of the whole society. Giving birth is a patriotic duty ... Those who refuse to have children are deserters, escaping the law of natural continuity" (cited in Hord et al. 1991: 232).

Along with those restrictions, Ceausescu set up a campaign that aimed to change the norms and values of citizens; such ideological campaigns can serve to strengthen any laws and restrictions. Through the media, through state pronouncements, through laws and regulations, women were depicted as responsible for producing children for the benefit of the country. All women were expected to bear and raise at least four children. But women who bore even more children were seen as state heroes; those who bore six, or eight, or ten children were given state awards and some small privileges for doing so well for the country. Thus, good women – those mothers who had a lot of children and raised them well – were lauded. And those who did not meet the government's standards – those who had too few children, or who sought abortion or other ways to avoid having an unwanted birth – were held up as enemies of the country, as deviants, and were often punished for violating regulations. Any childless person aged 25 years or older was taxed every month because they were not contributing to the nation.

The Romanian state also promoted the family as the center of these national efforts, the place where mothers took on their most important role, raising children. Ceausescu proclaimed: "The highest patriotic citizens' duty for each family is to have and raise children. It is inconceivable to imagine a family without children. The greatest honor and more important social role for women is to give birth, to give life, and to raise children" (Kligman 1998: 71). In its support of families, the state also made it increasingly difficult for couples to divorce. In the government's rhetoric, the family was a sacred place that could help the country reach its demographic, economic, and political goals. Citizens were barraged with messages making it clear that all efforts should be toward having more children, raising them for the fatherland, and thus contributing to Romania's future. And while women – as mothers – were the main targets, others too were part of the scheme: medical professionals were held responsible for increasing the birth rate – doing so became part of their job (Kligman 1992b: 19). Physicians at factories and other workplaces had to show that the workers there had fulfilled government-required birth quotas or were denied their salaries (Hord et al. 1991). Doctors sometimes refused to perform Caesarian sections because they feared being accused by the government of performing an illegal sterilization (Hord et al. 1991: 231). Thus, Romanian women and their families faced an all-out assault on their reproduction, involving both regulations and restrictions as well as strong and constant rhetoric. Reproduction came to determine women's status and place and their bodies were glorified as reproductive machines (Kligman 1992b). As we saw in China, this kind of rhetoric and campaign can make it difficult or impossible for women to imagine their own reproductive plans and future.

As harsh and constrictive as were the early campaigns, they did not stop the downward fertility trend. In the first two years after the abortion ban was enacted, fertility rose, as women faced the immediate consequences of these restrictions. But after those early years, people found ways around the ban, especially by finding abortion providers outside the law, and the fertility rate continued to decline. In response, the government enacted ever-harsher regulations and punishments, and stepped up its propaganda to try to convince women and families to follow state orders.

The consequences of these measures were far-reaching. During these years of reproductive control, maternal mortality rose, resulting in Romania having the highest maternal mortality rate (MMR) in Europe;[8] 87 percent of those deaths resulted from complications following illegal abortions of women desperate to prevent another birth (Benson et al. 2011). Children also suffered; many of them were born unwanted by their parents, and into families and communities dealing with dire poverty. Many children ended up as wards of the state, living in orphanages under terrible conditions (Kligman 1992a). Romania's assault on reproduction took a huge toll on women, and on families. Women suffered physically and emotionally. Because of lack of access to abortion, and with contraceptives not available, "sexual intimacy was fraught with fear and anxiety lest another encounter result in pregnancy" (Kligman 1998: 205). In Romania, as elsewhere, it was poor women who suffered the most from such state restrictions; they did not have the means to find illegal but safe abortions, or the connections to get one through normal means, and they could not travel away from the country. And while some contraceptives were available on the black market, the cost of that route – where the price of a condom was equivalent to an average day's wage (Hord et al. 1991) – put contraception completely out of reach for some.

This focus on reproduction in Romania was by all accounts a complete disaster. It did not achieve Ceausescu's population goals and poverty remained widespread, deep, and scarring. Women and children suffered great hardship, both physical and mental, as they tried to survive through the harsh conditions. It is estimated that a high percentage of children born during these years suffered from psychological and neuropsychological disorders (Hord et al. 1991) because they were born into extreme hardship, often to parents who did not want them or were unable to care for them properly. The legacy of these 23 years lasted long after the 1989 revolution that overthrew the government and resulted in Ceausescu's execution. The damaging effects of Ceausescu's reproductive policies were widely recognized, which led the new regime to dismantle the restrictions on contraception and abortion on its first day in power (Hord et al. 1991). Over the following year, Romania experienced huge changes in reproduction policy and outcomes. Maternal mortality declined dramatically; in one year, that figure was halved, from 159 deaths per 100,000 live births to 83 per 100,000 in 1990 (Hord et al. 1991) (see Figure 2.2). The new government, with help from international organizations and governments, worked to establish new health and reproductive services. But the long and brutal years of Ceausescu's regime left a long legacy of disrupted families, dire poverty, and reproductive terror.

Using Incentives and Disincentives in India

We turn to India for a different version of state involvement in reproduction. India is an important country in any study of population control for a variety of reasons. It has long had one of the largest populations of any country. In India, we also see the attempts of a newly independent state to wrestle with questions around population as it endeavored to develop its own approaches to development and economy, and tried to resist western action and influence. Throughout, geopolitics around the Cold War and India's population size and growth have drawn and sustained western interest, and it is often held up as the epitome of a country whose population needed control. As one scholar described it, "India was both the problem and a potential success story"; both "an experimental site and an ideological frontier in population control" (Rao 2010: 80, 78).

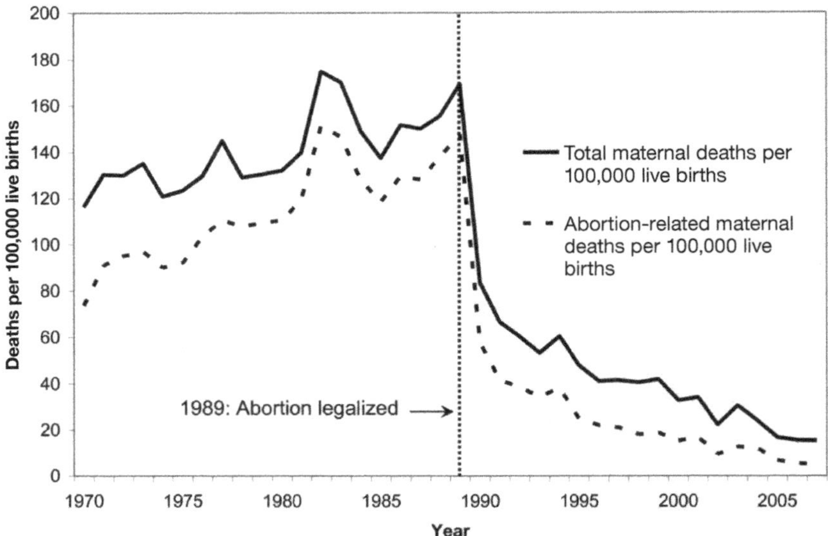

Figure 2.2. Romania: effect of abortion restrictions, and then their lifting, on maternal mortality rate
Source: Benson et al. 2011

In many ways, India is not like our earlier examples of China or Romania. Population control in India seems nowhere near as coercive. Indeed, India has often been put in a different category than those countries, with strong but not coercive policies. That its programs were seen as less extreme than both China's and Romania's mean that many countries look to it for guidance. India has a parliamentary democratic government based on a constitution and a rule of law. But even with those safeguards, we see the "violence of family planning" (Wilson 2018) played out in India too. While India has had a different history from that of Romania and China regarding population control and even its relationship to the West, we can nevertheless see familiar echoes of coercion and a focus on women's bodies to achieve national and global aims.

After India achieved independence in 1947, its leaders were challenged to manage and lead a country that had been under colonial rule for nearly 100 years, which had shaped most of its social, political, and economic institutions to the advantage of Britain. The new state leaders connected India's poverty to its colonial history and were committed to finding a path – an independent path – to the construction of a modern state. Population was very much a part of the planning of the new state, leading to the establishment in 1952 of the first national family planning program in the world. India was like many other countries in its belief that reproduction was central to state economic development goals. Indeed, in 1960, state leaders made the family planning program "the very centre of planned development" (Connelly 2006: 645, quoting the Indian Planning Commission, 1961). But India has also received an outsized amount of attention from the world, and its population policies show a complex combination of the Indian state maintaining its own pathway and western – particularly US – influence over those policies.

India's population size and growth were of concern to its new leaders, and, soon after independence, the state began promoting fertility control as a necessary part of planning at both the national and the individual level (Chatterjee and Riley 2001). The government opened up new clinics across the country, providing free contraceptives to low-income women, insisting that India could reach its population goals by providing increased education and access and through the development of an information campaign to convince parents that smaller families were best (Connelly 2006). In these efforts, Indian leaders hoped to avoid more targeted efforts at controlling reproduction and the often strong pressures from the West to do so. In 1965, US President Lyndon Johnson withheld food aid to India – in the midst of a potential famine – until India met US demands to apply incentives in its sterilization program (Gupte 2017). At the 1974 UN World Population Conference, India made headlines when it announced that the country would follow its own vision of economic/population balance. There, India took the stance that "development is the best contraceptive," thereby refuting the claim of many western demographers that, in order for a country like India to achieve economic stability or growth, it must first control its population.

By the late 1970s, as the country missed its hoped-for goals of fertility reduction and contraception use, Indian leaders began to re-evaluate their approach and turned to more targeted, top-down, and ultimately coercive approaches to reproduction control. They insisted that a "frontal attack on the problem of population" (Alok 1992: 84–5) would be more effective. The government began to establish numerical population targets, and instituted a program that included incentives and punishments with the explicit goal of reducing family size. The government now saw reduced fertility as necessary to reach its economic goals, a philosophy in close alignment with western ideas and not all that different from China's insistence that economy and population both need state planning. In 1976, Indira Gandhi declared an Emergency, allowing the state to assume power in excess of regular democratic processes; she proclaimed: "We must now act decisively and bring down the birth rates. We should not hesitate to take steps which might be described as drastic. Some personal rights have to be kept in abeyance for the human rights of the nation" (SLaW 1993) – a statement with eerie echoes of Romania's stance. The government began to rely increasingly on sterilization; with a more permanent contraceptive method, and with control of contraception out of the hands of individuals, the state hoped to reach its population goals more quickly. In the 1970s, sterilization efforts were stepped up to such a degree that the coercive tactics and subsequent disasters in the family planning program – particularly a program of forced vasectomies for men[9] – led to a public backlash that helped to bring down the Congress government in 1977. And, while India's government learned a lesson from that approach and loss of power, if we look at where the program traveled in the following years – with its continued targeting of the poor and minorities through women's bodies – the lesson seemed to be not to avoid coercion, but to be careful about just which groups get targeted.

Sterilization continued to be a central method of birth control in the government's family planning program, but since 1977 efforts have been focused almost entirely on women. In addition to a focus on sterilization, national and state officials used increasingly coercive tactics to meet sterilization targets. Individuals were sometimes forced to undergo a sterilization in order to receive a wage increase and even food or water. Local officials – "motivators" – would use incentives (such as cash) and punishments (such as wage penalties) to push people to undergo sterilization. One village woman explained why she agreed to be sterilized. Her husband had been targeted for sterilization, and told he would lose his salary if he did not consent. She then agreed to sterilization so her husband would not have to undergo the procedure. "We were poor then. What would we have done without his salary? ... I told myself I was doing it of my own free will. But it was government pressure" (SLaW 1993). Other incentives might be small amounts of cash, or sometimes as little as some lentils, suggesting how it is often women's poverty and lack of food that forces them to agree to sterilization. Declaring family planning to be "something like a war," Asoka Mehta, a Planning Commission official, argued that population growth was "the enemy within the gate ... It is war that we have to wage, and, as in all wars, we cannot be choosy, some will get hurt, something will go wrong. What is needed is the will to wage the war so as to win it" (quoted in Connelly 2006: 653). India might not have been a communist country, but the sacrifice of individuals' reproductive goals for the good of the society was part of state rhetoric in India too.

As happened in China, officials themselves were punished or rewarded depending on how well they reached the targets set by the government. Targets were set at the national level and distributed down to the local level. Local "motivators" often vied for "cases" – women who agreed to sterilization – offering an incentive that they hoped would convince a woman to undergo the procedure. Motivators were sometimes hired directly by the family planning program, but they were also often local village officials or even shopkeepers. If a motivator was not successful in bringing in the required number of cases, their salary could be withheld, or even worse. A shopkeeper might lose his shop. As one rural woman who had been targeted by a local motivator insisted: "The main issue is to stop women from having children whatever the circumstances or the ensuing problems" (SLaW 1993). And while the pressure on women was immense, so too was the pressure on those who were supposed to implement the program's goals.

India is also notable for the foreign involvement in its population programs. Even as the newly independent Indian state insisted that it would forge an autonomous road forward, decisions about family planning were also deeply connected to global politics that influenced India and its programs in fundamental ways. Especially in the early years of its population control programs, India was reluctant to receive aid from western governments and agencies, knowing that accepting it would bring regulations and structures that were shaped by foreign priorities, not their own. But for all its reluctance, India did receive such aid; funding came from a number of foreign governments and agencies, including several from the United States and Canada. Especially as India moved towards incentives and punishment, US advisors assisted in directing the new program, helping to put into place a strategy of rewards and disincentives, and encouraging India to "do ... the needful" (Narayana and Kantner 1992). In the 1970s, Indian leaders came to agree that population growth was a potential threat to economic development (Caldwell 1976; Connelly 2006; Malthus 1993 [1798]; Coale and Hoover 1958); this signaled India's acquiescence to western ideas of population and economy, and marked the state's focus on direct and often coercive intervention in reproduction and family planning as the necessary way to a strong Indian future. "Overpopulation sidelined all other factors, including historical income inequality, as the main reason for underdevelopment" (Sarcar 2021). Indian leaders saw good planning – in reproduction and population and all else – as a sign of a modern country (Chatterjee and Riley 2001); such an argument reflects a belief that countries and individuals who cannot or will not plan their reproduction are backward and unlikely to succeed in their goals. As the family planning poster shown in Figure 2.3 asserts, small families, like the one on the right, were shown as

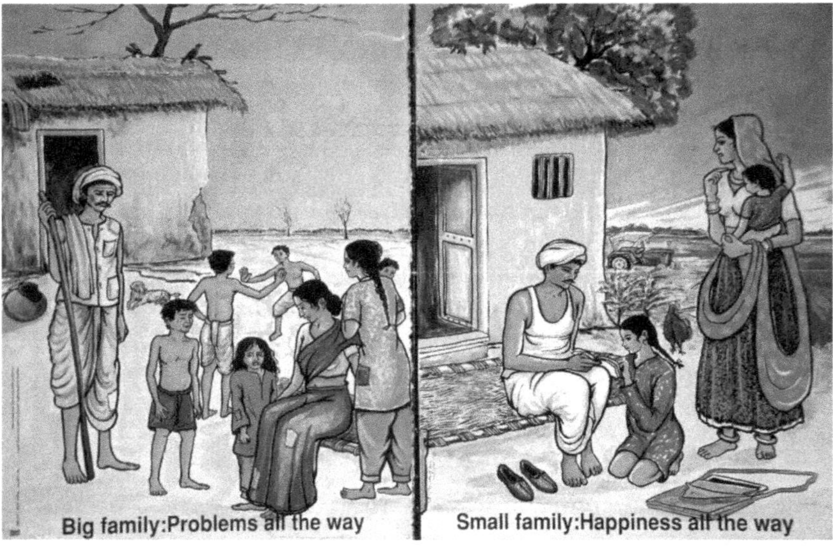

Figure 2.3. "Small Family Happiness": poster from the Mass Education Media Division of India's Ministry of Health and Family Welfare, 1992
Source: https://collections.nlm.nih.gov/catalog/nlm:nlmuid-101455001-img

successful – able to afford books (and, by implication, education) for their children, a good house, a tractor, even jewelry. The family on the left is depicted as poor, with holes in the roof of the house, barefooted children clothed in rags. The message is obvious: their poverty is caused by having too many children. "One or two, that's enough! Plan your family!" a slogan admonished (SLaW 1993).

Officials in other countries took great interest in India's population and its efforts to address the problems it encountered, for several reasons. India's independence coincided with the beginning of the Cold War, and both the Soviet Union and western alliances were looking to gain influence in the Global South. Both sides saw India as important in this contest, potentially tipping world balance, and made efforts to court the country. If India moved into the Soviet column, the US feared that even more of the Global South would align with communism, threatening the place of the US in the world. A noted demographer of the time stated that "the political survival of westernized groups is at stake" (Irene Taeuber, quoted in Connelly 2006: 635).

In addition, these world events occurred at a time of rising concern with "overpopulation" and, here again, India was seen as a key player. The West regarded India and other countries in the Global South warily, concerned that population growth in that part of the world would upset global balance. American biologist Paul Ehrlich published his hugely popular *The Population Bomb* in 1968, arguing that overpopulation would doom the earth. He opened the book with a clearly racialized description of Delhi that was meant to scare people about the dangers the world faced from countries "like India":

> The streets seemed alive with people. People eating, people washing, people sleeping. People visiting, arguing, and screaming. People thrusting their hands through the taxi window, begging. People defecating and urinating. People clinging to buses. People herding animals. People, people, people, people ... [S]ince that night, I've known the feel of overpopulation. (Ehrlich 1968: 1)

A recent analysis of that early work makes clear the role that race played in raising a fear of "overpopulation":

> The Ehrlichs took the cab ride in 1966. How many people lived in Delhi then? A bit more than 2.8 million, according to the United

> Nations. By comparison, the 1966 population of Paris was about 8 million. No matter how carefully one searches through archives, it is not easy to find expressions of alarm about how the Champs-Élysées was "alive with people." Instead, Paris in 1966 was an emblem of elegance and sophistication. (Mann 2018)

It was because of India's importance to Cold War politics, to western concerns about world population growth, and to the balance of global power, that the US became heavily involved in, and encouraged and supported, India's attempts to control its population. Indeed, the United States has been involved in small and large ways since the beginning of India's family planning program, advising the country's leaders on how to undertake a program whose aim is to reduce population growth and encourage lower fertility; it has provided technological and data assistance throughout the decades. Notably, the US has been supportive of even the most extreme aspects of India's program. In the midst of one of its most coercive periods, in the mid 1970s, Robert McNamara, then head of the World Bank, commented: "At long last, India is moving to effectively address its population problem" (Mann 2018). Especially in the early years, US financial support often came with an insistence that India develop a particular type of program – an "effective" and "vigorous" one (Connelly 2006: 652).

Throughout all phases of India's attempts to control population (and mirroring what happened in China and Romania), it was women who were targeted. Despite its earlier program aimed at sterilizing men, assumptions about women's role in reproduction remained strong. Women – who were the ones who actually got pregnant and bore children – were seen as the central players in reproduction, despite the importance of family influences. In addition, government programs and directives regarding reproduction were shaped by discourses around the role of women and gender in the formation and development of the new nation. Partly because of India's status as a previously colonized country, government officials emphasized the need to keep Indian culture strong and protect the nation's reputation, ideologies, and norms. Women's roles as culture bearers were seen as central to nationalist goals (Bumiller 1990; di Leonardo 1987). Once the Indian state came to believe that national success necessitated a smaller population, women were targeted as the most direct route to that goal. In this way, control of women's reproduction became linked to, and a cause of, the nation's future success or failure.

India has changed its policies since the early decades of its population program. But as we will see when we turn again to India's story in later chapters, the Indian state continues its attempts to control population through a focus on women and their fertility. Today, sterilization still accounts for three-quarters of all contraceptive use in India, the highest level in the world (Wilson 2015: 2). While foreign advisors now play a smaller role in India's program and policies, geopolitics and western influence continue to be involved. As we will see in later chapters, neoliberal capitalism, with its emphasis on free markets and individual rational self-interest, has had a strong influence in India on planning around economic development and population, as it has in many countries. As India leaned into that ideology, its path increasingly came to reflect the neoliberal ideas first developed in the west – that individuals are responsible for their way forward, and should gather and employ their own resources to find success in their own lives. After the UN ICPD in Cairo in 1994, India purportedly moved away from family planning targets to a "cafeteria approach," a program offering women choice among several contraceptive methods. When examined beyond the rhetoric, however, we still see the old ways of family planning targets, of program workers punished or rewarded for bringing in new "cases," and little availability of contraceptive methods beyond those that authorities consider to be the most effective: sterilization and long-acting hormonal methods such as Depo-Provera and Norplant. In its 2012 study of the India program, Human Rights Watch heard from many local health workers about the pressure and punishments they faced around sterilization targets. One worker described her work:

> I have to bring one woman every month for the operation. The MO [medical officer] or my supervisor says, "Go bring them from wherever you want, it's not our business. Find them. But you must bring one woman for operation every month. If you cannot even bring one woman in a month for operation it means you are not doing your work properly." They say they will complain about us. [Or] remove us from our jobs if we don't complete this target. We are told, "Until a woman agrees for the operation keep hounding her." (HRW 2012)

Most importantly, at the heart of the program today is a continued belief that women's reproduction needs controlling (Wilson 2015).

It is also important to note that, while all Indian women were subject to state control, some were targeted more than others. Rural women, poor women, women of lower castes and classes, and Muslim women all experienced heightened attention. Indeed, as the new Indian government worked to establish itself on the world stage, it had a certain image it wanted to project: strong, modern, and equal to western powers. These marginalized groups were seen as a drag on India's goals and success (Purohit 2019; Wilson 2018). We discuss these issues further in Chapter 5.

These examples of three very different countries underscore the contestations around control of reproduction and the role of the state in these contestations. In each case, controlling reproduction was vital to state goals, and in each case the state employed a range of tactics to bring reproduction into alignment with its own national agenda and domestic policies. Geopolitics played a role in all three, even if in different ways. In India, it was not only its colonial past but ongoing western anxieties about population growth and world balance that have played a role in the shape and scope of population control. In the attention it has received from world powers, India represents a large part of the world – that part of the world that is not heavily industrialized, continues to be poor, and has fertility and mortality rates higher than those found in the Global North. The US-dominated post World War II agenda promoted the invention of "development" and the "developing world" and, in the process, "the notions of 'underdevelopment' and 'Third World' emerged as working concepts in the process by which the West (and the East) redefined themselves and the global power structures" (Escobar 1988: 429). Western involvement in these development programs comes out of a combination of a mission to aid poorer countries whose economies are weak, and anxieties that these countries represent a demographic threat to the world – that higher population growth in poor countries in the Global South will cause a rebalancing of the world's power and upset western domination and white dominance. These anxieties – about population growth and size and the racial composition of that growth – echo Ehrlich's concerns from *The Population Bomb* of 60 years ago. India's history, its connections to and resistance to the West, and its subsequent alignments with outside powers, reflects these mixed influences. At the heart of state efforts has been a belief that management and control of reproduction are necessary to achieve its goal of becoming a strong and modern independent county.

But even in Romania and China, where leaders more explicitly sought to forge an independent path to modernity and asserted their own versions of population control, national population control programs have reflected geopolitical and domestic anxieties. Romania wanted independence, especially from the Soviet Union, and China worked to keep western influences away. In their attempt to find a place on the world stage, both countries, like India, saw population and its control as central to success. And in both cases, the state employed often brutal methods to wrest control of reproduction away from individuals and put it in service to state and country.

The history of population control in China and Romania underscores the power of reproduction, the reasons for contestations around its control, and the ways the programs adopted are nearly always targeted at women. But the lessons learned from these three countries apply even to those places where the state is less overtly or visibly in control; even where it appears that women control their own reproduction, we will see the state is still a powerful player in reproductive outcomes. But while the state is often a key player, and brings great power to control the reproduction of its citizens, women are rarely helpless or immobile on such matters. Even in the most restrictive of situations, women often navigate carefully and forcefully to seize and maintain as much control over reproduction as possible. We saw evidence of that resistance in each of the three countries described above, even in China and in Romania during the height of their population control drives. Even in places like village India, which might grab fewer international headlines than Romania or China, women work to maintain independence from the challenges they face from state processes or even family members. Reliable, accessible birth control is seen by all as giving women important power over the course of their lives, which is why there are struggles over reproduction everywhere. And while the state may be the key institution in these contests, other social institutions such as family and religion also play roles in reproduction and its control – as we will see in the next two chapters.

3
Religion and the State

Even as there are many examples of the ways that states explicitly push reproductive agendas, and influence women's access to and use of reproductive services, in most cases states are not acting alone. In this and the next chapter, we look closely at the role of two social institutions – religion and family – to understand how they too are involved in reproductive processes.[10] We will see that family, religion, and the state are distinct but intimately entangled institutions, and the relationships among them are rarely simple, but usually complex and fluid. Part of that interweaving can be attributed to the ways that state, religion, and family all arise from and are embedded in a particular society; societal norms and values play a role in the construction and maintenance of each and influence the distribution of power across groups and individuals. We focus on the two institutions of religion and family because they – along with the economy, which we address in Chapter 6 – touch the lives of all individuals in any society and often have powerful influences on reproduction. In this chapter, we look at religion, and take up family in the following chapter.

Religion is a key element of all societies, and is involved in how individuals understand the material and spiritual world. Here we focus on the ways that the structural and ideological elements of religion have played a direct role in reproductive issues. In many societies, religious institutions can be a political force, directly influencing state policies through support or disapproval of laws. Even without systemic religious involvement, religious ideology is powerful when it proscribes or encourages certain behaviors, including messaging to followers about expected or forbidden models of reproduction. Both Catholicism and Islam have historically been pro-natalist, and the state can sometimes act to lessen the impact of religious strictures regarding reproductive norms. But state and religion form a powerful partnership in other places, especially when they are in agreement about what is or is not acceptable in the society.

Religion's power is evident not only in those places where it has a formal tie to the state, such as Costa Rica (where Catholicism is the state religion) or Egypt (whose state religion is Islam), but even in countries that claim a separation between church and state, such as the United States. We explore these state–religion connections in several countries, each highlighting different aspects of this relationship. One notable feature of these examples is their great diversity. Religious doctrines, and even the same religious texts, are interpreted differently in different settings. Our examples make clear that the effect of a religion – Islam or Christianity, for example – on reproduction or on gender differs depending on the cultural, economic, and political context, pointing to how, even in a context of religious hegemony, it is often other priorities that have the upper hand in shaping policies around reproduction.

Poland: Church and State Collaboration on Reproductive Policies

Poland's history of reproductive and gender politics over the past several decades is instructive in how the state works with other social institutions to shape the lives and reproduction of women. After World War II, Poland came under the influence of the Soviet Union and communist control, and was a signatory to the Warsaw Treaty; in 1989, the regime was overthrown by the opposition movement, led by the Solidarity labor union, and a democratically elected government was established. While we might assume that democracy would bring more rights, Poland's experience underscores the complicated relationships between religious institutions, the state, and women's bodies.

Under the communist regime, Polish citizens had experienced hardships and restrictions. But many (Williams 2011; Matynia 1994) see that era as more supportive of women in some ways than the later, democratic regime. Under communism, women were pushed into work to support nationalist goals of economic development; consequently, the state put in place strong support networks for women in the form of child care, access to contraception, and easily available abortion. This allowed women to take better control over their reproduction, and gave them ways to handle the demands of their work and family lives.

The relationship between the state and the Catholic Church during those years influenced what has happened since. The Communist government maintained a clear separation between church and state, and saw the church as harmful to state goals. Communists attempted to erode the Catholic Church's ecclesiastical power and impose atheistic rationality over what it labelled "superstition." But the majority of the Polish population was Catholic, and the church was a powerful force during the communist regime, acting as "a national symbol of resistance" (Heinen and Portet 2010: 1007). To that end, as opposition to the communist regime grew, the church threw its support behind those who were looking for change. That powerful support left Solidarity, the labor union at the forefront of the resistance movement, in debt to the church, leading to a strong alliance between the new state and the church after the transition; indeed, once in place, the new government ushered in major changes based on church teachings, changes that have had a significant influence on reproduction, often to the disadvantage of women. Pressured by church officials, one of the first acts of the new government was to begin restricting access to reproductive services. Abortion was almost completely banned, and over the course of the next years, much of the formerly available support for reproductive services, such as family planning, and for women's work and family lives, such as child care and family supplements, disappeared. As it has developed a neoliberal approach to its economy, Poland has increasingly depended on private sources for services of all kinds, from child care to health services.

As we saw in Romania, China, and India, in Poland too it is women who have endured the biggest burdens under the new regime. Women are responsible for most child care and housework, even if they are also working full time in the paid labor force. Thus, the dismantling of support for work and family hits women particularly hard. But just as significant has been the ways the church has asserted its religiously sanctioned social norms: that the proper roles for women lie in the domestic sphere.

Thus, it was not the socialist or communist state, but a popularly elected government that championed democracy and the market, that effectively curtailed women's rights. The Catholic Church has long held a powerful position in Poland. But it was working together with the resistance movement and the subsequent government that allowed the church to assert such strong influence (Mishtal 2015: 21ff.). While both church and state in Poland are similarly interested in nation- and community-building and both want to expand their influence, there are also differences between them, especially in their sources of power. The state controls population through punitive means and actions such as targeted taxation laws. The church, on the other hand – at least in the modern era – exerts its power through a kind of moral governance. That collaboration has led to a powerful state–religion nexus: "Thus the status of the church as a moral authority was [always] of utmost importance ... but now ... the church's power has been fused with state power" (Mishtal 2015: 21).

Indeed, after 1989 the church led a "wave of moralization" (Mishtal 2015: 37). Arguing that the family had declined under the socialist regime,

> Priests and politicians were heard redefining Polish women's identities around traditional gender differences, casting their social roles primarily ... as mothers and wives, and calling for a return to the kind of "femininity" that was presumably lost when women entered employment outside the home during the previous decades. The wave of moralization simultaneously rejected women's rights and embraced a rights discourse in other ways that more closely aligned with the Church's teachings. The church spoke of the "rights of the family" and "marriage rights," and on the individual level it argued for women's "right to motherhood." (Mishtal 2015: 37)

Poland's more recent restrictions on IVF technology (Sussman 2019), which limit its use to married couples, reflect the ways that church doctrine has been incorporated not only into promoting motherhood, but into visions of what constitutes "proper" families and motherhood as well.

The pressure on women becomes even greater as Catholic arguments about proper gender roles and reproductive constraint combine with an argument promoted by the state that suggests that women have a responsibility to society to reproduce. In ways that echo the Romanian nationalist stance on population that we saw in Chapter

2, Poland's very low fertility and population growth rates are now being used as key measures of the nation's economic and political health. Worries about a "dying nation" and the need to increase Poland's demographic strength have been used by state officials to construct women as neglectful not only in relation to their families but also to the nation if they do not put family and motherhood first.

In recent years, there has been increasing, and increasingly public, opposition to reproductive restrictions in Poland. The Women's Strike (Stajk Kobiet) movement, begun in 2016, has organized massive demonstrations as Poland has further reduced access to reproductive services (see Figure 3.1). Poland already had one of the most restrictive abortion policies in Europe, allowing abortion only in cases of congenital anomaly, rape, incest, or serious threats to a woman's health, but the state pushed through a further narrowing by removing the clause permitting abortion in the case of congenital anomaly. In late fall of 2020, thousands of Poles took to the streets in protest (see this book's cover image); the show of force led to the government's delay in implementing the new law. More demonstrations have followed; in January 2022, large demonstrations protested the death of a woman unable to access an abortion even though her life was in danger. But the protesters want more. Many believe that this opposition movement has stirred up widespread disapproval of the government and of the role of the Catholic Church in Poland's politics more generally, and are looking for other changes, including increased government support for health care and education and a more independent judiciary (Henley and Strek 2020). Polls show that

Figure 3.1. Materials promoting the All-Poland Women's Strike (Strajk Kobiet)

more and more Polish citizens are leaving the church because they see it as intervening too far into political and social life in the country. In 1989, 90 percent of Poles approved of the church's position in the country, but that figure now stands at 41 percent, and continues to decline, particularly among younger Poles (Pawlak and Ptak 2021). However Poland's politics play out, recent events demonstrate the ways that reproductive politics are at the core of state legitimacy and opposition.

In Poland, then, we can see how state involvement in reproduction and women's lives is tangled with other institutions. Despite a formal agreement in 1993 that purportedly maintained independence of church and state, the continued close ties between them has meant laws have been imbued with the church's version of morality. In addition, reproduction has been tied to cultural nationalism and to national goals, which are sometimes reduced to demographic numbers, and an argument that too few children and people mean a "dying Poland."

One of the lessons we learn from Poland can be carried over to other places as well. Whether a government is left- or right-leaning, and even its rise from revolutionary struggles, do not set it on a particular path regarding reproductive politics. In Poland, it was after a pro-democracy oppositional regime was in place that we saw some of the harshest restrictions regarding reproduction. We see that in other places too. For example, in the past several decades, Ecuador has experienced changes in governments; its most recent leftist government has, like Poland's, also teamed up with the Catholic Church and run havoc over women's reproductive rights. There, women have been imprisoned for seeking abortions (Carpenter 2019). These and other examples underscore the power of alliances between church and state, and the ways those alliances can impact women's reproductive lives.

Brazil

The Catholic Church plays an important but different role in reproductive politics and outcomes in Brazil. In the poorer settlements of northeast Brazil in the 1980s, reproductive control was unavailable to families, and mothers faced a constant threat of losing the children they bore to poverty, starvation, and illness. There, as Nancy

Scheper-Hughes (1993) has documented, the church's influence came from internalized fatalism rather than from explicit state connections as we saw in Poland. In Brazil, their faith in God and the church have encouraged poor mothers living in shantytowns to face the loss of their children "without weeping," often showing little emotion around the many infant deaths they witnessed.

Scheper-Hughes focuses on the context that influenced these reactions. Because of increased sugarcane cultivation, the decline of subsistence crops, and a weakening of the industrial sector, these mothers had little income, no government support, and struggled to survive. Scheper-Hughes argues that the seeming indifference to their children's deaths – which happened frequently and at rates much higher than in the wider Brazilian population – does not reflect some innate cruelty or lack of caring on the part of these mothers. Rather, in the midst of extraordinary difficulties, they relied on religious faith to make sense of their lives. When their babies died, they believed that God had taken the child, and that the child was now an angel, and less likely to suffer. This religious faith was useful to them in their grief, given the government's clear indifference to the sufferings of the women, children, and others in these shantytowns. The government's disinterest in the hardships these mothers faced, as they desperately tried to provide for their children in a situation of dire poverty, was reflected in how these children's deaths were rarely even acknowledged or recorded. Here, religion serves to mitigate mothers' grief and hopelessness and helps alleviate a stronger reaction, one that might be directed at government authorities. The church did not provide women a path to social change, but merely a refuge from the "violence of everyday life." Scheper-Hughes points to the church's traditional "hostility toward female sexuality and reproduction" and its opposition to undertake action to address "gender oppression and ... the useless suffering of mothers and infants (1993: 529), underscoring how the Catholic Church both fails these poor women and makes it even less likely that any political change will occur. These women are thus failed, not because church and state work hand in hand, but because state authorities and the Catholic Church both turn a blind eye to their plight.

Like Christianity, Islam has had influences on reproduction and women in different ways across the world. Though some have argued that Islam discourages women from controlling their fertility, scholars have warned that thinking that there is some "fateful triangle" (Obermeyer 1992) between Islam, women, and reproduction ignores the ways that religion acts and interacts with the state differently in particular political, economic, and cultural settings. About those who resist contraception in Morocco, one population official argued: "Islam is not the problem here, but the premier problem is how people understand Islam ... There are many interpretations" (quoted in Hughes 2011: 429). The local setting may be particularly significant because Islam does not have a central authority to declare how religious texts should be interpreted. Obermeyer argues that because the combination of "variability in the social context" and "the flexibility of texts ... they can be used by the groups in power, and those in the opposition, to legitimate different positions on women and population issues" (Obermeyer 1994: 60, 66). We now look at two countries with strong Islamic influences, Morocco and Egypt.

Egypt: State Cooptation of Islamists

Egypt has a secular constitution, supporting freedom of belief. But, at the same time, Islam has been the state religion of Egypt since 1980, and a majority of Egyptians are Muslim. Nevertheless, in the realm of reproduction, religion does not play the prescriptive role we might expect given the place of Islam in Egyptian society; rather than religion, in Egypt, as in many countries, it is the state's economic and political concerns that most directly shape state involvement in reproduction. In Egypt's period of secular Arab nationalism of the 1960s, which was followed by a modernizing agenda of postcolonial nation-building, Egypt has followed a script on reproductive politics that is not very different from other, more overtly secular, countries.

State focus on reproduction and fertility levels came after the country experienced rising incomes and a growing economy in the 1970s that was followed by an economic slow-down, rising unemployment, and mounting external debt in the 1980s. It was at that time that Egypt – with prompting from western powers that were heavily invested in the economy – turned to a focus on reproduction, fertility, and population growth as key to economic stability and growth. International donors such as the US Agency for International Development (USAID) recommended the establishment of a new program focused on bringing fertility rates down and increasing contraceptive use. Although Egypt's TFR had declined from 6.6 in the late 1960s to 3.9 in the early 1990s, Egyptian officials and foreign advisors argued that it was still too high and deliberate efforts should be made toward changing reproductive outcomes. To meet the new government goals of decreasing the population growth rate from 2.8 in 1988 to 2.1 by 2001, contraceptive use rates would have to rise; the government aimed to have 51 percent of couples using contraceptives, up from 35 percent at the time (Ali 2002: 33). The government also began to push "more effective" contraceptive methods, encouraging women away from oral contraceptives/pills and toward IUDs and other long-acting contraceptives such as Norplant and Depo-Provera, over which women have less control (Ali 2002: 34).

What was the role of religion in all these plans and interventions? In spite of Egypt's status as a Muslim state, Islam had very little direct influence on the development of Egypt's program. The major force that drove the Egyptian state to expand its role in controlling reproduction was not religious but economic. Government officials and program officers "claimed that the rate of [population] increase would raise unemployment rates, accelerate the loss of agricultural land, speed up urbanization, and reduce the per capita investment on education. In short, all the indices of development and standard of living would be adversely affected" (Ali 2002: 33). While there was some organized Islamic resistance to the program in the 1980s and 1990s, the state adopted a policy of cooptation, striving to incorporate Islamists' objections to the program into its own goals regarding reproduction, arguing that family planning is compatible with Islamic ideology (Ali 2002: 156). The state also relied "heavily on the state-sponsored religious leaders (e.g., the shaykhs of Al-Azhar University) to interpret Islam as favoring family planning" (Ali 2002: 57). Within the program itself, family planning workers were trained in how to convince women that Islam did not prohibit the use of contraceptives. Thus, it was economic goals rather than religious understandings that were paramount in shaping the development of family planning in Egypt.

Egypt came to be considered a regional success in the area of population control, as its fertility and population growth declined; by 2008, its TFR had dropped to 3.0 and by 2014, 59 percent of women were using contraceptives (UNFPA Egypt). But after US funding dried up, and with social, economic, and political change occurring across the country, fertility rates increased to 3.5 by 2014, accompanied by higher population growth. Declaring that the two biggest threats to Egypt were terrorism and population growth, President Abdel Fattah al-Sisi announced a renewed focus on population and fertility in 2019. Promoting a message that "two is enough," the government hopes to provide services and messages that help to reduce the TFR from its rate of 3.5 in 2019 to 2.4 by 2030. At the time of writing, the Egyptian state has again worked to partner with Islamic leaders in this population work, and Al-Azhar, Egypt's top Sunni Muslim authority, has endorsed the program. But the state's move to bring Muslim leaders into its plans underscores the continuing wariness of many Egyptians to follow government policies around fertility decline. Taha Abou Hussein, a professor at the American University in Cairo, explained that "calls for birth control in Egypt are always resisted by the people, as many Egyptians believe that these calls are meant to change religious constants," and that population increase is not as harmful as the government contends (cited in Sabry 2021). The government's efforts to enlist Islamic leaders is an attempt to convince many Egyptians that the program is not just "a kind of harassment and restriction by the authorities," but rather an indication that Islam does not prohibit efforts to control fertility (Sabry 2021).

In many ways, and despite the 1971 Constitution declaring that "Islam is the religion of the state" (Article 2), Egypt's approach to reproduction and family planning is not very different from that of secular countries such as India, with a focus on economic growth and stability and the ways in which population and reproduction are connected to those goals. We will revisit Egypt's approach to controlling reproduction in Chapter 6, where we discuss the role of the US government and NGOs in shaping the program. But here, we see how economic goals have taken precedence over any religious concerns about fertility control.

Morocco: Women's Interpretations of Islam

In Morocco, we see a different relationship between state and religion. Morocco too claims Islam as its state religion and most of the population is Muslim. Morocco is a monarchy; the king claims direct descendancy from the Prophet Mohammed and is seen as the country's spiritual leader. It is the ways that Islam is characterized by the government as being opposed to the country's modernization goals that has led to religious tensions – including in areas of reproduction. But while Morocco shares with Egypt priorities of economic growth and population control over religious concerns, Islam in Morocco – as interpreted by Moroccan women themselves – actually bolsters women's readiness to use contraception.

In its efforts to achieve a modern country, the Moroccan government repealed a French colonial law that prohibited contraception in 1966, and has encouraged parents to use contraception to plan their families and have fewer children. The Moroccan state argues that planning and individual responsibility are necessary steps in the country's goal of economic prosperity, a discourse that is similar to that in several of the countries we have been discussing. But rather than soliciting the support of Muslim leaders as has happened in Egypt, state rhetoric positions Islam as an oppositional force to its own plans and frameworks for Morocco's economic and demographic future. A key factor that mitigates some potential opposition to state support of fertility control is that the king's religious legitimacy strengthens his political authority.

As in other places, poor and rural women, nearly all of whom are Muslim, struggle with seemingly contradictory edicts from the state and Islam about whether family planning is acceptable. But these women see connections between religion and family planning differently from how the state views them, demonstrating an interesting twist on the influence of religion. They do not believe their use of contraceptives is incompatible with their Muslim religious beliefs and express less concern about religious opposition to contraception than do Muslim women in other societies. Drawing from Islam's teachings of leading a good-quality life, women see a small number of children as a requirement to any financial or social success. Hughes Rinker describes how one rural woman relied on her own interpretation of Islam to justify her family planning. Contraceptive use allowed her and her family a better chance of economic survival:

> Nawal clearly and simply stated that God knows what is happening in her life, and therefore it is acceptable to use contraception to space her pregnancies. If she did not plan her pregnancies, she may not be able to physically, emotionally, or financially handle being a mother to

> children who are too close in age. According to her, God understands what people can and cannot bear and provides for them accordingly … For Nawal, Islam has taught her to control her fertility in order to make the most out of what God has given her. (Hughes Rinker 2013: 120)

In her discussion, Nawal referenced the Qu'ran to underscore how she was following Islamic principles of properly caring for her family and thus acting as a "good" Muslim woman.

In Morocco, then, women's faith influences their own reproductive decisions, and because of how they interpret Islamic teachings, they end up making decisions that support the state's own goals of smaller families and controlled population growth. As Hughes Rinker explains concerning rural women's assessment of contraception: "They did not discuss reproduction and medical practices in terms of rights, control, and power as the government … does, but replaced these terms with a vocabulary of religious beliefs and practices as well as motherhood" (2015: 237). The irony is that even though the state is concerned that religion might negatively influence its own development goals, it is their adherence to religious beliefs that makes it more likely that mothers and families will accede to state entreaties about family planning (Hughes Rinker 2015; Hughes 2011).

The lessons from Morocco and Egypt are twofold: even though Islam is an important force in both countries, it plays a different role in each, underscoring how the role of religion in population programs is shaped by social, political, and economic context. In addition, even within one society, different sectors – in Morocco, ordinary women and the state – interpret Islam differently and thus establish their own stance on Islam's relation to reproduction in different ways.

Islam's influence in Morocco reminds us that religion's role is not always predictable. Despite the state construction of Islam as opposed to modernity, individuals there draw from Islamic teachings and writings to support their own interest in using birth control and limiting the number of kids they have, in the end supporting state directives. Morocco also reminds us that even when women find ways to take some control of reproduction, that does not necessarily mean challenging gender structures or norms. Most women there continue to consider motherhood to be their own most important and proper role, and see family planning as helping them to be good mothers. In all places, it is clear that state economic and political goals are as likely as religion to shape reproductive programs and outcomes.

Morocco, Egypt, Brazil, and Poland are all examples where there is little separation between state and religion. Even so, religion's influence differs in each. The Catholic Church bolsters the state's reproductive agenda in Poland, but, in Brazil, it is the silence of the church that causes poor women to suffer the high cost of losing their children to poverty. In Egypt and Morocco, Islam is an important part of state rhetoric around population and reproduction, as the state in both countries works to find ways to temper the wariness that many Muslims feel toward fertility control programs.

US Reproductive Politics and the Role of the Religious Right

We only have to turn to debates about abortion in the United States to see that, even in countries where there is purportedly a clear and explicit (constitutional) separation between church and state, religion can influence laws and policies. In the US setting, the state does not operate alone in shaping reproductive access, as we saw in a country like Romania. Nor do we see the (Catholic) church seizing power and influence as it does in Poland. Nevertheless, state policies, religion, and control of reproduction – in the form of access and availability of contraceptives and abortion and reproductive health services – are strongly linked in the US. While certainly not all opposition to abortion comes from religious groups, or even from individuals with strong religious beliefs, it is nevertheless true that much of the funding and institutional support at work opposing abortion in the US comes from religious groups (Kotch 2019). Some Christian churches – predominant among them, the Catholic Church – have taken public stances against abortion. The Catholic Church opposes abortion in all circumstances and has given strong – financial and ideological – support to the anti-abortion movement. Some Protestant – especially evangelical – churches also oppose abortion in similar ways. But the Pew Foundation, a nonprofit and independent NGO, found that a majority of American adults from many faiths – including Jewish, mainline Protestant, historically Black Protestant, Muslim, Orthodox Christian, Hindu, and Buddhism – support legal abortion in all or most cases (Masci 2018). As tensions grow over reproductive rights, many religious denominations, churches, and religious groups are becoming more visible in their support for abortion rights. As one leader of the National Council of Jewish Women explained about efforts for religious groups to work together: "We're going to start together as diverse groups of faith, to pray and learn and sing together ... That feels like the right way to send the message that we are doing this work because of our faith and not in spite of it" (cited in Meyer 2021). The stances of these religious organizations mirror that of the general population. Polls show that 59 percent of Americans and 67 percent of American women disapproved of the Supreme Court's decision overturning Roe *v.* Wade, the 1973 decision that provided constitutional protection for abortion (Pandey 2022).

Nevertheless, Christianity has had a profound influence on reproductive politics in the US. Some of that influence comes about because those that do oppose reproductive freedom – in particular, Christian conservatives (the "Christian Right") – have been able to exert an influence larger than their actual representation in the population. The National Council of Jewish Women leader quoted above explained: "For too long, we've allowed a small but loud group from the religious right to dominate the narrative, and it's time we reclaim it" (Meyer 2021). But the Christian Right has established a well-organized and well-funded movement against laws and policies that would give women reproductive access and freedom. Abortion – its access and even its legality – has been shaped by an alliance of grassroots organizations, evangelical and other Christian churches, and Republican lawmakers, an alliance that connects religion, state, and reproduction in powerful ways. Linda Kintz points to

> the organizational genius of this movement, one that depends on highly efficient networks of prayer meetings. The Christian right's organization at the electronic grassroots level, its ownership of a broad spectrum of media and broadcast networks, and its operation of its own law and journalism schools, are among the most sophisticated practices in contemporary politics. (1994: 52)

In recent years,

> the anti-abortion movement has tried almost everything possible to try to stop legal abortion – it has attempted to amend the Constitution, change the composition of the Supreme Court, decrease the number

> of medical schools teaching abortion, stop women from entering clinics, reduce the number of professionals performing or assisting in the performance of abortions, and promote and culture of shame and stigma for women considering abortion. (Cohen and Joffe 2020: 9–10)

The efforts of anti-abortion activists resulted in the Supreme Court's overturning of Roe *v.* Wade in June 2022, allowing new state bans on abortions. Consequently, abortion is now legal only in some parts of the US. Yet even before the Court's decision, access to abortion and even contraceptives had become increasingly restricted in the last decade, with many efforts focused on state and local levels. By the time of the Supreme Court ruling, some 19 million women of reproductive age were already living in "contraceptive deserts" in the United States, residing in counties that do not offer a full range of contraceptive methods (Power to Decide 2019). The Court ruling has meant that abortion will be illegal in about half of the states in the US (Nash and Cross 2021). These restrictions affect women of color and poorer women most directly for at least two reasons: these groups are overly represented in those seeking abortions (Cohen and Joffe 2020: 13) and they are also least able to find the resources to navigate successfully around the roadblocks to abortion.

Even without a well-organized and well-funded religious movement, we would likely still see that religion plays a significant role in reproductive politics in the US. That comes about because, despite claims that state and religion are separate, the history of the US is one entwined with Protestant Christianity. From its founding through the present, Christianity has shaped most aspects of social life in the US (Bernstein and Jakobsen 2010). Thus, even the most "secular" of processes are steeped in a history that has been imbued with Christian principles and values. These values have influenced everything, including the importance of work, the acceptance or rejection of different family forms, and gender norms and expectations. Political leaders are often measured by their adherence to Christian beliefs, suggesting another entry point of religion into the state. The role of religion – what it is and what it should be – in American law and society remains a contentious issue. It is true that most Americans are not practicing Christians – not going to church or praying regularly – and the percentage that do has been steadily declining. But 70 percent of Americans still identify as Christian (PRRI Staff 2020), with only 9 percent saying they are atheist or agnostic – compared to 19 percent of Belgians saying they do not believe in god (Pew Research Center 2018); about 50 percent of Americans say that the Bible should influence American law (Lipka 2020).

Those opposed to reproductive advice about and access to abortion are able to draw from this continuing – if not always overtly public or acknowledged – Christian influence in American life. Arguments about the "moral majority" or a "Christian" embrace of motherhood are more powerful in a society where about a third of Americans believe that being Christian is essential to being a "true" American, a figure that compares to only 9 percent of people in Spain believing that being a Christian is necessary to being a Spaniard, despite Spain being a predominantly Catholic country (Stokes 2017). For example, the Christian Right has been effective in arguing for "family values" and their importance to American society, and in using those arguments to push their own agenda. They argue that family is central to US society's strength and stability; their support for a particular version of family – and against what they see as deviant forms (same-sex marriage, children outside marriage, blurred gender roles, or even comprehensive sex education in schools) – links Christianity and US political and social life in ways that are difficult to shut down or to counter as effectively as that initial messaging. For a politician to take a stand against family values seems to suggest a lack of support for something most Americans would see as important. "The conspiratorial fantasy that an overbearing state was actively working to insert itself in the 'traditional,' heterosexual family dominated conservative politics for more than 30 years, promoted in grassroots newsletters, conservative religious publications, right-wing talk radio, and GOP campaigns" (Young 2018). The naming of an anti-abortion stance as "pro-life" also makes clear the ways the Christian Right has been able to tap into rhetoric that, at least at first, seems to reflect broadly shared (Christian) values.

Christianity is thus a powerful force in American life; in a setting where Christian principles and beliefs have shaped the landscape, it is easier for some groups – like the Christian Right – to yield power and influence beyond their actual numbers. The US provides a way to understand the power of moral governance, the role of social norms in shaping reproduction, and the ways that religion shapes reproductive politics even in those countries where it is claimed that religion is constitutionally separate from the state (Razavi and Jenichen 2010).

Resistance

Efforts to restrict reproductive services and access do not go unchallenged. Many, perhaps most, acts of resistance happen quietly, and often privately, as individuals seek to reach their own reproductive goals by bypassing state laws or restrictions. Some of these everyday acts of resistance can be seen as "weapons of the weak," but the majority are actually some of the most effective ways to resist strictures that go against an individual woman's reproductive goals (Scott 1987, 1990).

We also see public, visible displays of resistance, efforts to push back against state, religious, or community rules that are seen as unfair and often unrepresentative of what most want. We saw that, in Poland, such resistance, which started as protests against restrictive abortion laws, has moved beyond reproductive issues and focused on more general state practices, such as state support of health care or small business. In Ecuador, where abortion is criminalized, groups such as Las Comadres provide women with medication to induce abortion. At the same time, Las Comadres and other groups are working to decriminalize abortion and thus provide easier access to the procedure for all women (Carpenter 2019). In 2018, after a long and difficult struggle that involved grassroots activism and coalitions of concerned parties, the citizens of Ireland overturned the existing restrictions on abortion and legalized the procedure in that largely Catholic country.

As we consider how religion and state have worked together and against each other to influence reproductive processes, it is worth noting how popular resistance to oppressive target-driven population control by the state can take religious overtones: Islamism in Egypt, Islamophobic Hindu majoritarianism in India, and, in the case of Poland, religious inflected resistance to "Godless" communism. Connections between state and religion are dynamic and fluid, as different players – individuals, communities, religions, or states – use religion to support their goals.

In the US, as powerful as the movement has been to restrict abortion access, resistance to anti-abortion actions has been ongoing for many years. Some of that resistance has happened at the state level. Over the last few years, as the threat to abortion legalization at the federal level became more real, several states, including Maine,

New York, Vermont, and the District of Columbia, asserted their states' rights and put into place protections that would mitigate any federal ruling against abortion access. Other resistance can be found at the most local level. For example, the Mississippi Reproductive Freedom Fund (MRFF), founded and led by Black women, works to support pregnant people and parents, but also acts to help fund abortion access. Mississippi has been one of the most restrictive states regarding abortion and abortion access and 91 percent of women in Mississippi live in counties that have no abortion services (Guttmacher Institute 2021). MRFF gives women a path to pursue their reproductive needs when they otherwise might not be able to (Grant 2019). In other areas of the US, small local groups, as well as national organizations such as Planned Parenthood, have also acted to make abortion access as widespread as possible, especially as access has been increasingly diminished across the US. For example, Planned Parenthood and other groups have opened clinics just over the borders of states that have outlawed abortion, allowing women in those states easier access to abortion. These changes may help to mitigate the effects of any legislation – especially at the local level – that narrows abortion access.

With these examples of the influence of religion on reproduction and women's lives generally, we can see that it is rarely religion per se that is key, but, rather, how religious texts, tenets, and even history, are interpreted. Interpretations – whether in Christianity or Islam or any other religion – differ across the hundreds of historical moments and current settings. The nearly 40 countries that are Muslim majority are located in the Middle East, in Northern and sub-Saharan Africa and in South and Southeast Asia and, as we might expect given that range, the restrictions, laws, expectations, and norms around reproduction vary greatly (Varley 2012; Obermeyer 1992). The same is true with Christianity, which has myriad sects and interpretations of key religious texts. Among the countries that support Christianity as a state religion, we see very different approaches to reproduction and its control. Even in places like the US, which claims a separation between church and state, religion can play a key role in shaping the reproductive landscape. While we are thus cautioned from assuming that religion has a single influence on reproduction, we also see how it can combine with other forces – political, economic, family, or other – to influence women's lives, reproduction, and its control. The leftist or rightist leanings of the state do not necessarily track with a particular stance on reproductive rights, gender equality, or the influence of religion. Where religion and state share assumptions about reproduction, gender, and ideal roles of women – as in Poland – it can mean that it is less likely that individual women are able to find ways to meet their reproductive needs.

In other places, religion institutions are silent on issues of reproduction, with significant consequences as well. In Egypt, state cooptation of most Islamic leaders on reproduction and family planning has allowed rhetoric about economic priorities to dominate social discourse around population and reproduction. Silence on the part of the powerful Catholic Church in Brazil can be interpreted as complicity on the part of the church in the neglect of poor women in northeast shantytowns. Women there have little way to confront state abuse and come to interpret their hardships as divine intervention rather than state neglect. In the US, religion's influence is often masked as concern over "family values." In any society, we can expect religious institutions to wield power in reproduction, especially in how it aligns with or opposes state population goals and controls. Resistance is similarly shaped by local politics, and takes many forms, as women and their families seek to reach their reproductive goals.

4
State and Family: Cooperation and Contestation

Like religion, family is a social institution that is vital to all societies but, while found everywhere, it differs in definition, form, and function across space and time. Nevertheless, however defined, family is the social institution that often plays an immediate role in shaping women's lives. Families can mediate the effect of other processes and institutions – including the state – on individuals and often acts as a link between the private and public processes of reproduction. But families are not necessarily simply safe havens or unified groups always working toward a shared purpose. They encompass hierarchy, nodes of power, and their own norms and values that shape the lives of individuals within them; in many societies, women claim an unequal place in these hierarchies. Thus, in the realm of reproduction, different family members – marriage partners, women, men, different generations, or others – may or may not share similar goals or desires. Given the importance of reproduction to all aspects of family, it is to be expected that this institution is a key player in contestations around reproduction, both within the family itself and with other institutions, including the state; those contestations leave women forced to navigate yet another set of competing and sometimes difficult tensions around reproduction. The examples we present here focus on how state and family – and women as family members – work both sometimes with and sometimes against one another to influence reproductive outcomes. How the state conceives of, supports, or restricts different family forms, structures, and processes has great influence on families and family members. But families influence state policies as well, as they work to carve out their own version of a future.

We begin with a look at how access to contraception and birth control has helped to transform family structure and relationships in many societies, often giving women more independence from patriarchal constraints; those changes underscore the power of reproduction in shaping societies and families. A second section looks at how maternalism is part of many state programs in Latin America. We also look at families in Japan and in Norway, countries that we rarely associate with explicit control of reproduction or population. Nevertheless, state regulations in both these countries, though indirect, play a powerful role in shaping families. For our last example, we return to China to describe a situation where state and family reproductive goals are often in conflict with one another and where women reside within those conflicts. In all these examples, we see the ways that individuals navigate reproduction as both a private and a public process, and how family and state remain deeply involved in these processes and in women's lives.

Birth Control, Family Constraints, and Women's New Lives

Women and others have long worked to control their fertility, using available means either to avoid or stop pregnancy, or to get pregnant and carry a pregnancy to term. As the history of birth control methods makes clear, women used potions, herbal remedies, or physical intervention to avoid or stop pregnancy (Jütte 2008). The development of modern, more reliable contraception, and its increasing accessibility, allowed women to bring reproduction more easily under their own control, often leading to enormous shifts in family relations. Reproduction and its control had been central to most families and communities, with those holding the most power – usually males and elders – having a dominant say in reproduction; the introduction of family planning into these families and communities often meant a disruption in – and concomitant struggles over – those long-existing family processes, hierarchies, and power structures (Gordon 2007), a further testament to the importance of reproduction and its role in social institutions like the family.

In the United States, the Food and Drug Administration (FDA) approved "The Pill" in 1960 and it quickly became widely available. Writing about the impact of newly accessible and reliable birth control, Letty Cottin Pogrebin, founding editor of *Ms.* magazine, recalled:

> The impact of The Pill was ... radical. It meant sex need not lead to pregnancy. But it wasn't just another form of contraception, it was an equalizer, a liberator, and easy to take. For the first time in human history, a woman could control her sexuality and determine her readiness for reproduction by swallowing a pill smaller than an aspirin. Critics warned that The Pill would spawn generations of loose, immoral women; what it spawned was generations of empowered women who are better equipped to make rational choices about their lives. (CNN 2010)

In the US, the timing of the widespread distribution of birth control that was both reliable and under women's control, including The Pill, coincided with women's movement into the labor force, which had begun during World War II and continued thereafter. By 1950, one-third of all women worked for wages, sometimes in part-time work, sometimes after their children had started school, and sometimes full time. Women from working-class families had long worked for wages, as did African American women, but there was an increasing acceptance of women working outside the home across most classes and racial/ethnic groups. Reliable birth control played a part in these changes, allowing "challenges to traditional sources of male supremacy ... and [allowing] women [to] gain personal dignity from limiting their fertility and earning money" (Solinger 2019: 142). As Linda Gordon (2007: 8) argued, "there has [always] been a strong connection between women's emancipation and their ability to control reproduction."

Although it often occurred later than in places like the US, accessibility to birth control has had an equally profound influence across the world, transforming the lives of women and families in ways that have been nothing less than transformative. In some places, reliable birth control has been welcomed by entire families, allowing them to plan their futures and manage their economic situation. But in other places, where fertility desires have differed among family members, the introduction of birth control has often shifted the balance of power within families. Where women's own preferences differ from those around her, access to family planning methods, especially to methods that are under her own control, can give women independence from family control and familial demands, again underscoring how control of women and control of reproduction often go hand in hand.

An example of the impact of family planning access on women's lives can be found in Uganda. In 2020, the total fertility rate for the country as a whole was 5.54. While one of the highest in the world, that figure reflects a drop from 6.26 in 2010. Some women and their husbands believe that how many children they have should be up to God and that any interference in the form of birth control indicates a lack of religious faith (Potasse and Yaya 2021). But also important in understanding Uganda's reproduction rate is the number of women who would have preferred to have fewer children. The estimate that some 40 percent of the female population face barriers to accessing birth control suggests the difficulties that Ugandan women have in trying to manage their reproductive goals. Rural women have the greatest trouble accessing reproductive health services or obtaining contraceptives because of factors such as economic barriers and the distance to clinics.

Gender inequality plays a significant role in these processes, especially in rural Uganda. Such inequality can come at a community level, as when the government is not willing or able to fund reproductive services, or at the family level, when husbands will not permit their wives an independent decision on contraceptive use. Many rural women report that family members, especially husbands, make it difficult for them to use contraceptives. Ugandan husbands often see wives bearing many children as a sign of respect, and are reluctant for their wives to use contraception to limit births (Potasse and Yaya 2021). A (male) participant in one study done in Uganda's Kingdom of Buganda region explained: "This place belongs to a culture named Buganda whereby men have the tendencies to determine the number of children the wife should produce, so that is one hindrance" (Potasse and Yaya 2021: 6). Because men control family finances as well, it is can be difficult for women to find an independent way to get access to contraception, which might involve fees for transportation to a clinic, and/or the cost of contraception itself. As one health administrator described, "A woman doesn't have a voice ... A man has to decide. Even if a woman was doing something, earning, it's the man who is responsible. It is the man who is the owner of everything. The woman cannot own children, cannot own animals, you name it" (Heinz and Roth 2019: 197). Under these conditions, many women welcome NGO-sponsored programs that provide reproductive services. Women have used those services sometimes with, but sometimes without, their husbands' knowledge. Many clients spoke of how family planning allowed them to manage the size of their families or permitted them to space their births to protect the health of their children. One commented about using family planning to space her births:

> I am using family planning methods. Child spacing so I can get time off to rest my body and take care of the young kids as well. So, by the time I give birth, this one is at least of age. I'll give birth again when my child is in school, that's when I will have the next one. I want that time in between so that I can work and prepare for the next one coming. (Heinz and Roth 2019: 209)

Many studies have found that women's contraceptive use and the control it gives them over reproduction is positively associated with higher education, with labor force participation, and with women's access to money. While access to contraception is clearly necessary for all women, it is what tends to accompany that access that gives women newfound independence within the family. Studies from across the world indicate that contraceptive access and use often comes with other changes, including urbanization and rising income levels (Mason 1986), but also with changes specific to women: higher education for girls and women, increases in women's labor force participation, and women's greater access to money (Balk 1994; Riley 1998; Kishor 1995). Education for girls can open new opportunities for women, and give them access to information and services that allow them greater control over their lives. A study done in Nigeria found that women who had received even a single year of education had more say in decisions in their families (Caldwell and McDonald 1982). Even that small amount of schooling gave a woman more access to community information and resources and made her more likely to assert herself within her family. She was more likely to insist on taking a sick child to a clinic, even against the advice of elder family members. If there were reproductive health services in the community, she might be able to translate that stronger voice to gain better access to reproductive health and methods of fertility control, a connection between women's autonomy and reproductive control that research has found in many societies (Haile and Enqueselassie 2006; Jejeebhoy 1995; Morgan and Niraula 1995; Biswas et al. 2017). While autonomy is defined differently in different places (Riley and DeGraff 2018), it often measures women's ability to move about the community on their own, without male supervision; to participate in decisions regarding the household or children; and to have access to and control of money in the family.

But in the societal shifts that occur during such transitions, women can also lose out, as the power that motherhood gives them can be undermined by the demands of a new society. Buchi Emecheta captured the importance of a changing context in her novel, *The Joys of Motherhood*. In that story, Nnu Ego, a village woman in Nigeria, experiences societal changes at first hand. In her village, motherhood is a necessary and highly desired role, and having many children gives women power. Children were women's wealth, their source of support, their joy. It is a reminder that women have often seen motherhood as a source of power, giving them a support system in their children, and the power to shape the lives of the next generation (Blackwood 2000; Wolf 1972). The meaning of motherhood undergoes abrupt change when Nnu Ego moves to Lagos, and she and her new husband struggle to feed and support their growing family. In the city, having many children is a burden and motherhood is not a revered status; there, the ability to find an income is most important. Nnu Ego's story depicts how motherhood is interpreted in these different contexts. In the village, wealth flowed from children to parents, with more children meaning that parents were usually better off (Caldwell 1976). But in an urban environment, where a market economy shapes life, children become a liability; too many children can sap a family's resources and ability to survive. The number of kids Nnu Ego has to care for, combined with the precarious place she and her husband hold in the expanding labor market, makes her life very difficult. As is true for women in many such situations, Nnu Ego focuses her efforts on helping her children; her income is used to give them the education and training they need to participate in the new market economy. At the end of Emecheta's story, with Nnu Ego's help, her children have found success, with good careers. But Nnu Ego herself does not fare well. By the end of the story, she has lost any of the status, authority – or joy – that motherhood might have brought her in the village. She ends up dying alone in the city. Her story exemplifies how the ideal number of children a woman has depends on context, and that with urbanization and a growing and spreading global economy, parents are likely to think about the ideal number of children differently; limiting family size and putting resources into fewer children might make more sense in the new economy. *The Joys of Motherhood* is a fictional tale, but one found in many communities across the world, as women's lives and expectations often undergo profound and complex change as societies shift and move toward a market economy, and attitudes toward fertility adjust to the new situation.

While we know that family planning programs can help women control their own reproduction and change their lives and their families in profound ways, we are still trying to understand what other benefits accrue from these programs and reproductive services more broadly. We assess programs further in later chapters, but here mention one recent controversy over how to evaluate a family planning program's success. A follow-up study undertaken in Matlab, Bangladesh, was carried out to assess the long-term effects of contraception adoption on women's lives (Barham, et al. 2021). The researchers revisited an innovative program established in Matlab in the 1970s, which was created to understand what kind of family planning initiatives might work best in highly religious (Muslim), poor rural communities. In one area of Matlab, women were provided with easy access to contraception, mostly through home delivery. In another area, women's access was not so easy or convenient. The new program was considered a success; where women had easy access to contraception, they quickly adopted family planning, and the number of children they had fell. The program's success influenced other programs across the world.

When they revisited Matlab 35 years later, the researchers expected to see long-term effects of these family planning programs and the smaller families that resulted. Instead, they found that women who had used contraception did not have vastly different lives from those who had not: the former were neither wealthier, nor even healthier than the latter. These findings surprised some, especially because it seemed to undermine some of the arguments in favor of strong access to family planning, in particular the economic benefits that are likely to accrue. Some researchers pointed out that it was only one study, or one location, and that other research has underscored that family planning can have significant effects on women's economic and social well-being. Other research (e.g., Lam and Duryea 1999; Joshi and Schultz 2013) has shown that, even if the women who use contraception and had fewer children were themselves no better off than women who had more children, their children nevertheless benefited, receiving more education and higher cognitive scores: "The increased time and resources available to women when they have fewer children are mostly invested directly into their children" (Lam 2021: 30). But the Matlab researchers themselves made an important point about the findings; as one of them, Randall Kuhn, explained: "The main translation of our results is that you shouldn't expect [family planning] programs to improve women's economic wealth ... It should be enough that they reduce family size. If you want them to improve women's economic well-being, you would need to do a bunch of other things" (cited in Luscombe 2021). Indeed, despite the program's successes in decreasing fertility levels, critics point to how the organization of the program did not disrupt gender inequalities in the area:

> Door-to-door delivery to women in purdah was an effective means to get contraceptives to village women, but that approach fail[ed] to disturb and may even [have] reinforce[d] the patriarchal structures that keep women isolated and vulnerable ... Contraception cannot solve the larger problem of women's subordination, which ... should be addressed more directly. (Schuler et al. 1995: 137)

If the goal is to better women's lives, then access to reproductive health services is important, but such services alone are not sufficient. Other programs that enable women to fully participate in community life, by providing access to education, to good jobs, and to positions of power, are also important.

We are not arguing that access to reproductive health services is not key. But, as we will see in later chapters, family planning programs are often supported because of the economic benefits they are thought to enable – to women themselves, but also to communities or societies. The politics – local and global – that often come with these family planning programs mean that these programs can sometimes act as Trojan horses, bringing new ideology and connections to the global economy, some of which may not be completely welcome. This study of Matlab results reminds us that women should have access to reliable reproductive health services, including contraception, not because it might serve some distant goal but because it gives them control over their own reproduction. As Kuhn has argued, "Family planning is wonderful because it gives people control [over] their own bodies and because it leads to fewer unwanted pregnancies" (cited in Luscombe 2021). Even as women's new independence over reproductive decisions can shake up family authority, access for its own sake is an important accomplishment.

Motherhood in Latin America

As further evidence of the ways that family and state are linked, we turn to Latin America to consider maternalism. Maternalist ideologies construct and view women as having – or potentially having – unique values associated with motherhood, including nurturance, caring, and self-sacrifice. Maternalism has existed for centuries, in many societies, and is used by different groups for their own agendas. Often eliding the differences between mothers and women, maternalism has been used to support increasing women's power in the public sphere (bringing the domestic into the public). For example, some women argued for the right to vote – in the US or in Chile, among other places – reasoning that, because women are more peace-loving and responsible than men, women as voters would make society better. At other times, maternalism is used to bolster arguments that women need to be kept in their place at home and in the family, an approach that may "have the effect of re-traditionalizing gendered roles and responsibilities" (Molyneux 2007: iii). We saw that kind of stance in Poland, where some church and state officials have argued that women, as mothers or potential mothers, need "protection," which justifies cutting back their rights to paid work or reproductive services.

While it is prevalent in many parts of the world, maternalism and actions based on that ideology have a long and deep history in Latin America; Ramm asserts it is "a mother-centered region" (2020: 20). Kin networks are very strong both for poorer families, which find them necessary for survival, and for richer families, which build strong business or political networks from them. As is true in any society, gender plays a significant organizing principle in families, in kin networks, and in society more generally. But in much of Latin America, family ideology and the strong influence of religion come together to construct gender in ways that often equate women with motherhood.

> Catholic teachings define gender roles as complementary, and motherhood is asserted as the essence of women's nature. Motherhood

> is conceived as self-sacrifice and self-abnegation, and women are expected to "choose" motherhood as their destiny so as to comply with God's will ... Hence women should devote their lives to their families, and families are seen as an antidote to individualism and social conflict. (Ramm 2020: 21)

Thus, women are expected to sacrifice their own interests as they devote themselves to their families and see them through any difficulties. Such ideologies reduce women's roles and identities to that of mother, closing off alternatives. We look at how "women's primary private responsibility [gets translated] into public policy" (Koven and Michel 1993, cited in Ramm 2020: 13) by looking at what has happened in Chile over the past few decades.

In Chile, family has long been considered the foundation of the nation, where important socialization and social reproduction takes place. Chilean governments, whether left- or right-leaning, have regularly built policy on that assumption, and with a maternalist lens: that women, *as mothers*, need to be protected and supported. Consequently, some measures of women's health (maternal mortality and health, for example) have improved and remain strong (UNICEF 2022) and women who are trying to balance work and family responsibilities can benefit from state support. But at the same time, these policies both limit women's claims to equality and restrict the number of women who are to be supported by state policies. Thus, when Chile supports mothers, it underscores and heightens an essentialist version of gender, one that sees women and men as fundamentally different, and defines women through their role as mothers.

In the Salvador Allende era (1970–3), the socialist government touted the need for gender equality and for giving women more say in society, but these measures were built on maternalistic principles. "Allende's conservative view of women as mothers ... resulted in generous policies for mothers and less initiatives promoting gender equity" (Goldsmith Weil 2020: 76). An illustration of how a maternalist approach can both support mothers and undermine women can be seen in the Allende government's programs, which were directed at women. In an effort to reduce child malnutrition, Allende began a milk program, which has continued to operate – under very different political regimes – for decades. It promised to provide a daily half liter of milk to every child under the age of 15. The program was controversial and not always successful; it was often mismanaged and not everyone wanted the milk (Goldsmith Weil 2020: 78). But importantly for its legacy, it was based on a premise that the state should provide the resources for improving the health of mothers and children. The program has been deemed a success in the ways that it has helped reduce child mortality and malnutrition and increased mothers' connections to local health centers. The maternalist premise on which the program was modeled continues to undergird state programs in Chile today (Alvarez Minte 2020). Chile has provided generous state support for mothers, but, at the same time, it has been a country where women have had the least access to reproductive services in the region; that too was reflected in the Allende government approach, when it suspended internationally funded birth control programs, which also had long-term consequences. In Chile, women's health care is focused on providing support for pregnant women, but much less attention has been paid to the provision of wider reproductive health care and services such as family planning. Abortion has been completely banned and criminalized in Chile since 1989; only in 2017 did a new law begin to decriminalize abortion and to permit it in some limited circumstances, such as rape or when the mother's life is in danger (Aljazeera 2021). Challenging Chile's long history of maternalist state policies, Gabriel Boric, the newly elected president in 2022, made attention to gender equity – not motherhood – one of his campaign promises. Among his promises to address gender issues, he has vowed to work toward increasing all women's sexual and reproductive rights, including access to contraception and abortion (Saez 2022).

When we look closely at the use of maternalism and reproduction, we see that, while it can and has been used by feminists to claim a place in society, or to push back on some oppressive laws, it is also frequently used by the state to discipline women. Key to these maternalist policies are how they support not gender equality, or even all women, but rather a specific version of gender and motherhood: "mothers at the service of the state" (Molyneux 2007). "Respectable mothers, who are formally married, are conventionally considered to be deserving of social protection. By contrast, unmarried mothers have been marginalized from receiving social benefits. Unmarried mothers are traditionally labeled as immoral, as their sexuality is not controlled by a formal male partner" (Ramm 2020: 16). State policies reinforce these conventions and, at the same time, discipline women and their sexuality and reproduction.

Resisting Family Pressure in Japan

In Japan, the state has had a large hand in reproduction, but less for its direct rules regarding numbers of children than for how it has prioritized the economy – and a particular economic model – over the needs, desires, and challenges of families, women, and men. Thus, in its *absence* of family policy, we can trace how the state informs reproductive outcomes.

In recent years, the media, government officials, and ordinary citizens have expressed concern about Japan's population crisis – labeled by different names: a baby crisis, a marriage problem, a women problem, an aging problem. Each of these terms highlights a perceived cause or consequence of the overall phenomenon: Japan's very low fertility. In fact, fertility began to fall in Japan shortly after World War II, when it began its decline from a TFR of 4.5 to 2.0 by 1957 (Tsuya 2017). The TFR continued to decline in the 1970s, and now hovers around 1.3 (see Figure 4.1). Fertility at this level has a number of consequences, including very fast aging of the

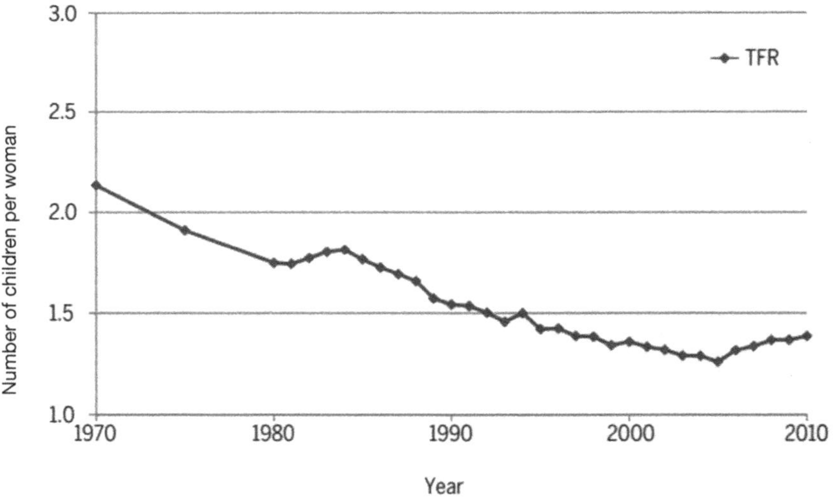

Figure 4.1. Total fertility rate (TFR) in Japan: below-replacement fertility has continued for decades
Source: Roberts 2016: 42

population and, over time, a decline in overall population. Many see this situation as a population "crisis," with some referring to it as a "demographic time bomb" – ironically – invoking the earlier alarmist language of the demographic nightmare of *over*population. In the media and in academic research, many discuss how this demographic situation will likely hurt the economy and Japan's standing in the world. Even those who use less alarmist language still agree that Japan's aging population needs addressing; in 2015, 27 percent of the country's population was aged 65 and above, and that proportion is projected to grow to 40 percent by 2060. That kind of age composition suggests a shortage of workers in the labor force, and an acute need for facilities and staffing to care for the elderly. But while there is widespread agreement about the challenges of an aging population, and even the need for a stronger safety net, there is more disagreement about what has led to such low fertility and, in particular, what should be done about it. Gender and family are at the center of these disagreements, but so is the role of the state in setting economic and social priorities: should it be the economy, or the welfare (and survival) of the people that gets first priority?

Many countries across the world have experienced fertility decline. In most cases, lower fertility comes about because individual women are having fewer children than did their mothers and grandmothers. But the fertility decline in Japan and other countries in Asia over recent decades has come about at least partly because women are postponing marriage until their later childbearing years, or not marrying at all. Indeed, Japan's marriage rate has also been declining, and reached a new low in 2020 (Hisanaga 2021). Thus, while this might result in a "baby crisis," especially because Japan sees little childbearing outside of marriage, some declare this evidence of a "woman problem." Some pundits point to evidence that women are not fulfilling their family and national obligations to establish families and bear and raise children, while others argue that this is evidence that women are resisting Japan's traditional focus on narrow gender roles, which ignores women's needs and limits their opportunities.

However the interpretations are couched, what is clear is that individual and family goals are inconsistent with and actually damaging to the goals of society and state, and underscore how reproductive goals, outcomes, and interests are constructed by different social institutions, often in contradictory ways. Similar disagreement can be seen in arguments about the most effective way to respond to the crisis of low fertility. Some focus on the need to care for a growing proportion of elderly people, and argue for widening state support for this group, through subsidies, increased provision of services, and newly created institutions to house and care for Japan's aging population. Such increased state contribution would directly challenge what has widely been viewed as a family responsibility. Others focus on women's resistance to marriage and childbearing. Whereas in 2000 only 10 percent of women aged 35 to 39 had never married, by 2020, that had reached 25 percent (Rich 2019), reflecting a sharp change in how women are thinking about marriage. But there are disagreements about what these lower marriage rates mean. Seeing the increased numbers of women in the labor force, some argue that the state needs to provide more and better child care facilities, and create other ways for women to balance family and work demands. But others see women's refusal to marry and have children as resistance against strict and unequal gender roles. Evidence for this perspective comes from the division of labor in families; even when women are working outside the home, they continue to have near-total responsibility for the home and for childrearing (see Figure 4.2), with men making some of the lowest contributions to family work of any country in the world (Roberts 2016). One official in Oita Prefecture argued that men will have to do more if Japan wants to reverse the fertility decline, explaining: "Women won't have children unless their husbands share child-rearing chores" (Kazue 1995: 15). Other observers focus on how single women contemplating their future are opting out of those unequal responsibilities, seeing their single lives as providing better opportunities for personal growth and a balanced work/private life (Rich 2019). This perspective suggests that the state could make marriage and motherhood more attractive to women by changing the demands of the labor market.

More support for the influence of the labor market also comes from attention to men and their own reluctance to marry. As we can see in Figure 4.3, while the proportion of women never marrying by age 50 has risen in recent years, even more steep has been the rise in the proportion of men who never marry. By 2010 it had reached over 10 percent, a significant rise from its level of around 2 percent in 1970. Explanations for men not marrying usually point to the changing shape of the labor market. Since the mid-twentieth century, the best and most sought-after jobs in Japan have been "regular" jobs, most of which are filled by men; they provide men with benefits and,

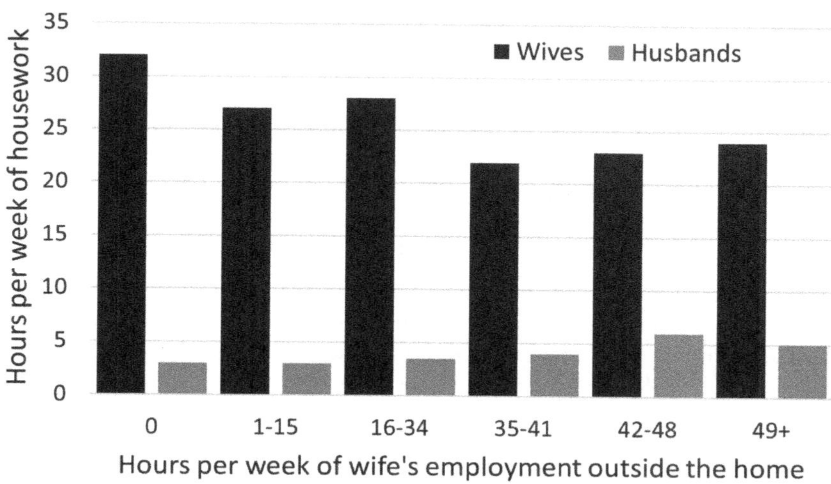

Figure 4.2. Wives' and husbands' average housework hours per week by wives' weekly employment hours, Japan 2009
Source: Compiled from Tsuya 2017

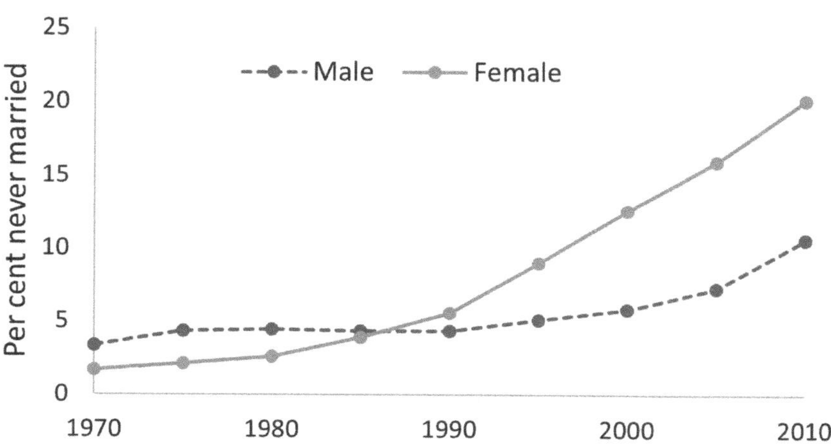

Figure 4.3. Trends in proportion of those never married at age 50, Japan
Source: Roberts 2016: 6

essentially, lifelong employment. Landing such a job means a man is ready to marry, knowing that he will be able to provide for the family (Semuels 2017). But changes in the economy in recent decades and the ways in which Japan has tried to grow its economy have resulted in an increasing number of men being unable to achieve such job security; instead, they are hired into irregular, often precarious, jobs that come with a low salary that makes it difficult to plan for the future. Without financial security, they themselves are unlikely to see marriage as possible, but they are also much less likely to be seen by women as potentially good husbands and fathers, another reason some women eschew marriage. Women themselves are usually in irregular jobs throughout their working years, in most cases expecting to quit employment to raise a family. Indeed, the shape of the job market makes it very difficult for anyone to combine work and family. The model worker in Japan is a man, without household responsibilities. One of the complaints about regular jobs is how men are not able to devote time to their families, even if they wanted to. Employers' expectations that workers will be available in evenings and on weekends, working long days and traveling frequently, make it difficult for men to have any time for their families (Semuels 2017). Thus, it is both women and men who are unable or unwilling to marry and form families in Japan in the current economic situation. And that lower rate of marriage, combined with reluctance within marriage to have more than one child, is a major contributor to Japan's low fertility.

The state has responded, but in limited ways. Its major efforts have been focused on ways that might allow couples to balance work and family life. These include direct payments to parents who bear a child, parental leave initiatives, and increased investment in child care facilities. But many believe these efforts do not go far enough (Inagawa 2018). Child compensation payments are not available to all workers. The parental leave regulations lack teeth, and many parents are unable to access parental leave compensation, especially workers in small companies, which is where a large proportion of women work (Tsuya 2017). Child care facilities have increased, but waiting lists are long, with many parents still unable to secure a place for their children. One respondent in a study on families in Japan argued that raising children has become too difficult: "Women's burden is too high. Economically also, it's not easy. If you want to get work, you can't find a daycare center. Every door is shut (*happo fusigari*). We have to do something about women's burden. It's too great" (Roberts 2016: 48). Most importantly, these state measures have not resulted in any measurable change in the fertility rate, suggesting just how ineffective they have been.

Many argue that it is women who are bearing much of the pressure of Japan's crises. In recent years, the state has been asking women to bear the burden of solving the nation's economic and demographic crisis. Under a policy dubbed "womenomics," former Prime Minister Abe encouraged women to "increase their labor force participation ... shoulder the brunt of childcare and housework, find a spot in daycare for the baby despite lengthy waiting lists, put up with a corporate culture that is unfriendly to parents, and hope that the in-laws or their own parents do not fall ill, less they be requested to provide eldercare" (Roberts 2016: 48). Considering the list of women's responsibilities and the near impossibility of being able to meet all of them, women's resistance to marriage and motherhood becomes more understandable. One researcher has argued: "Women do not want their bodies to be used as instruments of population policy which is why they are indifferent, at best, toward government concerns about the dwindling population" (Kazue 1995: 19). Indeed, as another feminist, Ashino Yoriko, argued in the early years of these debates:

> What's wrong with the low birthrate? ... Japan's emphasis on economic growth has forced an unwanted life on its women. If the country's concern with efficiency goes too far, women and the elderly and the handicapped will end up being unwelcome members because they won't contribute to the nation's economic progress. (Cited in Kazue 1995: 20)

From her perspective, Japan's low birth rate is really about the priority that Japan has put on expanding and growing its economy, often at the expense of its people.

Support for Families in Norway

In some ways, Norway makes an interesting contrast to Japan, adding another perspective on how gender, low fertility, families, and the state interact in effecting demographic outcomes. Ashino

Yoriko, the Japanese feminist quoted above criticizing Japan's focus on the economy, also argues that, in places like Norway, state interventions are less focused on increasing the birth rate or growing the economy than on improving the welfare of its people. While some see the description "nanny state" in reference to Norway and other countries as negative, others are more accepting of how it describes a focus on social welfare rather than more narrowly on the economy and economic growth.

Norway has been closely watched by many who are concerned about too-low fertility. Research has shown that fertility is more likely to increase when there are higher levels of gender equality (Myrskylä et al. 2011; Dommermuth et al. 2017). In Norway, gender equity is an explicit component and focus of state policies, partly because of an apparent belief that gender equality is an important goal in itself, as Kazue argues above. But Norway is also attentive to the effects on fertility and population that gender parity regulations might have. Norway's support for gender equality includes a wide variety of programs, such as state-funded child care for all, generous parental leave policies, and efforts to bring more women into high levels of government, to attention to gender inequality in the workplace. These all have the potential effect of making it easier for women (and men) to balance full-time labor force involvement and family, and that balance, many argue, is key to raising fertility rates. For decades, some parental leave has been offered to both parents, and parents could design their child care according to their own circumstances. But in the early 1990s, Norway also explicitly targeted fathers in their regulations, adding "daddy leaves" that were not transferable: fathers had to either take the offered (paid) leave, or lose it. (Mothers also received nontransferable leave, but they had long taken advantage of such leave, while fathers had not.) Norwegian officials hoped that such interventions would encourage more involvement in parenting by fathers, and that that involvement would lead to more gender equality within families and in society more generally (Apolitical.com 2018).

More fathers did, in fact, begin to take parental leave; between 1992 and 1997, after the new rules took effect, the percentage of men taking leave rose from 2.4 to 70 percent (Apolitical.com 2018). In addition, changes in the law have influenced how much time men spend on leave; when the length of state-sponsored leave increased, men spent more time at home. The influence of state support in this area may be evidenced by how some three-quarters of men currently take the exact amount of leave time stipulated by law. Beyond the actual time men spend with their young children, the policies seem to have influenced gender norms more broadly. Margunn Bjørnholt, a Norwegian sociologist, observed that "fathers started taking leave, and it has probably had an effect in terms of the cultural norms around parenting … in Norway today, it would be very hard to insist on just being the breadwinner and not caring about the children" (cited in Apolitical 2018). Others have argued that these directed leaves have had further results; women are able to rejoin the labor force more quickly after childbirth, and, because they are able to balance family and work, they are more likely to opt to have more children, thus increasing Norway's low fertility rate.

But it should also be noted that while these policies seem to have influenced gender, families, the workforce, and fertility, they have not led to complete gender equality. Women in Norway are still much more likely to take longer parental leave than men, leading to the "motherhood penalty" that is seen in most societies, whereby women lose their status and place in the labor force because of time taken to care for children. In addition, women also do the lion's share of housework in most families (Lammi-Taskula 2006). And some research has shown that the gender differential in housework has a major impact on fertility decisions. Women in gender-unequal households are much less likely to have a child at all, let alone more than one (Dommermuth et al. 2017). Such findings suggest that gender equality is indeed related to fertility levels, but it is gender equality at both the society *and* family levels that matter. Government support for working mothers helps women lead more balanced lives, but their continuing "double day," working both outside jobs and responsible for most of the housework, discourages them from having (more) children. Many other countries are watching Norway and other Nordic countries to learn more about how gender equality – and the state's role in facilitating such gender equality – play out. In all industrialized societies, women have a heavier burden than men trying to balance family and work, and that discourages them from having more children, or sometimes any children. While states in some countries like Norway have chosen to intervene in these processes, attempting to find ways that support women and their families in their reproductive goals, others, like Japan, are more reluctant to step too far into family processes like reproduction or division of household labor and child care. The ways in which reproduction is both a private and a public issue makes it likely that the proper or most effective role of the state in these processes will remain contested.

Caught between Family and State in China

The gap between state and family goals around childbearing and reproduction has been glaring over the past several decades in China. As we saw in Chapter 2, in 1980, China instituted a very restrictive and well-enforced policy that limited the number of children any couple could have; the state's goal was to use "birth planning policies" to slow China's population growth (Riley 2017b). Urban couples were allowed no more than one child and most rural couples were able to have only two children. Urban families found these restrictions easier to cope with than did many rural families, even if they disagreed with state regulations. In urban areas, because most workers could expect to receive a pension and other government support, parents were not as dependent on their children and did not perceive the number (and gender) of their children to be as threatening as did rural families. There, where government support was scarce, parents and families believed that, without the right number and gender of children, their very survival was in jeopardy; consequently, resistance to the state's policies was much stronger and more widespread in rural than in urban areas.

Women became caught between family and state in these struggles over reproduction. For centuries, men of all ages were favored over women, who were subordinate in all aspects of their lives. Women were expected to marry men chosen by others, and to live in their husband's family's house and village; one of their most important duties was to produce sons for their husband's family. But even though women's and men's interests were not always aligned in these families, in most, women and men both wanted children, including sons. Men wanted children who would carry on the family line and contribute to the family economy as they got older. Women wanted children who would form a woman's "uterine family," family members who were devoted to their mother and would take her side in family disputes (Wolf 1972). Often, both fathers and mothers wanted sons because it was sons who would take care of their parents

– fathers and mothers – in their old age. Thus, while there was great gender inequality in Chinese families, women found ways to make their families work for them, even within the confines of a strict patriarchy (Kandiyoti 1988).

But most of the elements that allowed women to take a carefully negotiated position in their families were stripped away when birth policies were implemented, leaving women caught between two powerful social institutions and inflicting an enormous burden on the birth planning process. When the state imposed birth restrictions on families, it was women who were targeted and directly subjected to scrutiny and monitoring. When punishment for violating policy was enacted, it was women's bodies that bore the punishment, in the form of forced abortion or IUD insertions. At the same time, the family expected and encouraged women's resistance, hoping the family could elude state officials and produce the desired son. Thus, women were encouraged and expected to take bodily risks in order for the family to achieve its own goals, and resist the power of the state (White 2010).

Today, China has overturned its birth restrictions. Worried about an aging population and too-low fertility, the state is encouraging couples to have more than one child. Though the state goals have changed, it is still women who are targets of state campaigns. While many government messages are directed at young couples, it is women who bear the brunt of these campaigns. Because women do much more child care and housework than men in China (Riley 2017a), even though they are well represented in the labor force, it is they who struggle to balance family and work.

While the clash between family and state goals is often not as obvious and clear elsewhere as it is in China, there are often differences between these social institutions in many societies. Few countries have as heavy a hand in policies surrounding reproduction as does China, but nevertheless, state interest in fertility and population is often in contention with the reproductive goals and desires of families. In state support of or disagreement with family goals, women can get caught, pressured from different sides to meet expectations and bearing the burden that attention and pressure to conform to others' reproductive goals inevitably brings.

Looking at the ways that religion, family, and state work together and against each other around issues of reproduction underscores how individuals "make their 'voluntary' reproductive choices in an institutional context that severely constrains them" (Blake 1994:168). Social institutions are not always aligned with each other in their reproductive expectations, but they are all powerful influences on the lives, decisions, and bodies of citizens in any society. When acting in conjunction with one another, whether directly or indirectly, the force they bring to bear can be significant. Individuals regularly find ways to navigate these powerful currents; indeed, we have seen resistance even in the face of restrictions, harsh punishment, or bodily harm. Nevertheless, the examples in these last two chapters underscore the ways that the lives of individuals are rarely able to escape the constraints and opportunities created by religion, the family, and the state, and the powerful control they exert over reproduction in any society.

5

State Management of Reproduction in the Making and Unmaking of Communities

One of the central reasons that states seek to control reproduction and women is the role that reproduction plays in the construction and maintenance of the nation-state around particular images and goals. In that process, reproduction is both a conduit to such control and shaping and a way of conceptualizing alternative visions. From this perspective, "reproductive politics-as-a-way-to-solve problems reflects a belief that the social, economic, political and moral problems that beset our country can be solved best if laws, policies, and public opinions press women to reproduce or not in ways that are consistent with a particular version of the country's real needs" (Solinger 2019: 13). These visions nearly always involve calculations about how population might impact national economic outcomes, as China's birth planning efforts demonstrate, or demographic strength relative to neighboring countries, as we saw was the case in Romania. But they also nearly always involve population composition: who is bearing children, who is not, and who should or should not be. Central to the imagined nation or community (Anderson 1991) are considerations of race, ethnicity, gender, religion, and class. That is, the policies that are developed and applied to reach population goals are applied differently to different communities. Are immigrants included in the vision of the nation's future? Are all religious groups equally welcome as citizens? What role does race or ethnicity play in that imagined community? In these processes,

> regulation of sexual and reproductive practices has been informed by an ideal of nationhood that at once unifies and excludes. Practices

> such as marriage, sexual intimacy, abortion, assisted conception, and adoption have all been regulated in the name of a national need for cultural distinction and not simply in terms of their own rightness or wrongness. (Fletcher 2005: 368)

Women, "as biological and cultural reproducers of the nation" (Sekhon 1999: 226) are always in the sights of those trying to influence the demographic future. It is women's bodies that undergo pregnancy and bear children, and it is women who do most of the work of raising children in any community. Shaping reproduction means controlling women. That control hinges on whether a woman (and her family) is perceived as belonging, or a threat to, the imagined nation.

And as these processes are key for states, so too do they play out in communities. Reproduction is part of the way in which communities envision and shape the community to fit their goals of what it should look like, who is part, and who is not part, of the community, and how it might look in the future. Demographic form and size are regularly perceived as key to the survival and future of any community; that is true from both outsiders' and insiders' perspective. Reproduction is both a threat and a source of power. The stakes can be very high.

As we will see, population policies follow those imaginations and target differently those perceived as helping the state or community to reach its goals and those seen as threats to them. Reproduction is also important to those who might be resisting these processes, who are vying for a place in the community, or working for survival of a marginalized community. Through explicit and less direct measures, some women are encouraged to have more children and others to have fewer.

In this chapter, we take up how reproduction is part of the making and the unmaking of communities. We will explore these processes in several contexts, including Italy, Palestine, and in smaller communities too. But we start the chapter focused on the United States, where reproduction – its control, and resistance to dominant ideologies – has played a key role throughout its history. As we will see, these processes are refracted through lenses of race, ethnicity, class, and religion, as Americans have worked to imagine and shape their future.

Shaping Reproduction and Population in the US

The United States has no explicit national population or family planning policies, per se. But reproduction has been shaped and controlled in important ways by US policies. Some of those policies have had explicit reproductive goals; in others, reproduction is less explicit, but often equally powerful. These policies – some enacted at the federal level and others within a state – tend to target specific groups, including poor and nonwhite women and communities.

We begin this section by looking at one of the major ways that the US has tried to preserve or change the demographic shape of the country, through immigration. Some people – those deemed likely to help the US reach its demographic, economic, or cultural goals – have been allowed to migrate and take up residence. Others – those deemed outsiders, unassimilable, or dangerous – have been prevented from entering the US, or, if already in the US, constrained in their legal or social access to citizenship. In addition to immigration policies, other measures have sought to control the reproduction of groups within the US. Those include immigrants, but we also look at how three marginalized groups – the poor, Native Americans, and African Americans – have been the target of reproductive control throughout the entire history of the United States.

Restricting Who Comes and Stays: The Role of Immigration in Constructing America

Policies of immigration and reproduction have been used in attempts to shape the US into a particular image, or meet an imagined notion of what the country should look like. Over the past century and a half, laws have made it easier, harder, or impossible for different groups to immigrate and make a home in the country. Some legislation has targeted specific groups or countries. In 2017, the US put into place restrictions on immigration from seven "Muslim majority" countries (Executive Order 13769 and, later, EO 13780); the Trump administration's rationalization was that this ban would reduce terrorism in the US. Highly controversial both within and outside the country, the order was rescinded in January 2021. But this law was not something new; such immigration restrictions have existed in the United States for centuries. The first such law was the Chinese Exclusion Act of 1882, which forbade most Chinese from immigrating to the US. What is similar between these two acts, more than a century apart, is the extent to which they reflect how particular groups have been targeted in immigration laws and regulations in ways that are meant to shape who is allowed to enter and settle in the United States.

Even more common than a law aimed at one group have been the ways that immigration laws have been used to shape the racial composition of the US more generally. Particularly notable was the Immigration Law of 1924, which focused on national origins and was a direct attempt to keep the country white. It gave permission for white western Europeans to immigrate, but severely restricted those from nonwhite countries – especially Asians and those from Southern and Eastern Europe[11] – to legally move to the United States. While this and other US immigration laws are purportedly national-origin based, they are shaped by concerns around race and ethnicity. The 1924 law and those that followed "remapped the ethno-racial contours of the nation"; they were developed out of a belief that "the American nation was, and should remain, a white nation descended from Europe." These immigration laws were powerful: they remade "immigration law into an instrument of mass racial engineering" (Ngai 2004: 17, 27). Controlling who becomes a new American or how immigrant communities and families were allowed to contribute to their adopted country was and continues to be an attempt by leaders to maintain a dominantly white nation. At the core of the exclusions put into place have been racist beliefs about a group's character or beliefs, or a fear that whites might lose their dominant demographic position.

In addition to preventing the entry of immigrants from certain countries, immigrant populations have been subject to other restrictions. While the Chinese Exclusion Act and the Gentleman's Agreement (1907/8) denied the entry of Chinese and Japanese migrants, respectively, the US also targeted Asians already in the US, denying them the ability to become naturalized citizens. As non-citizens, they were restricted from owning land and from accessing other resources that would allow them to develop strong families and communities. These restrictions on reproduction stifled the growth, futures, and even survival of Asians and Asian communities in the US and remained in place until 1943 for Chinese and 1952 for Japanese.

Most immigration laws are not only raced but gendered as well. While restrictions on who and how many immigrants may enter the US is one way to limit immigrant numbers, another focus has been on the control of immigrant reproduction, a focus that usually targets women. Often depicted as "hyper-fertile" and having "too many children," immigrant women have been drawn as a threat to the white majority; their presence and their role in building ethnic communities has been seen as dangerous and needing control. Indeed, while the 1882 Exclusion Act kept most Chinese from immigrating, it was actually an earlier act, the Page Act of 1875, that had equally longlasting impacts on Chinese communities. Arguing that Chinese women were potentially prostitutes and thus dangerous to the American public, it forbade the entry of nearly all Chinese women. At the same time, Chinese living in the US were not allowed to marry nonwhite Americans. The combination of these laws made it nearly impossible for Chinese to form families and have children. Without any way to create families, and with no possibility of having children, Chinese communities in the US grew increasingly older and remained predominantly male for decades (Peffer 1999). Here, we see how targeted immigration laws can actually produce communities and reinforce discriminatory attitudes and practices. That so many Chinese in the US lived outside families made them seem even more alien and threatening to white Americans, who saw their living arrangements as deviant and un-American – living arrangements that were the result of the discriminatory immigration laws themselves.

But Asians and other immigrants in the US who faced such discrimination still found ways to build strong communities. Once allowed to do so by law, immigrants became naturalized American citizens. Second and third generations followed, as immigrants from places like China, Japan, and Mexico settled down in the US and began to have children. It was these generations – the children and grandchildren of those original immigrants – that worried many white Americans. They watched as increasing numbers of community members were born in the US and were thus American citizens. For example, in 1900, only 10 percent of Chinese in the US were American-born, but that grew to 21 percent by 1910 and over 40 percent by 1930. By 1940, American-born Chinese made up more than half of the overall Chinese population in the US (Molina 2014: 75). As US citizens, they were entitled to own land and to use all the resources of the country, like all other US citizens. White Americans found these community members even more threatening, seeing them as "aliens within."

The perceived threat of these immigrants, and the way it threatened the white dominance of the nation, led to a further focus on reproduction. For example, in the 1910s and 1920s, many officials in Los Angeles voiced concerns that Japanese in the area were having too many children. Health officials published data on fertility at the time, and in an effort to raise alarms about the dangers of Japanese fertility, they presented those data in a way that made births to Japanese look higher than they actually were (Molina 2006: 55ff.). These officials tied this "excess" fertility to economic threats supposedly posed by Japanese, pointing out how the unbalanced birth rates of whites and Japanese had the potential to allow the latter to dominate agricultural production in the future. In a public speech, one health official wondered aloud: "Will it be the cultured, civilized, educated American women or must we depend upon the foreign, ignorant, uncultured, and half-civilized?" (cited in Molina 2006: 57). Here, it was not Japanese immigrants who were of most concern, because – as non-citizens – they were not permitted to own land. Rather, concern was focused on the next generations of Japanese, who had automatic (birthright) citizenship, and could buy and own land. This rhetoric came to be tied to larger issues of "race suicide," "race betterment," and "yellow peril" discourses; white officials often went public with arguments that, if white fertility rates did not increase, whites could lose their place in American society, be "overrun" by Asians and other immigrants, or even disappear altogether. Following this rhetoric, white officials tried to encourage whites to have more children and to discourage immigrants from having so many.

Around the same time, the reproduction of Mexicans in Los Angeles was also being closely watched, with similar concerns of their "too-high" fertility rates, and with fears that it would lead to an outnumbering of white Los Angelinos. Mexican women too were depicted as "overly fertile" (Molina 2006: 146) and, by bearing so many children, using up resources, and posing an economic threat to white Americans. These concerns led to mass sterilizations in California in the 1930s; the campaign was supposed to improve society by keeping some (the "feebleminded") from reproducing. But the targets were much more often nonwhites, including Mexicans. How many Mexicans were targeted in these programs is not known, but, as we discuss further below, data and documents from the era indicated that Mexicans were sterilized at high rates and against their will (Molina 2006: 147).

These actions against Japanese, Chinese, and Mexicans in the US suggest how American officials had begun to move from controlling population primarily through exclusion at the border to targeting what were increasingly seen as internal threats: outsiders within. As immigrants bore children who were American citizens, it was these citizens, seen as "perpetual foreigners" because of their race, who became the targets of concern and action. The view of them as "aliens" – a group that is not and never will be real Americans (Ngai 2004: 5ff.) – evidences how race, not citizenship, was at the base of these state and local actions.

In recent rhetoric about immigrant mothers, we can see the continuing underlying concerns that many Americans have about immigrant reproduction, as fertility levels have dropped in the US, and even though the fertility of immigrants (or "foreign-born") has dropped more sharply than that of native-born Americans, and the gap between the two groups is narrowing; in 2010, native-born women had a TFR of 1.69 compared to a TFR of 2.02 for immigrant women (Camarota and Zeigler 2021). Thus, while immigrants have regularly been seen as an economic or racial threat throughout US history, it is immigrant women who are distinctly targeted for their reproductive threat. It is their bodies that are seen as producing "foreign citizens" and contributing to a changing American demographic landscape.

Coming from a continuing interest in keeping the US white and a worry about "alien" reproduction and growth of the nonwhite population, attention has also focused on who should be allowed citizenship. A recent debate about "anchor babies" highlights the rhetoric and its underlying "genderacing" (Kim et al. 2018) around the perceived threat of nonwhites to the nation. This term has been used in accusations that immigrant women – Mexican and Chinese – come to the United States strictly to bear children so that the family may eventually gain legal citizenship. Automatic US citizenship ("birthright citizenship") is given to anyone born on American soil, so – the argument goes – these babies will "anchor" the family's claim to future citizenship. Some Americans see these processes as threatening to white America, arguing that this privilege allows immigrants to sponsor relatives and others, will give immigrants access to land and voting rights, and allow immigrant groups to build families and communities. Some have gone so far to argue for repealing birthright citizenship, which has been guaranteed by the US Constitution since 1868. One scholar explicitly connects such ideology with concerns about reproduction: "The fear of sexually active and fertile brown immigrant women posing as an invading menace serves to buttress racist immigration restrictions designed to control unwanted populations" (Kim et al. 2018: 322).

This kind of anti-immigrant rhetoric has far-reaching consequences. For one, it influences how immigrant women access necessary social, economic, and medical services for themselves and their children. Because they are concerned that Americans may see them as taking more resources than they deserve, they are less likely to seek help for their children, whether that is in schools, medical facilities, or the society at large (Huang 2008), leaving their children and themselves even more vulnerable to the poverty and discrimination they face every day.[12]

This discourse reflects how, within the negative language about immigrants, there is a gendered discourse that depicts immigrant women as particularly threatening to the self-image and desired racial composition of the US. Gender and reproduction are thus linked as a dangerous combination; though immigrants might be seen as an economic threat, women can threaten the very identity of the nation. "Immigrant bodies have become the economic, demographic, and political battleground for America's future" (Huang 2008: 406).

Controlling Reproduction within the US

While immigration regulations have been used in an attempt to shape the US into what some imagine to be an ideal – white – nation, many other US policies – some direct and many more indirect – have focused on other communities and women within the country's borders; along with immigrant groups, the poor, Native Americans, and African Americans have also been targeted. There are some similarities and overlaps among the targeting of these marginalized communities. For example, because race has always influenced socioeconomic class, women of color have been overly represented in many of the actions targeted at the poor. But while the goals of the state interventions were sometimes similar, there were also differences that reflect the distinct place each group has had in the nation's racial structures and history.

In addition to direct action, influence on reproduction has taken many other forms. It includes how some Americans are encouraged or discouraged from having children; the support or lack of it for families and children; the provision or shortage of reproductive health services for different communities; and even tax laws that have made having and raising children more or less difficult for some people. Direct actions have sometimes garnered more attention (and resistance), but less direct policies may actually have had even more influence, both because they are more widespread and because they are often harder to recognize and may thus not elicit strong resistance.

Controlling the poor

Often marginalized because of their lack of access to resources such as health care, good education, and housing, throughout US history, the poor have also been targeted around issues of reproduction. The history and experience of this group makes clear the double-edged sword of contraceptive services: these communities both lack access to birth control and, at the same time, experience more surveillance over their reproductive decisions.

Johanna Schoen (2005) examined the history of birth control and sterilization in North Carolina over the last century, and provides evidence for these competing narratives of birth control programs there. In that state, poor women, especially those in rural areas, have had less access to birth control – including contraceptives, abortion, and sterilization – than have women with more resources. That lack of access has meant difficulty managing reproduction. But at the same time, some poor women experienced a different set of problems, as their marginalized position resulted in their being coerced into sterilization. Schoen's story of two women's experience around sterilization demonstrates how it is the context of these programs and procedures that shapes the outcomes and undermines women's ability to control their reproduction.

In 1965, Nial Cox was an 18-year-old Black woman who underwent sterilization. She did so because, if she had not consented, her family would lose their welfare benefits, upon which this poor family depended; that was in spite of the fact that Nial herself was not receiving anything from the welfare program. Why would government officials target someone like Nial? She was African

American, unmarried, and gave birth to a child outside marriage. For those reasons, and using arguments based on pseudo-scientific theories about race, the state classified her as a "mentally deficient Negro girl" (Schoen 2005: 75) and thus subject to a North Carolina eugenics law that allowed sterilization for women who were found to be mentally diseased, feebleminded, or epileptic.[13] Nial fit none of those labels, but under state law, her status of unmarried mother, combined with her poverty and race, made her an easy target. Nial was one of more than 8,000 people sterilized between 1929 and 1975 in North Carolina under the state's Eugenics Board. We can understand more of how the state interpreted the law when we know that 85 percent of those 8,000 were women, half of whom had given birth outside marriage. These laws were also racialized: in North Carolina, 23 percent of sterilized patients in the 1930s and 1940s were Black, 59 percent between 1958 and 1960, and 64 percent between 1964 and 1966 (Schoen 2005: 108). During those years, Blacks made up well under 25 percent of North Carolina's population (see Figure 5.1).

Nial's story contrasts with that of Shirley, who sought to be sterilized but was denied the procedure. Shirley was a white married woman. She had two children from a previous marriage and a third after her divorce; because she struggled with mental health issues, Shirley placed all three children for adoption. In 1957, she married again, a Marine who was often stationed overseas. Shirley continued to have serious mental health challenges, and did not want to get pregnant, feeling she was unable to properly care for children. Her husband, however, disagreed. When Shirley decided to undergo

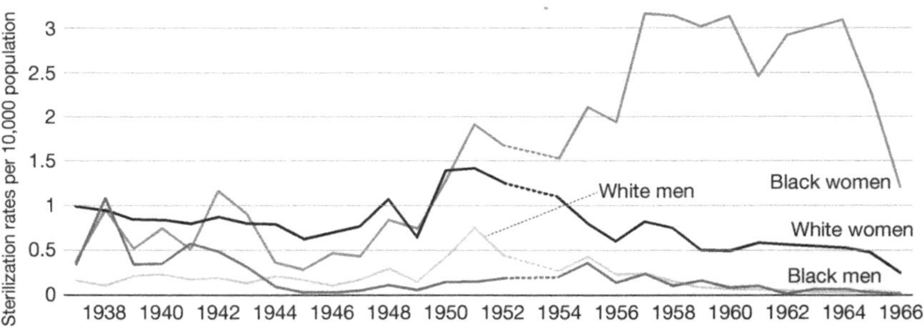

Figure 5.1. Forced sterilization rates in North Carolina, by race and sex
Source: Stern 2020

sterilization to prevent any future pregnancies, her husband would not sign the consent form. During the previous years, as Shirley spent years in and out of mental health institutions, he had been unavailable and not present. In spite of the evidence that sterilization might help Shirley recover from her illnesses, and despite the frequent absences of her husband and Shirley's own urgent pleas for permission, the state Eugenics Board denied her petition to be sterilized, arguing that her husband's desire for more children and his belief that his wife might someday recover outweighed all the available evidence and Shirley's own demand to undergo surgery.

The stories of Nial and Shirley demonstrate how sterilization in North Carolina could be both coercive and liberating. "Although the risks of major surgery accompanied female sterilization, the unreliability of other contraceptives and inaccessibility of abortion made sterilization an attractive option for women from all class and ethnic backgrounds." But, just as importantly, "it was not the technology of sterilization itself that determined whether women saw the operation as oppressive or liberating but the context in which the technology was embedded" (Schoen 2005: 78, 79). And in the same way, women had either less or more access to the technology depending on how authorities perceived their status in the community. Shirley was denied sterilization because she was white and married, and because her husband's desires were given much greater weight than her own. Nial was forced to undergo sterilization because her status – as a poor, Black, unmarried mother – was perceived to be of greater threat to the white male authorities. In neither case was the woman able to execute her own decision or choice. Coercion was used in both cases, since the outcome in each was imposed by state authorities and not freely chosen.

In spite of the way these laws were interpreted, often to women's disadvantage, women in North Carolina navigated their way through them and sought their own reproductive goals. One strategy they used to gain permission to undergo sterilization (or in some cases, abortion) was to find a way to be declared mentally ill or feebleminded. We saw that, in some cases, like Shirley's, even years of mental illness and hospitalization was not able to trump husbands' dominance in these decisions. But in other situations, a woman might feign mental illness and convince a doctor to declare her unfit – just so that the state would permit her a desired, chosen, sterilization. Freedom from repeated pregnancies and the challenges of raising many children often meant that "it mattered little under what pretenses their operations were approved, as long as they were approved. These women expressed relief and gratitude after being sterilized" (Schoen 2005: 124). What these stories from North Carolina show is how poor women, and particularly those of color, were denied control of reproduction in many ways. Some, who did not want it, were coerced or forced to undergo sterilization. Others, who sought sterilization, were denied. The poor were more likely to be targeted, and to have fewer resources to resist state decisions, in either case.

What happened in North Carolina happened in many other places. In the first half of the twentieth century, 32 states had eugenics programs that allowed health officials to declare individuals "unfit" to reproduce and thus to sterilize them, without consent (Novak and Lira 2018) and some 60,000 people across the US were sterilized through eugenics programs (Novak and Lira 2018). Most often targeted were women of color, and inevitably poorer rather than richer women. In California, where a third of all such sterilizations took place, it was Latinos who were most likely targeted. After California passed a eugenics sterilization law in 1909, 20,000 compulsory sterilizations were performed before it was revised in the early 1950s. Under the law, medical officials were able to authorize sterilization for individual women and men who were classified as "feebleminded" or had conditions "likely to be transmitted to descendants." From 1920 to 1945, medical officials were much more likely to recommend Latinos than non-Latinos to be sterilized under this law (Novak et al. 2018) (see Figure 5.2). Early in that period, it was Latino men who were at higher risk: from 1920 to 1926, Latino men had a 23 percent greater risk of being recommended for sterilization than non-Latino men. From 1926 to 1945, Latinas had a 59 percent greater risk of being recommended for sterilization than non-Latinas. These differences persisted, even when one accounted for (controlled for) differences in age. Virginia and West Virginia also had eugenic sterilization laws, allowing the state to sterilize those who were "high functioning retardates" but also those who were convicted as petty criminals (Flavin 2009: 34). New Jersey allowed the state to sterilize women who had had illegitimate or biracial children (Flavin 2009: 34).

The context in North Carolina and across the country changed with the introduction of more effective means of birth control in the

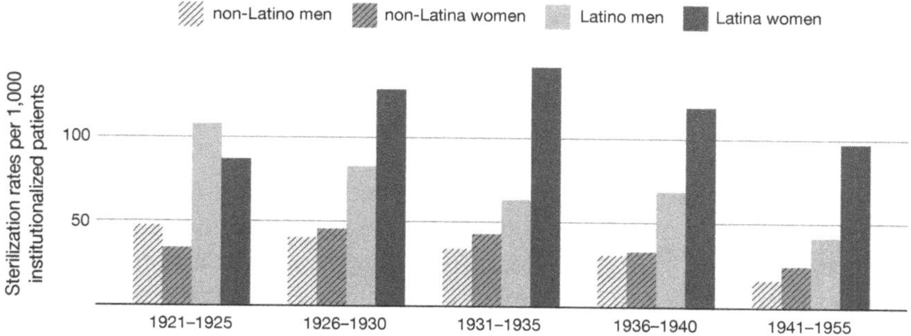

Figure 5.2. Forced sterilization rates of institutionalized patients, California
Source: Novak and Lira 2018

1960s and 1970s. With the possibility of controlling reproduction without resorting to sterilization, both individual women and state programs began new efforts in the area of family planning. Eugenic sterilization laws were repealed in those years, in North Carolina and other states.

But the dismantling of such sterilization laws and the actions connected to them did not change the targeting of marginalized communities. There is evidence that many of these early patterns of differential targeting of sterilization continue today. There have been several recent "no procreation" cases in the US where a judge rules that, if a woman wants to win back custody of her existing children, now in foster care, she must not get pregnant and is sometimes threatened with sterilization (Flavin 2009: 29). These cases are controversial, as they violate the right to bodily integrity; for that reason, these kinds of decisions and suggestions are often made off the record, or privately. But studies have found that sterilization rates are higher for women of color in the general population as well. One study (Volscho 2010) found that Black women had a 75 percent higher rate of sterilization than white women, and Native American women a 123 percent higher rate. That study controlled for potential mitigating factors such as education, number of children, marital status, and income. Another study (Shreffler et al. 2015) added a further factor to its examination of differences in sterilization: whether or not women regretted having the procedure – adding that factor gives us clues as to how the women themselves saw sterilization. This study too found sterilization rates to be higher for African American women than for white women, but Black women were also less likely to regret sterilization, less likely to see it as interfering with the children they wanted to have. There were different results regarding Native Americans; women from this group are also more likely to be sterilized than any other group of women in the US and those differences do not disappear when socioeconomic status, age, and fertility history are accounted for. But Native Americans are also more likely to regret having undergone the procedure. The researchers also found that Latinas, though less likely to be sterilized than white women, were also more likely to state that sterilization prevented them from having the children they wanted to have. Asian women have the lowest overall sterilization rate, but they are also the group that is most likely to report being pressured to undergo sterilization. As the authors of the study clarify: "We do not have concrete evidence that coercive practices are taking place among Native American or Hispanic women, but certainly higher rates of sterilization surgeries and regret are cause for concern" (Shreffler et al. 2015: 44). While these two studies show some differences, and, in each, patterns differ across racial groups, what is clear is that race continues to play a strong role in sterilization practices in the US.

Native American reproduction in the context of settler colonialism

"Colonial politics have always been, and remain, reproductive politics" (Theobald 2019: 4). Indeed, the control of reproduction within marginalized groups began early in the history of the United States – reproduction among Native Americans was a major concern of white American settlers from the early days of their arrival in North America. One of the main goals of white settlers was land acquisition, which in turn led to a focus on reproduction among Native women. As Evelyn Nakano Glenn argues, "In settler colonialism, the object is to acquire land and to gain control of resources. To realize these ambitions, the first thing that must be done is to eliminate the indigenous occupants of the land" (2015: 55).[14] Elimination involved a variety of mechanisms. In the early years of white settlement, Native Americans were killed as they defended their lands from white attacks; enslavement was also used as a way to contain Native Americans.

While Native men were seen as a threat in these Indian Wars, it was Native women's reproductive capacity – the ability to sustain the survival and growth of the community – that made them seem even more threatening to white goals, especially in the long term (Theobald 2019: 5). State control over Native reproduction took many forms over the years. Toward the turn of the twentieth century, the government began to use other means besides direct warfare in its efforts to eliminate indigenous people. It began with programs designed to bring about cultural assimilation ("Americanization"); to achieve this "social death," it was necessary to "kill the Indian, and save the man" (Glenn 2015: 57). The targeting of women and children reflects the recognition by all involved of the role played by biological and social reproduction in sustaining any community and how assimilation can be another strategy of elimination of cultures or communities (Glenn 2015).

Native family structure was also targeted. Many indigenous communities had developed a system of flexible family and child care arrangements that served to protect children in the case of a parent's death or ill health and provided a broad group of kin to support children (Theobald 2019: 26ff.). But whites found such family organizations uncivilized, and punished any deviation from a nuclear family structure. Relatedly, rather than the complementary gender roles that were found in many Native American communities, with women and men both contributing to the health of families and groups, whites insisted that men be "proper," "civilized" husbands and fathers, and take charge of the (patriarchal) family and its members (Theobald 2019: 38). That change meant that Native American women lost much of their power and status within families, and did not have the same access to community resources as did men. Perhaps most brutal was the removal of children from their families, and their placement in boarding schools. Whites believed that, in this way, Native children would lose their Indian ways, would be subject to less influence from their mothers, and would more easily learn American values and habits. At these schools – often far from their families – children were not allowed to speak their native language, and were taught how to dress, act, talk, and think as "Americans." Reports of abuse and early death were widespread (Dejong 2007). The brutality of child removal was two-pronged. Families were shattered and children lost their ties to their communities. In addition, the fear of these child removals resulted in the acquiescence among indigenous groups to many other demands by whites. For example, under threat of losing their children, Native American women often agreed to procedures such as sterilization.

The US state began a more systematic focus on contraception and sterilization later on. In 1970, Congress passed the Family Planning Services and Population Research Act, which made contraception available to women. It was meant to address both "overpopulation" concerns and a lack of access to contraception for some groups. While these concerns were largely focused on countries in the Global South, there were worries that the fertility rate of some women in the US was also too high. Much of the unease about overpopulation was racially based, a concern that fertility of nonwhite populations both outside and inside the US was a threat to white dominance. In 1970, the TFR was much higher among Native American women than among white women (respectively, 3.29 as opposed to 2.42 average number of children per woman). Because Native American women were having more children than most other Americans, the government – mostly through the Indian Health Service – targeted Native communities, trying to convince women to use contraceptives and have fewer children. "The basic rationale for the new law was that through an aggressive effort by the government to make family planning services fully available and affordable, couples would have only the number of children they desired, and that as a result, the rate of US population growth would decrease and ultimately stabilize" (Stith Butler and Wright 2009). Significantly, the targeting of this population occurred at a time when overall Native American population numbers could not reasonably be considered a threat to white Americans. The Native American population was under 800,000 in 1970, making up less than 0.5 percent of the overall US population (US Census Bureau 1973); that figure reflects the decimation of the population due to white settlement, aggression, war, and death from the introduction of new diseases by white settlement in North America.

As we saw for poorer communities, contraceptive access in Native communities had both positive and negative consequences. Even as the 1970 Act provided contraceptive access to Native women seeking birth control, it also signaled the beginning of a program of coercive sterilization of Native women. Some estimate that 25 percent of Native American women were sterilized in the six years between 1970 and 1976 (Lawrence 2000). These sterilizations – in number and how they were performed – were so alarming to people, both inside and outside Native communities, that it prompted a government investigation into what was happening. And while the subsequent 1976 government report (Investigations of Allegations Concerning Indian Health Services) avoided a full-out condemnation of the system, it pointed to many irregularities around these sterilizations, among them: that women were not fully informed about them before agreeing to undergo such a procedure; that women gave their "consent" while they were in labor or right after giving birth, when they were not fully aware of what they were signing; that doctors were performing sterilizations on women under the age of 21, even though the US Department of Health, Education and Welfare (HEW) had strictly forbidden that; and that the 72-hour waiting period between a decision to undergo sterilization and the procedure was not enforced in many circumstances (Lawrence 2000: 407ff.).

Race and racism played a central role in doctors' behavior. As one scholar put it, the main reasons doctors gave for promoting sterilizations were "economic and social in nature." (Lawrence 2000: 410), and in many ways their ideas and behavior align with other measures that had been used to change or eliminate indigenous family practices. By performing sterilizations and preventing "excess fertility" of women of poorer means, some doctors rationalized their actions by arguing that they were helping both the society and individual women too. They voiced commonly heard arguments that, when poor, Black, or Native women had too many kids, it was bad for them (they could not get ahead) and bad for society (which would have to support these children if their parents could not). Other doctors argued that Native American women (and other women who were also targeted at that time) were unable to responsibly and reliably use other methods of birth control and the only way for them to prevent pregnancy was sterilization.

These arguments point to how embedded racism and classism were central parts of the reproductive abuse of Native American women. For these women, who were considered incompetent, and whose fertility was not under control but needed to be, sterilization was easily enforced and justified. The reproductive services offered to Native American women similarly reflected racist beliefs that they were incapable of making good decisions: they were not given full information, their consent was often coerced, and their reproductive losses were not taken seriously. And because parents lived with the constant fear that their children would be removed and placed in foster families or boarding schools, some only consented to sterilization because of the hope that this would allow them to hold on to their children.

For Native women, of course, the loss of ability to bear children, or more children, was often heartbreaking, and disrupted lives, families, marriages, and communities. In communities whose very survival is in jeopardy, bearing the next generation is paramount, providing economic strength and tribal sovereignty. For women, motherhood – as "lifegivers and mothers" (Theobald 2019: 25) – is a key part of their lives; reproduction was key to their status, position, and power in the community. The abuse around biological and social reproduction that Native Americans experienced over decades and centuries has contributed to the devastation of these communities and tribes and has meant that they continue to struggle to regain their vitality and even survival.

Devaluing African American women and motherhood

When looking at reproductive control over the course of US history, the control of reproduction during slavery obviously stands out as a brutal practice that has been shown to have centuries-long reverberations. There are some similarities between the experiences of Black and Native women, but some key differences as well. While desire for land acquisition led white settlers and the state to try to reduce reproduction among Native American women, in the case of African Americans, slavery was as much about production as reproduction. One of the main purposes of controlling reproduction among enslaved women was to produce more labor for slave-owners. Owners thus wanted their enslaved women to produce as many children as possible, even though they were not willing to provide even basic maternal care to ensure healthy births (Ross and Solinger 2017: 19). Children born to an enslaved woman were the property of the slave-owner, and a mother had no say over whether she would be separated from her children, whether they would be sold away from her, or even whether she would be able to control such an immediate and basic process as being able to nurse her babies (Ross and Solinger 2017: 20). Even after slavery ended, African American women were not able to gain control over reproduction. Constrained by racist practices, they had little access to good medical care during pregnancy and childbirth, and were able to get little – and often no – support from government programs designed to aid "deserving" mothers during the late nineteenth and early twentieth century (Ross and Solinger 2017: 30). Legal scholar Dorothy Roberts (1998a) points to the "dark side of birth control" in her history of African American reproduction and its legacies. Many activists who were involved in providing increased access to contraception among African American women were eugenicists, who targeted Blacks because they believed they were biologically inferior. Roberts points out that Margaret Sanger, an early pioneer of birth control in the early twentieth century who has been both celebrated and vilified for her efforts, played a role in this targeting. Roberts explains:

> It appears that Sanger was motivated by a genuine concern to improve the health of the poor mothers she served rather than a desire to eliminate their stock [as other eugenicists wanted]. Sanger believed that all their afflictions arose from their unrestrained fertility, not their genes or racial heritage ... Sanger nevertheless promoted two of the most perverse tenets of eugenic thinking: that social problems are caused by the socially disadvantaged and that their childbearing should therefore be deterred. In a society marked by racial hierarchy, these principles inevitably produced policies designed to reduce Black women's fertility. The judgment of who is fit and who is unfit, of should reproduce and who should not, incorporated the racist ideologies of the time. (1998a: 81)

It is how these events and processes continue that may be even more important, because it suggests just how much that earlier history continues to resonate today, how US involvement in slavery has shaped American society through to the present and the continuing effects of racism and hostility toward Black mothers and Black women's reproduction (Nelson 2003). In the media, Black women are depicted as overproductive, producing children they cannot support, and as drug addicts and uncaring, irresponsible mothers (Roberts 1998a). As Roberts notes, women's bodies are targeted by government policies and restrictions, but poor mothers – and especially poor Black mothers – are a special target. Roberts has substantiated the myriad ways that Black women's motherhood – particularly poor Black women's – has been devalued for centuries. They are derided as matriarchs who destroy Black family life because of their dominating ways, and seen as irresponsible mothers who do not pay attention to their children, as "welfare queens" who continue to have children to fatten their government checks, or as hyperfertile, unable (or unwilling) to control their fertility. As Khiara Bridges describes it:

> The welfare queen is discursively constructed as a marriage of contradictions: she is uneducated, yet informed enough to make lucrative her reproductive capabilities. She is stupid, yet smart enough to shift to the government the costs of maintaining her (luxurious or at least undeservedly excessive) lifestyle to the tune of billions of dollars a year. (2011: 211)

Black motherhood has repeatedly been depicted as deviant by the media and government officials in many – often contradictory but always harmful – ways. An irony of the degradation of Black motherhood is how it has occurred even while, at the same time, Black women have cared for white children throughout US history, as slaves or as free Blacks – a classic example of stratified reproduction. Black mothers have also experienced the "overpolicing" of their families, and in the process, are much more likely to be declared "unfit mothers" and to see their children removed and placed in the foster system (Roberts 2002). "State mechanisms of surveillance and punishment work to penalize the most marginalized women in our society while blaming them for their own disadvantaged positions" (Roberts 2012: 1476).

It is because they are so devalued that Black women have been targeted in a number of US campaigns that purportedly protect a fetus from harm. For example, in the early years of women being charged for using drugs during pregnancy, Black women were overrepresented: of the first 52 women charged between 1989 and 1992, 32 were Black (Roberts 1997). While some have argued that such restrictions are really about protecting children, criminalizing mothers is ineffective at base, and also highly racialized. Studies have shown that Black women are much more likely than white women to be charged for substance abuse during pregnancy, even though rates of substance abuse are actually similar in both groups (Chasnoff et al. 1990). Roberts (1997) argues that this portrayal of Black mothers as addicted and as harming their babies is just another way of presenting them as terrible mothers, alongside the matriarch and the welfare queen. The message is that Black women do not deserve to be mothers and should be discouraged from playing that role.

That racism and discrimination persists today. The US maternal mortality rate is much higher than in any other wealthy western country (see Figure 5.3) but Black women in the US fare even worse (see Figure 5.4). Compared to white women, Black women have a much higher chance of dying during pregnancy and their babies are more likely to be born underweight and early, and to die in infancy. Because these higher rates prevail even when we compare Black and white women of similar education or socioeconomic class, researchers attribute most of the differences to the effects of racism. Some of that can be seen in the interactions between health providers and Black patients, where Black women's complaints or concerns are less likely to be taken seriously, and where there is less rapid and extensive intervention into any pregnancy complication (Mutambudzi et al. 2017; Bryant et al. 2010). But the effects of racism go further. There is increasing evidence that Black women's higher rates of maternal mortality and complications and the higher infant mortality rates for Black babies is likely at least partly due to the racism that Black women experience throughout their lives. Studies show that such experience increases hormones to levels that can be harmful during

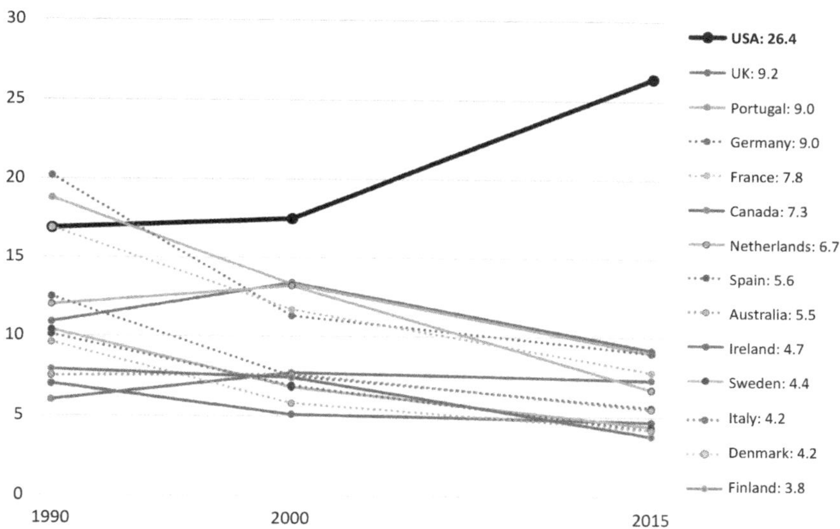

Figure 5.3. Maternal deaths per 100,000 live births, various countries
Source: Compiled with data from GBD 2015 Maternal Mortality Collaborators 2016

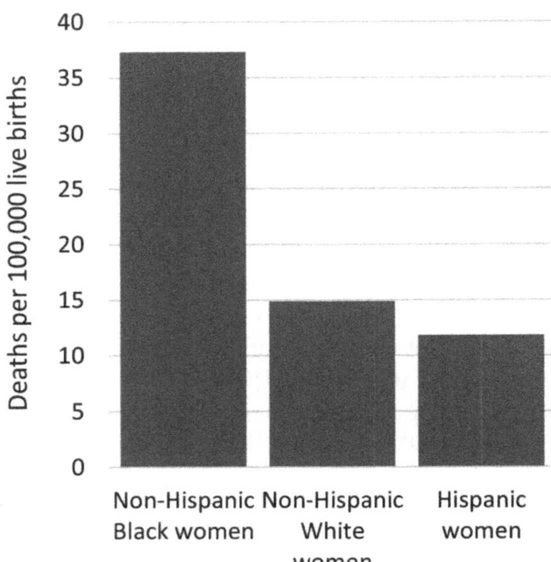

Figure 5.4. Maternal mortality statistics by race/ethnicity, USA 2018
Source: Compiled with data from National Center for Health Statistics

pregnancy, and cause pregnancy complications, premature birth, and lower infant birthweights (Clark and Anderson 1999; Collins et al. 2004: Rosenthal and Lobel 2011; Taylor 2020). Here, we see that the burdens that racism places on women have physiological consequences. It is a clear case of structural violence where ideology and institutional practices by state and nonstate actors result in terrible consequences.

As we saw above, Black women are also more likely to be targeted for sterilization than are white women. Other methods – such as Norplant or IUDs – are also more likely to be pushed on poor Black women. Some doctors argue that these are better methods for women who are not able to use other contraceptives reliably (Burrell 1995); women do not have to "worry" about pregnancy after the implantation. But what it does is make it difficult for women to maintain control of reproduction.

There is an uncomfortable irony here. Black mothers are surveilled more closely than white mothers, with health and social workers more likely to suspect them of behaving in ways that will result in their having too many children or act in ways that will negatively impact their children. At the same time, Black women actually endure heavier burdens – in health facilities and throughout their daily lives – that include less or poorer access to health care that might allow them healthier pregnancies, births, and children. Thus, Black mothers face scrutiny, surveillance, and coercion, without the actual social and economic support they need. As we have seen repeatedly for marginalized groups, efforts to control the reproduction of Black women were often done in conjunction with – and often using the very same laws that benefited other (white middle-class) women – more reproductive access (Ross 2016).

Black women have resisted this treatment. As individuals, Black women have navigated contraceptive access, pregnancy, childbirth, and other reproductive processes alongside the racism and ineffective and harmful treatments they are regularly offered. In addition to this individual work, as we will detail below, Black women have also begun to organize as a group to call for a long-demanded and wider version of reproductive justice, beyond a narrow conceptualization of bodily autonomy derived from a focus on the right to contraception and abortion. The new focus insists on taking the treatment and history of marginalized groups into account, and insisting that all factors, challenges, and needs for bearing and raising healthy children must be addressed to achieve reproductive justice. Originally organized by Black women leaders, the movement now includes a broad array of coalitions among women, working to push back against a system that has targeted and mistreated women of color for centuries.

Reproduction in US Empire-Building

Just as reproduction played a role in the settler colonialist goals of white settlers in North America, it was also intricately tied to US empire-building beyond the US mainland. We focus here on the evidence from Puerto Rico, but similar kinds of processes took place in other sites of the US empire, including Hawai'i, Guam, and the Philippines.

The United States acquired Puerto Rico after invading the island and winning the 1898 Spanish-American War; the island was made a US territory and Puerto Ricans became US citizens in 1917. But the relationship between Puerto Rico and the United States has never been easy or settled. Since acquisition, there have been debates about the island – concerning what caused the widespread poverty that Puerto Rico has experienced, what its relationship to the US should be, and whether or not Puerto Rico should be independent from the US. Reproduction has been involved in all these debates (Briggs 2002). As the US worked to bring Puerto Rico problems under control, many argued that its poverty was caused by "overpopulation" on the island. As we have seen in earlier examples, this argument, especially during the mid-twentieth century, was racialized and classed: it was poor, nonwhite women whose fertility was considered too high and as posing a threat to white dominance. *Which* women were having "too many children" was as important as *how many* children were born. Some Americans were using these familiar tropes to claim that Puerto Rican women were hypersexualized and producing too many babies without the financial means to support them.

This focus on population growth led the US government and private foundations to promote family planning and to set up a system of family planning programs throughout Puerto Rico. Organizations like the Rockefeller Foundation began programs on the island, promoting contraception, experimental health interventions, and other strategies. Clarence Gamble (heir to the Proctor and Gamble fortune) had been interested in issues of population in the US and around the world, and in the 1930s turned his attention to Puerto Rico where he established clinics across the island. Gamble saw Puerto Rico as a kind of laboratory where family planning methods and programs could be tested; believing that it was high fertility that caused Puerto Rico's poverty, his organization targeted working-class women.

Through these debates and programs, Puerto Rico became a sort of poster child of the problems of overpopulation. "The notion that through overpopulation poor women were responsible for the economic ills of the island simultaneously served to mask US capitalist extraction and to provide an occasion for further US involvement" (Briggs 2002: 108). It took attention off the US state's role in Puerto Rico's weak economy and widespread poverty, and, instead, constructed those problems as caused by individual Puerto Ricans' reproductive practices. This discourse had long-term consequences. Even though the evidence from Puerto Rico did not support such a connection between poverty and population growth (in fact, income was growing even as population was increasing), nevertheless many became convinced that Puerto Rico's poverty was caused by its high fertility. "The island's women, as one official put it, 'kept shooting children like cannon balls at the rigid walls of their economy'" (Earl Parker Hanson, quoted in Immerwahr 2019: 246). Such a stance allowed the US to avoid any responsibility for the deep poverty and inequality of Puerto Rico caused by its imperial relationship to the island.

Because of these racialized beliefs about Puerto Rican fertility, enhanced by ideologies of colonialist superiority and modernity, Puerto Rico also became a site of contraceptive testing. American researchers held clinical trials of birth control pills in the 1950s and 1960s, and other forms of birth control were tested on the Puerto Rican population during those decades as well (Immerwahr 2019: 248ff.). While contraceptive testing sites existed in other parts of the world, Puerto Rico served as an acceptable testing ground because it was under US control but off-shore, because of the racial composition of the population, and because of its status as a population out of control.

Resistance to US involvement in Puerto Rico has also involved population issues. Nationalists, who worked for independence from the US, also drew on arguments about reproduction. For example, in the 1930s and 1940s, nationalists argued for a return to a social model they contended had existed before Americans had arrived; their vision was of a male-dominated society where women's primary role was motherhood. Highly influenced by the Catholic Church, they argued that family planning interrupted women's natural role and led to madness (Briggs 2002). They believed women should not be "deprived" of having all their children around them; that is what makes them proper women and that role will stabilize society. Others who opposed US involvement in Puerto Rico, including leftists and feminists, also saw population as key to the island's future success. Their goal was to help working-class families, reduce poverty, and improve women's lives. Believing that lower fertility would result in less poverty and stronger economic development, they supported the dissemination of birth control throughout the island. They hoped that in this way, Puerto Rico could assert itself as a modern – or at least a modernizing – country.

Puerto Rico is important in any discussion of reproductive politics in the US for several reasons. Reproduction was a major issue for all involved in the establishment of and opposition to the American colonial government on the islands. Questions about reproduction – whether it was too high, needed to be controlled, was a positive or negative force for both the island and the women who lived there – were debated and acted on. These actions included programs that originated in the US and were exported to Puerto Rico – family planning programs, clinical trials of contraceptive methods, and ideology that linked overpopulation to poverty as the reason for the island's troubles. But reproduction was part of the very meaning of Puerto Rico to Americans. Like policies targeted at Native Americans and Blacks, we can see in US maneuvering around Puerto Rico an attempt to define who is included and who is excluded as Americans, the role of race in those constructions, and the ways that reproduction is seen as central to control of these communities and their place in the larger American social, economic, and political landscape.

Marginalized Groups beyond the US

We see some of the same processes around immigration and marginalized groups in other countries beyond the United States, of course. The inequalities – around race, ethnicity, religion, class, or something else – produce and are produced by policies, government acts, media portrayals, and norms and values that nearly always involve aspects of reproduction. Just as in the US, in some cases, attention is focused on who should be allowed entry into a country. In others, it is that the reproduction of a marginalized group is targeted differently from that of mainstream populations. We demonstrate the pervasiveness of such actions through an examination of several places: Japan's and Italy's attempts to deal with low fertility and migrant populations; Singapore's efforts to create a larger elite class through reproduction; and India's reckonings with religious difference.

Migrants in Japan

In Chapter 4, we saw how many people in Japan are concerned about the country's low fertility rates, and are suggesting or implementing new policies to address them. But related to those demographic issues is a concern about immigration. Immigrants might help Japan solve some of its labor shortages caused by fertility declines, but

Japan has long been hesitant – and is sometimes downright hostile – about admitting outsiders. Nevertheless, pressures from an aging population and increasing problems in labor supply have opened the door to an increase in migration. But because immigration remains widely unpopular in Japan, immigration rates and numbers are very low for an industrialized nation; immigrants total just under 2 percent of the total population. Japan refuses the entry of refugees and limits immigrant arrivals to those who might fill specific needs of the Japanese economy. Even that is done reluctantly. Immigrants in Japan continue to have outsider status – citizenship is conferred only if parents are Japanese (*jus sanguinis*); being born in Japan (*jus soli*) does not lead to citizenship, and even third- or fourth-generation descendants are not usually granted citizenship. Discrimination against immigrants – again, even those who were born and have grown up in Japan (and are thus, technically, not immigrants) – has been extensive and well documented in hiring, in housing, and in education opportunities. A recent government survey from the Justice Department of foreign-born residents in Japan found that 40 percent "said they had been stopped from moving into housing because they were foreigners. Some of them had even seen notices saying foreigners were not accepted" (Hurst 2017). Even as Japan faces potentially severe demographic challenges, with an aging population and a shrinking labor force, its citizens are reluctant to dislodge its long history of ethnic and cultural homogeneity (Green 2017). Similar concerns are found in places as different as Italy, Singapore, and India.

Demographic nationalism in Italy

In Italy, the connections among reproduction, race, and immigration are also quite clear and powerful. Like the US, Italy is a country with concerns about who immigrates and how that immigration will shape the demographics of the nation. But – like Japan – Italy's worries are coupled with a low overall fertility rate. Publicly voiced concerns about this began in the 1990s; the TFR had reached a new low of 1.2 in 1992 (Krause 2012), which was, at the time, one of the lowest in the world. Pope John Paul II bemoaned the "crisis of births," arguing that it was a serious national challenge (Krause 2018: 75). Government officials, church leaders, and the general public all expressed alarm, worried about a declining and aging population with not enough children being born. Much of the rhetoric focused on women, who were being accused of not doing what they should to reproduce the nation. In the past, as we reported in Chapter 1, "responsible" behavior was demonstrated by control of fertility, by not having "too many" children (Schneider and Schneider 1996); indeed, in the past, southern Italians were criticized for their out-of-control fertility (Krause 2006). But in this new era, some argued, women needed to step up, be less selfish, and marry and bear (more) children. There were theories of how Italy had got to this point of such low fertility, most of which were focused on women's roles and plans. Perhaps, some mused, it was because now that women were in the labor force, they did not have the time or energy to raise children (Krause 2005). Given the predominant role they have played in their households, in raising children, and in taking care of the family, paid labor and care labor were not easily compatible. Or perhaps recent changes in gender expectations had given women more decision-making power in their families (Mills et al. 2008), and that led to fewer kids. But research has suggested that fertility decline could not be easily connected to those purported changes. Over the course of at least the twentieth century, many women had worked, often in small, family-run businesses, and had long been combining work and family care. And women continue to hold primary responsibility for household and child care tasks. Krause (2005) has argued that we need a more nuanced understanding of gender relations, as Italians – both women and men – figure out the changing gender roles and expectations in contemporary Italy.

How women and gender are viewed as entangled with the problem of low fertility is further complicated by Italy's attention to immigration. At the same time as Italy was watching its fertility levels decline, migrants were moving there in response to labor shortages in order to work in low-skilled jobs. In fact, much of Italy's demographic "crisis" is more accurately described as a concern about who is having children, and who is not. As in the US, there is a concern about what the nation should look like, and who is counted as a "real" citizen. Some perceive the low fertility rates of white Italians and the higher fertility rates of immigrants as leading to "the end of Italian culture" (Krause 2006), an argument that rests on the belief that immigrants can never be real Italians. These concerns about immigrants are also about race and religion, as many immigrants are not white (they are from northern Africa or from China, for example) and many are not

Catholic, but Muslim. That the fertility rate of immigrants is twice as high as that of Italy-born women has fueled rhetoric about a dying culture (Marchesi 2012). In this situation, "alarmist discourses encourage a form of demographic nationalism in which the national population is depicted at risk from internal sources – low fertility and rapid aging – as well as from external ones – increasing immigration" (Krause 2006: n.p.).

Because of this recent demographic history, Italy has sought ways to control not only immigration, but also reproduction – to encourage some women to have more children, and some to have fewer. Hoping to prod native-born Italians (but not immigrants) to bear more children, cash-incentive programs have been proposed or enacted. In 1999, in the city of Milano, for example, a newspaper suggested the city should offer a cash bonus to any woman who had lived in the city for at least 15 years (Krause 2006). In 2003, the national government promoted higher fertility through cash bonuses to those women who had a second child or beyond; however, these bonuses were offered only to European citizens – and, explicitly, not to immigrant women (Marchesi 2012).

In the midst of "replacement anxieties" (Marchesi 2012) – the below-replacement fertility of Italian women and worries that Italians are being replaced by immigrants – it is, again, women's bodies that are scrutinized and criticized for their failure to follow expected norms whereby Italy-born women are not providing the nation enough children, and where immigrant women are deemed as having too many children.

Designer genes in Singapore

Singapore is another country that has sought to shape the demographics of the country by encouraging some women to give birth, discouraging others from doing so, and by strictly restricting the reproduction of immigrant women. The situation for immigrant women in Singapore reminds us that stratified reproduction and discrimination against migrants takes place in the Global South as well as in the Global North.

After independence in 1965, Singapore sought to bring fertility and population increases under control, and began to implement policies to discourage families from having too many children – such as providing paid maternity leave only for the first two children, giving tax breaks for the first three children but none thereafter, or giving lower priority in schools for later-parity children. In 1983, Singapore went even further to shape reproduction: declaring a need to focus on the eugenic quality of births and tying education to eugenics, the government began to encourage well-educated women to increase their fertility (the "Graduate Mums Scheme"). College-educated women who had at least three children were rewarded with priority school admissions for their kids, tax breaks, and other incentives. These policies targeted women rather than men because female university graduates were more likely than male graduates to marry someone who was also highly educated (Cutler and Greene 1987). Indeed, the government argued that these policies would also encourage more educated women to marry. At the time, 16 percent of women college graduates remained single compared to 5 percent of men, and discourse focused on how educated women were less interested in family, more selfish, and not interested enough in contributing to the nation's health (Palen 1986: 7). Poorer women were also targeted, but in their case, it came from an attempt to keep them from reproducing: the government offered women from low-income or low-education brackets incentives if they agreed to undergo sterilization.

Both of these efforts – dubbed "designer genes" – were widely unpopular in Singapore, with educated women protesting against efforts to make them give up their careers in order to be mothers. And very few couples signed up for the sterilization program, in spite of the cash incentives offered. In addition, many argued that these programs were racially motivated, an attempt to increase reproduction among the Chinese population (who were more likely to have higher education) and decrease reproduction among the Malay and Indian populations. But the main reason these policies died out was that Singapore soon decided that, rather than favoring a reduction in fertility, the declining fertility rate and its consequences suggested it should instead be focusing on increasing fertility among all groups (Palen 1986: 10).

Around the same time, Singapore's labor needs resulted in a new wave of temporary migrants who came to do low-waged and low-skilled work in the country; many came from other Asian countries, like the Philippines. These migrants have regularly been subject to poor treatment by employers, and lack any protection or support from either the Singapore government or their own.

Restrictions on their reproduction underscores their treatment as second-class people. Foreign women living and working in Singapore (often providing care work in private homes) are not permitted to marry a Singaporean citizen without government approval. In addition, Singapore does not permit these foreign workers to reproduce: pregnancy results in deportation. To ensure that they are following policy, foreign workers undergo twice-yearly examinations, when they are examined for pregnancy, syphilis, and TB (Cheang 2021). In these ways, foreign workers provide needed labor while being barred from any reproductive freedom or from occupying a real place in society.

These two programs – one encouraging higher fertility among the elite and among certain ethnic groups and the other forbidding migrant reproduction – provide a quick glimpse of how a state attempts to manipulate reproduction for its own goals. Here, Singapore was hoping to use restrictions on reproduction to help shape the nation into one populated by (the correct number of) successful, educated people.

Reproduction and religious nationalism in India

We saw in Chapter 2 how coercion has been part of India's population programs for decades. Millions of women have endured physical brutality, bribery in the form of disincentives and incentives, and other measures as the country has sought to control its population through its focus on women's bodies. Many programs targeted poor women. The ascension of Narendra Modi and the Bharatiya Janata Party (BJP), together with its support of Hindu nationalist rhetoric, has brought growing calls by the right wing for new population programs to target Muslims in India in order to secure population "stability" and to protect the country against those who purportedly threaten its future.

In this campaign, some in the BJP have argued that Muslims present a demographic threat to India's and Hindus' future. Muslim fertility, they argue, is higher than that of Hindus; unless Muslim fertility is curbed and Hindus start having more kids, Muslims will "overtake" Hindus. But that kind of alarm belies the fact that Hindus make up around 80 percent of India's population, and Muslims less than 15 percent (Purohit 2019). In addition, the fertility of both Muslims and Hindus is declining. As Figure 5.5 shows, the gap

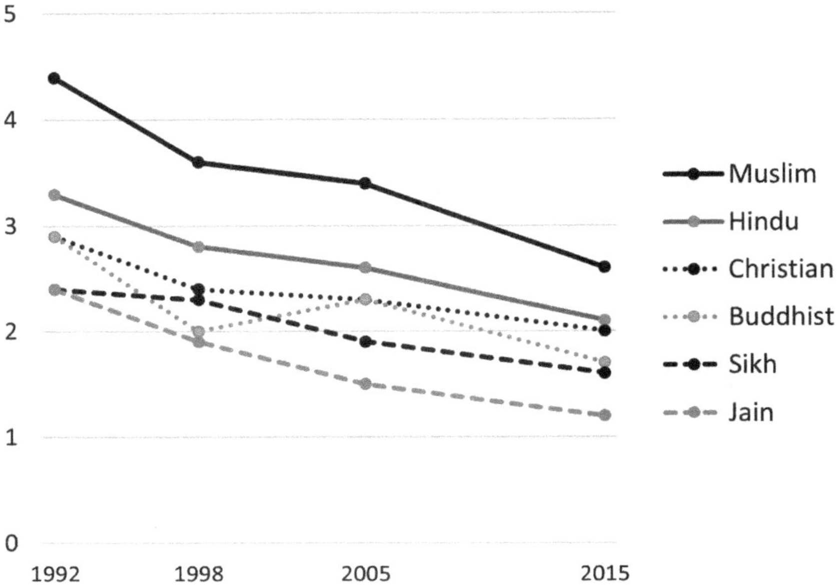

Figure 5.5. Average number of children a woman is expected to bear in her lifetime, by religion, India
Source: Compiled with data from Pew Research Center

between Muslim and Hindu fertility levels is narrowing. From 1992 to 2015, Muslim fertility declined from 4.4 to 2.6, which was a more rapid decline than seen among Hindus, which went from 3.3 to 2.1 during the same time period (*The Hindu* 2021). There is thus little chance that Muslims will come to dominate India demographically. Rather, the rhetoric reflects the interest on the part of some Hindus in maintaining their political, religious, and economic dominance. "Even as the myth of large Muslim families remains as false as ever, political leaders affiliated with the RSS [Rashtriya Swayamsevak Sangh, a right-wing, Hindu nationalist organization] raise the slogan of '*Hindu Khatre Mein Hain*' [Hindus are in danger of being wiped out]" (Sarcar 2021). The concerns expressed about overpopulation are, as in many other places, really about who should be having children and who should not.

In Uttar Pradesh, a northern state with a large Muslim population, the chief minister from the BJP has called for a "two-child policy," which would prevent anyone who has more than two children from receiving a variety of public goods, from access to government jobs to state aid given to poorer families. While he and other officials argue that such restrictions will benefit all people in the state, most understand the underlying motivation as "a veiled attempt to mobilize Hindu voters by tapping into an age-old trope about India's Muslim population ballooning out of control" (Shih 2021). It is one of several concerted efforts to secure India as a Hindu state, and prevent Muslims equal access. As one scholar explains, this kind of alarmist rhetoric "is an often-articulated Hindu nationalist trope that's acquired a ferocity ... It's not very different from the right wing, White American anxiety that Whites will become a demographic minority in the United States. In America, the issue is immigration. In India, the issue is fertility rates" (Shih 2021, quoting Ashutosh Varshney). There are further similarities between the American and Indian rhetoric: the rhetoric used by some Hindu nationalist groups constructs Hindus as a monolithic community and attempts to represent Muslim as "foreigners," despite the indigeneity of Indian Muslims. As India debates whether to enact new population policies, who is being targeted, whose reproduction is constructed as needing controlling, should be a focus. Mohan Guruswamy, a former BJP member, argues that this kind of rhetoric is a "code that everybody has internalized ... When they say, 'Those people are breeding,' who are they referring to? Muslims and lower castes" (cited in Shih 2021).

Some Hindu nationalists are also proclaiming concern about "love jihad," an assertion that Muslims are trying to out-populate Hindus through intermarriage with Hindus. In 2020, the state government of Uttar Pradesh passed a law to prohibit coercion of a bride or groom to convert to their spouse's religion. While ostensibly protecting against coerced religious conversion, in practice it is actually being used to prevent interfaith marriages between Hindus and Muslims and to provide justification for physical violence against Muslims involved in these marriages. It is evidence of how the far-right Hindu nationalist group has felt further empowered to carry their anti-Muslim agenda into communities, identifying and attempting to stop interfaith marriages (Frayer 2021).

As many have pointed out, any "two-child" population policy or restrictions on interfaith marriages are focused on the most marginalized groups – Muslims, rural women, the less educated, and those of lower castes. Some have argued that these groups need attention, because they have the highest fertility. Demographer Alaka Basu

(2020) asks us to step back from that kind of argument and instead recognize that it is the "precariousness of their lives … their very poverty, illiteracy, and lack of opportunity that tilts their cost-benefit calculus in the direction of children being the primary source of security – to protect them in times of crisis, in old age, in conflict, in natural disasters." A different approach would address those larger problems rather than simply trying to restrict the number of children women have.

That demographics is playing a central role in current political debates in India is not surprising. Population – its size and growth, but also its composition – is part of how states, nations, communities, and individuals imagine themselves. In India, people on all sides of these debates recognize that reproduction and the control of reproduction lies at the center of national politics; attempts to restrict, grow, or control sectors of that population have long been strategies to securing political power. What is happening in India mirrors a process that has been happening across the world for a long time: the threat that dominant groups see in the reproduction of marginalized groups, and the efforts undertaken to control that reproduction.

These attempts to control reproduction come out of many concerns and ideologies. One concern is numbers – that if a minority group continues to have higher fertility than the dominant group, sheer numbers will change that power structure. But concern over reproduction of marginalized groups is often rooted in a racialized imaginary of the nation or community, and policies are then embedded in racism and discrimination with an intent to control or even eliminate the minority group. Those in power believe that controlling the reproduction of Native Americans, African Americans, or Indian Muslims is a central and necessary way to control the community and bring about a particular version of a future.

Reproduction: The View from Marginalized Communities

Even as states and larger collectives have worked to restrict the reproduction of groups that are seen as less desirable, marginalized communities have also used reproduction as a form of resistance to their place and treatment by dominant groups or by governments. But as we will see in two examples, from Mexico and Palestine/Israel, using reproduction as a defensive tactic is not an easy thing to manage. And women – who bear the burdens of childbearing and rearing as men do not – can get embroiled in these struggles, caught between the pressures of the dominant society and their own community. In these kinds of struggles, "the positionings and obligations of women to their ethnic and national collectivities also affect and can sometimes override their reproductive rights" (Yuval-Davis 1996: 17). That Yasser Arafat, founder of the Palestine Liberation Organization (PLO), was known to declare, "The womb of the Arab woman is my strongest weapon (Khawaja 2018)," makes it clear how women's bodies can be weaponized in political and ethnic conflicts.

Women and the struggles of an indigenous village in Mexico

An example of how reproduction as a tool of resistance has gendered components for marginalized communities can be seen in what happened in a village in Mexico in the 1980s (Browner 1986). Because of its concern about population growth and its threat to the country's future, the Mexican government worked to provide family planning across the nation, including to the small village of San Francisco, in Oaxaca. But many of the villagers – indigenous Chinantec – felt that such efforts to control their population was a threat to their survival. However, there were clear gender differences about these issues within the village. The men were more likely to believe that the village should produce as many children as possible, at least partly because they saw population size as the best way of resisting government efforts to marginalize or eliminate indigenous populations and communities; a large population would also be protection against incursions by neighboring villages that wanted their land. But women – who were the ones directly impacted by extensive childbearing and childrearing – wanted to limit the number of children they had; they saw pregnancy as a health risk, and raising children as burdensome. Many women wanted to be childless. Men and women struggled over these issues. Women who had no or "too few" children were seen as selfish and unwilling to sacrifice for the greater needs of the community. Nevertheless, when the Mexican government introduced family planning programs to the community, women did not go to the government clinic for help in preventing births. Even though the clinic provided easily available contraceptives, they saw such a move as too public and risky, and too connected to Mexican government agendas. But they did seek out traditional ways to prevent births, relying on local medicinal plants. San Francisco men responded by trying to prevent women from using any kind of birth control; for example, they chopped down a tree whose bark, they believed, was being used to prevent births.

These events highlight the ways in which reproduction can have contradictory purposes and meanings, often connected to gender. For women, more pregnancies and children meant more threats to their own health, and increased burdens of childrearing. But for men, reproduction represented one of the only ways to preserve their culture and identity against the powerful Mexican state. Whether women are able to achieve their own reproductive goals will depend not only on how well they are able to navigate pressures from the state, but also on how much power they have relative to men in their own community; these different pressures and expectations can be contradictory and difficult to navigate for all community members.

Fertility of Palestinians in Israel

Reproduction also plays a central role in struggles and conflicts between Palestine and Israel, part of how people construct and interpret their own and others' lives within Israel and in the Occupied Territories. As Kanaaneh has argued:

> The very definition of the Zionist state, as of most other nationalisms, is based on demography and numbers, but the settler colonial history of the creation of the state of Israel heightens this obsession, as well as its consequences ... The calculation of the ratio of Jews to "Arabs" and the other violent separation, rigidification, and essentializing of these identities is a cornerstone of the imagined community of Israel. (2002: 18)

As such, the relative sizes of the Palestinian and Israeli populations have been a source of enormous attention and concern on both sides. In 2020, the Palestinian population – including those residing in the Occupied Territories – was 5.1 million compared to the estimated 8.1 million Jews living in the state of Israel.[15]

Palestinian fertility levels have been much higher than those of Israelis in the past; differences were greatest in the 1960s when the Palestinian TFR was 9.23 and Israelis had a TFR of 3.39. Those TFR differentials produced "intense demographic anxiety" (Steinfeld 2015: 2), which continues to the present, even though the TFR differential has almost entirely disappeared. In fact, the TFR of Jews is now estimated to be slightly higher than that of Palestinians – 3.05 and 3.04, respectively (see Figure 5.6), although the TFR in the Occupied Territories is higher, at 4.1 (Khawaja 2018).

Since its founding, higher fertility rates among Palestinians have been seen as a threat by Israeli Jews (a "demographic time bomb") and as a source of strength in Palestine. However much the Israel/ Palestine conflict is about land ownership and settlement, the number of people that each side can claim to have has played an important role; if one side claims a demographic majority, it may be better able to dominate the country. Israeli leaders have frequently bemoaned the relative shrinking of their population. Some scholars have argued that Israeli authorities have used unreliable statistics about the size of the Palestinian population and growth rate in order to raise warnings of ultimate disaster and a Palestinian takeover and to garner more support both within and outside Israel (Faitelson 2009). A Palestinian "take-over" is not likely, because, of course, claims to land and the ability to settle it are about much more than

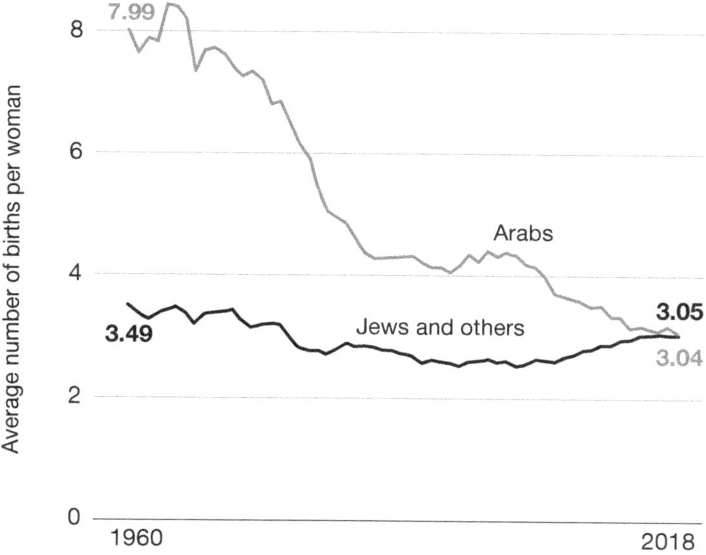

Figure 5.6. Fertility rates in Israel
Source: Aderet 2019

numbers of people; Israel has many more resources – including money, land, alliances, and military strength – than Palestine, all of which are deployed in the constant conflicts and battles in the area. Nevertheless, reproduction is still a focus. In an effort to combat this perceived threat and to boost the relative numbers of Jews in the population, the Israeli state has put into place programs that encourage Jewish citizens to bear more children and other programs that encourage Palestinian citizens to use birth control to reduce the number of children they have (Kanaaneh 2002: 35).

Palestinians too draw on population numbers and the importance of reproduction in their political goals. A common Palestinian saying reflects how reproduction also plays a central role there: "The Israelis beat us on the borders, but we beat them in the bedrooms" (Yuval-Davis 1987: 80). Yasser Arafat's argument, quoted above, about the importance of Arab wombs, underscores the ways that this political, religious, and ethnic conflict is played out with women's bodies – both Israeli and Palestinian – as they are contested and claimed by both sides.

Palestinian women are caught between competing expectations and forces. A large population and high fertility are largely seen as helping the Palestinian cause. But at the same time, Palestinian women also listen to the claim that modern women have few children, and that out-of-control fertility will mean Palestine is less likely to see success in the current world. In this discourse – found throughout the world, as we have seen – a responsible mother is one who has only one or two children and who puts her energies and resources into raising those children to be educated and successful in their future careers. This kind of rhetoric has been especially powerful in Israel, where the state has constructed Palestinians as reproductively backward; in this construction, it is their high fertility – rather than discriminatory state policies – that is the cause of their lower social and economic status in the country, which also has the potential to destabilize the state (Kanaaneh 2002: 252ff.). As they resist such labeling and blame, Palestinians turn to many tactics, including, ironically, one that fits some Israeli goals: some Palestinian women argue that by having fewer children – acting in a "modern" way – they are more likely to be accepted by Israelis and able to take their rightful place in the region and the world. But others see such an argument as succumbing to an Israeli model. No matter what stand Palestinian women take on reproduction, they endure pressure and conflict as they attempt to negotiate the conflicting expectations of those around them. Whether women should contribute to Palestine's goals through higher or through lower fertility, their reproductive behavior, and their central role and responsibilities as mothers, they remain in the crosshairs, easily judged for having too few or too many children, depending on the observer.

> Reproductive practices and discourses have become important markers of self and other ... partly because they are a central framework in Israeli definitions of self and Palestinian other ... Palestinians increasingly define themselves in terms of fertility and use reproductive control as a measure of modernity – or, alternatively Arab authenticity. (Kanaaneh 2002: 255)

Conclusions

Looking at reproduction from the perspective of communities underscores just how important a role it has in key issues: the size and racialized composition of the nation and whether that composition mirrors the imaginary of the nation; the size and power of a marginalized community; the ability of a community to survive. How communities respond to the challenges that are inflicted by the nation-state or other communities can determine what the future holds for all. Through it all, the gendered nature of these attacks on reproduction, and even the resistance to such attacks, underscores how reproduction connects women's lives with state policies and issues, even beyond those directly addressing reproduction. We have seen that reproduction is considered by many as a key tool in maintaining or dismantling a community. How reproduction of marginalized or small communities is viewed will, of course, depend on the position of the observer.

Smaller communities with ethnic, racial, or religious differences can be seen as a threat to the status quo hierarchy for those in positions of power, or even just part of the mainstream. We have seen that, across the world, dominant groups use their position to construct what they see as a demographic threat. They find ways to curtail reproduction – whether that is biological reproduction, as in the case of migrant women in Singapore, or social reproduction, as in the case of Japan in not allowing migrants to attain citizenship. But in other cases, strategies on the part of the dominant group include both biological and social reproductive constraints, as we saw happening in Native American, African American, and US poor communities.

Small or marginalized communities themselves recognize the centrality of reproduction too, of course. As we saw in San Francisco, Mexico, or among Palestinians in Israel, community members often see maintaining control over reproduction as necessary for their very survival. Such control can affect not only the community itself, but larger entities as well. As Ruth Fletcher argues, "women and men have reproduced children in ways that contest and change the dominant norms of their collectivities. Reproductive activities change the contours of nation and the agendas of nationalisms as much as they respond to them" (Fletcher 2005: 370). In Palestine, contested reproduction – control, numbers, and access to reproductive services – reflects the deep tensions between Palestinians and Jewish Israelis, as each group struggles for power in Israel. It is not surprising that fertility rates are much higher among Palestinians and Jews living in Israel than among those who live outside the region,[16] more evidence that in some high-conflict situations, higher fertility levels can be seen as a kind of defense against other groups (Kaufman 2021).

In the US, Black women too have resisted the kinds of attention their communities have received around reproduction issues. Some have formed coalitions to formalize a challenge to the dominant version of reproductive politics and access, and to advocate for reproductive justice. SisterSong is a social movement founded in 1997 as a coalition of 16 communities made up of women of color, with a goal of having their voices heard in a campaign that has often focused on issues of concern to white middle-class women. Sistersong argues that while reproductive rights are important, they have mainly focused on access to abortion and family planning. Women of color need more than access to abortion and activists within this movement have pointed to the problems with a reproductive rights agenda based on choice (D. Roberts 2015). Choice is not a useful concept for women who do not have access to reproductive services, or who experience such discrimination and racism that they are unable to navigate health services. Loretta Ross, one of the founders of Sistersong, argues that "the prochoice movement, largely directed by middle-class white women, is oblivious to the role of white supremacy in restricting reproductive options for all women, and as a result, often inadvertently colludes with it" (Ross 2016: 58). Expanding the goal to achieve reproductive justice brings in a social justice component. To achieve reproductive justice, women must have not only access to abortion and contraceptives, but the resources needed to decide whether to have children or not to have children, and to be able to "parent ... children ... in safe and sustainable communities" (Sistersong Collective). That expansive perspective on reproduction recognizes the ways that systemic inequalities and racisms have interfered with marginalized women's ability to control their own fertility; those larger systemic issues must also be addressed. Importantly, Sistersong directly confronts how reproductive control has been racialized in the US, and seeks to keep that racialization on the agenda as it works toward a fuller reproduction agenda.

Sistersong's agenda and arguments serve as a reminder of the complexities of reproductive politics. Often the very access to contraceptives or abortion that allows some women newly acquired control over their reproduction can be used – by the state, other organizations, or medical personnel – to constrain or even block reproductive control for other women. Women can find themselves caught between competing pressures, as they attempt to navigate through the gendered, classed, and racialized landscapes of their lives. In addition, a reproductive justice focus reminds us that whatever control women do or do not have over reproduction, it generally lies outside the grasp of any individual, but, rather, is part of social institutions, including the state.

6
Control of Reproduction in a Neoliberal World

While states remain powerful in shaping reproduction, the contemporary world has also been strongly influenced by the rise of neoliberalism and global capitalism. These forces have led to many changes that influence the lives of individuals around reproduction, including the withdrawal of state support for families, social welfare programs, and regulation of businesses, and the larger role of nonstate actors – private corporations and NGOs – in these areas. In this chapter, we focus on what the rise and spread of neoliberalism has meant for women's lives and for reproductive politics. We will see that, in the neoliberal era, reproduction remains as important as ever, but reproductive processes are shaped as often by these nonstate actors as they are by the state, although generally in conjunction with the state.

After addressing what neoliberalism is, we then turn to an exploration of how neoliberal capitalism has influenced reproductive processes in two countries where the US has played a dominant role, the Philippines and Egypt. We then explore how neoliberal ideology and rhetoric have been absorbed by other organizations.

How widely accepted neoliberalism has become is seen clearly in the actions and outcomes at the International Conference on Population and Development (ICPD), which took place in Cairo in 1994. Often referred to as "Cairo," the conference was seen as a watershed moment for reproductive politics across the world and one in which feminists played an important role. But as we will see, the Cairo agenda was heavily influenced by neoliberal assumptions and ideology, which limited how effective the conference was in changing ongoing reproductive politics. We end the chapter with an examination of The Girl Effect, an international program focused on girls and young women. We argue that although recognizing the importance of girls is a positive change, The Girl Effect and programs like it are motivated by the market and part of a neoliberal agenda; these programs have coopted feminist language and aspirations for egalitarian change, with arguments about empowerment, choice, and autonomy, but here in service to the market. Girls are targeted because girls will help communities to achieve the neoliberal goals of good investment and robust economic returns.

The examples we present here remind us that, even as states continue to play a role in managing reproduction and in women's lives generally, neoliberalism and the spread of global capitalism have meant that extra-state players – corporations and nongovernmental organizations (NGOs) – have become increasingly important in reproduction in most parts of the world (Harvey 2005; Metcalf 2017).

What is Neoliberalism?

Neoliberalism has been a potent global force for decades, but it often goes unnamed, is not widely seen for the powerful force it is, and is still not widely understood. The British writer and political activist George Monbiot (2016) points to its relatively unnoticed power:

> The ideology that dominates our lives has, for most of us, no name. Mention it in conversation and you'll be rewarded with a shrug. Even if your listeners have heard the term before, they will struggle to define it ... What greater power can there be than to operate namelessly? ... So pervasive has neoliberalism become that we seldom even recognise it as an ideology. We appear to accept the proposition that this utopian, millenarian faith describes a neutral force; a kind of biological law, like Darwin's theory of evolution. But the philosophy arose as a conscious attempt to reshape human life and shift the locus of power.

Neoliberalism is a set of ideologies and practices that first gained traction in the US and the UK in the 1970s. The first wave of neoliberalism was bolstered by wealthy states and NGOs, and was meant to create an oppositional pathway to socialist developmentalism in the Global South. At its core is a dedication to global capitalism and a belief that a free market economy – without state interference – is the best way to achieve individual and societal economic growth and success. At the societal level, neoliberalism supports open unregulated markets, privatization of services and social programs (such as health care), financial liberalization, and the shrinking of social welfare programs in the name of economic efficiency. It is built on the belief that "competition – between people, cities, regions, nations" produces the best results (Harvey 2005: 65). The market – capitalism – the argument continues, is the best way to solve global or national problems (Boyd 2016: 151).

The changes brought about by the turn toward neoliberalism shifted the role the state had played in previous eras. Before the 1970s, economists and others involved in government assumed that the state should have a strong role in most aspects of society. The state was expected to regulate the market in ways that would allow economic stability. That support would help in other areas, including employment, economic growth, and the welfare of citizens. In addition, the state would provide social insurance, providing for the welfare of citizens in the form of direct aid through health care, education, and by bolstering weaker communities. Neoliberalism brought a withdrawal of the state from many social and economic activities and has meant it is absent in supporting and shoring up social programs or services.

A neoliberal program is often targeted at the societal level, but the adoption of this ideology and these programs has huge impacts on all aspects and levels of a society, and affects the intimate affairs of individuals. These approaches mean that individuals cannot rely on the state for help to achieve financial success or growth or to help them in times of need. Because the state is no longer responsible for care of its citizens, they must be in charge of taking care of themselves. Thus, responsibility for economic success lies with the individual, who, like the national and global markets, should focus on developing their own "capital," whether that be economic investments or education. Neoliberalism holds that success is available to all, as long as they choose the right path. From such assumptions comes a belief that those who succeed (i.e. the rich) have done the right things, and those who fail (i.e. the poor) have made the wrong choices, and thus individuals have only themselves to blame (or credit) for their situation.

The US and the UK were the earliest proponents of neoliberalism. Margaret Thatcher famously declared that there is no such thing as society, only individual men and women. Therefore, "all forms of social solidarity were to be dissolved in favor of individualism, private property, personal responsibility, and family values" (Harvey 2005: 23). While the US and the UK were involved early, governmental and international organizations such as the World Bank and the International Monetary Fund (IMF) soon took up these practices and ideologies. It quickly became hegemonic in any economic planning and assessment across the world and permeates the discourse of development. The spread of neoliberalism has been shored up by the collapse of the Soviet Union and China's embrace of state capitalism, leading to an expansion and consolidation of neoliberal capitalism as the dominant global formation.

As dominant richer countries got involved in the economic development of poorer countries, they set certain conditions. In return for loans that might be used to jump-start their economy, richer countries and organizations like the World Bank stipulated that poorer countries must agree to "structural adjustment programs" (SAPs), that are based on neoliberal principles. To receive any help from richer countries, or World Bank or IMF loans, they had to agree to open their markets, privatize the economy, dismantle most market regulations, and practice "austerity measures" by dismantling their social welfare programs. Given that a major goal of the neoliberal agenda "is to ease conditions for profit-making" (Harvey 2005: 5), it follows that poorer states can easily lose out as they get pulled in to this system. Indeed, many writers attribute the growing inequalities within countries and between the Global North and South to the spread of neoliberalism (Monbiot 2016). International bankers and rich countries earn profits from these unequal relationships and the dependency of poorer countries. International corporations also have a strong hold on those governments, as "the boundary between the state and corporate power has become more and more porous" (Harvey 2005: 77–8). The impact on individuals in poorer countries is often acute: under these policies, individuals are left with few social services, struggling to find ways to survive in this increasingly hostile economic environment.

Neoliberal ideology can be found well outside the state as well, as civil society actors, often representing public/private partnerships, fill in for the now-absent government programs in areas like health care and economic support. As we will discuss below, NGO programs – including feminist ones – are often embedded in this kind of logic; because women's health NGOs make up a large proportion of feminist NGOs (Murphy 2012: 6), the impact on reproductive services is often extensive. In addition, some institutions, like the World Bank and the UN, have appropriated terms from feminism and are now using them for achieving neoliberal goals; for example, "the term 'empowerment' has been eviscerated of its original political content ... and 'agency' joins 'choice' in a coupling of concepts that permits little ... talk about power, inequities or indeed any structural constraints at all" (Cornwall et al. 2008: 3). As we will see as we examine the rhetoric and programs enacted through the 1994 ICPD in Cairo, even when feminists are involved in policymaking, the outcomes are often still deeply embedded in neoliberal ideologies.

Neoliberalism and structural adjustment policies have been particularly devasting for women. Women are more likely than men to be poor, likely to have a more tenuous hold in the labor market, and more likely to be responsible for children. They are, therefore, more dependent on the support that governments sometimes provide to struggling families. Women are also more vulnerable than men to the trade policies enacted under SAPs – it is the sectors of the economy that employ women, such as teaching or nursing, that get dismantled. Women are also vulnerable because they are overrepresented in other sectors of the economy as well: in export processing zones that employ cheap labor and provide little labor protection; and in smaller, poorly paid domestic industries like textiles that are often undercut by the import of foreign goods that are demanded in the SAPs (WGNRR 2004: 16–17).

We see the impact of neoliberalism, and the power of rich countries to enforce it, in countries like the Philippines and Egypt, and in the new roles that NGOs and corporations have stepped into.

Debt and Economic Crisis in the Philippines

The Philippines provides a good example of how global capitalism and neoliberalism have influenced all aspects of life in many countries of the Global South, from the very top – Philippine relations with other countries like the US – to the most intimate – women's relationships to family members. Women's reproduction – both social and biological – is fundamentally shaped by these processes. The effects on women and their control of reproduction is further undermined by the role that the Catholic Church plays in family and political life in the Philippines.

The Philippines is a poor country; its gross national per capita income of US$3,850 in 2019 puts it in the lower tier of Asian countries in terms of its economy. As is true in many places, families struggle to find a way to survive and create a better future for their children and grandchildren. But in the Philippines, those paths have been considerably restricted by the country's history of colonialism, its relationship to the US, and by the ways that SAPs have further constrained the options for the country and its people.

The Philippines has a long history of colonialism, first under Spain's rule for 400 years, and then under US rule. While the Philippines was declared officially independent from the US in 1946, the country has experienced a neocolonial regime ever since, as the US has maintained its influence through its military presence and its control of the Philippine economy. After independence, the Philippine government borrowed heavily to expand its economy, and has been in a debt crisis ever since. That debt and the constraints that have come with it have resulted in the "virtual surrender of the country's economic sovereignty" (Pineda-Ofreneo 1991: 6). The IMF, the World Bank, and the US government all stepped in to "help" the Philippine economy, making loans to the government to fund economic development. But these foreign groups also stipulated the terms of the agreement:

> In exchange for SAP loans, the Philippines was forced to open its doors to global competition via the development of export industries through the cheap manufacturing of goods. The economy had to abide by the stabilization program of the IMF which stipulated that the government must withdraw subsidies for farmers and consumers, open the economy to foreign goods and services, reduce support for small producers, and privatize state utility services, the national railway, and social security pension funds. (Parreñas 2005: 15)

These loans and subsequent debts have created an economic crisis in the Philippines.

This economic crisis, now decades-old, has burrowed deep into Filipino society, starved domestic growth and survival, produced enormous inequality within the country, and left a large proportion of the population in poverty. When foreign entities forced the country to open its markets, Philippine businesses found themselves unable to compete with foreign markets, unable to attract customers, and have no protection against that competition and take-over. Foreign dominance in the economy and economic deregulation has also reduced wages in the Philippines, making it difficult for many to earn enough for basic survival. The disappearance of state support for many aspects of social life has been just as devastating. Those services have been eliminated partly because of the large percentage of government spending that goes to debt service to foreign entities, making it difficult for the government to support such services. But as part of the stipulations of their loans, those foreign groups have also explicitly restricted how much support the government can give to public services such as health, education, and welfare. For poorer people in the Philippines, this debt crisis has meant severe hardship in a variety of forms. As a consequence of these processes that began in the early 1970s, by 1988, about half the country lived in poverty, as defined by official standards (which uses a standard of enough to feed a family of six each month). But others estimated that the poor actually made up 70 percent of the population; in this estimation, the poor included those who "cannot buy for their families recommended nutrient requirements, cannot permit two changes of garments, cannot permit Grade 6 schooling for the children, cannot cover minimal costs of medical care and cannot pay for fuel and rent" (Pineda-Ofreneo 1991: 13). The lack of state support hits the poorest the hardest, as they cannot afford to access alternative – private and costly – services.

Unable to find a way to support themselves and their families within their own country, millions of Filipinos migrate to other, wealthier, countries to try to earn enough money to support their families. The need for labor in the Global North, increased globalization of the world's economy, and the ways that SAPs have gutted economies like that of the Philippines has led to increased migration from poor to rich countries. The wages from migrant labor can sometimes fill in for missing government programs, providing children with education, health care, and better food and housing. Women have been especially caught in this system of poverty, inequality, and migration, with mothers often leaving their children behind as they seek work in other countries. As one scholar explained, "women … [take on] the role of shock absorbers in the absence of any other form of social security" (Imrana Qadeer, cited in Sexton and Nair 2010: 39). Many of these migrant women become part of a "global care chain," a process we will explore further in Chapter 7. What we want to underscore here is how neoliberalism and the gross inequalities between rich and poor have influenced the reproduction of Filipinas, caught up in a system where their labor is bought and sold across world.

The Philippine government and economy have become reliant on the remittances of migrants. Those remittances were estimated to be about 10 percent of the country's GDP in 2020, down from a high of almost 13 percent in 2005. In 2004, three-quarters of migrants seeking work abroad were women; since that peak year, that proportion has decreased, but women still comprise a higher percentage of Filipino migrant workers than men, making up about 56 percent of migrants in 2019. Women contribute to the state's economy at home too. Women comprise 70 percent of the workers in free trade zones in the Philippines, which produce most of the country's exported goods and are competing most heavily on the global market (Parreñas 2003).

Women have been both encouraged in and vilified for their overseas migration and labor force activity. On the one hand, their remittances have made it possible for their families and communities to survive and sometimes thrive, without government support. Because of the lack of government support for public services, migrant women's wages are often the only way that their children can get good schooling, that their families have the assurance of a regular and proper food supply, and that they might be able to buy a house. From this perspective, they are valued as devoted family members, mothers, daughters. Indeed, migrant laborers are regularly lauded as heroes for their contributions to the economy (Tanyag 2017).

But there is also a competing message about migrant women, one that draws on ideologies of the importance of family and proper gender roles to criticize migrant women. Thus, at the same time as "the state applauds the economic contributions of women … it also morally convict[s] these women for threatening 'family solidarity'" (Parreñas 2003: 30); by working outside the home and, especially, by leaving their families to find work outside the country, women migrants are depicted as not upholding – and even as violating – key principles of Philippine society. State rhetoric argues that strong families are the core of a stable and robust Philippine society, and the state has enacted laws to support what it sees as proper families. In the process of passing the 1985 Family Code, one government official argued that "we must have strong marriages and strong families in order to have a strong nation" (Parreñas 2005: 35). But it is a particular version of family that is promoted by the state: a strictly gendered nuclear family in which a father works outside the family to provide financial support and a mother stays at home to take care of the house and children. In this discourse, "maternity, understood to include the care of the family, is one of women's primary duties to the state" (Parreñas 2005: 36). Such rhetoric mirrors that of the Catholic Church, an institution with enormous influence on Philippine norms, values, and laws that has played a key role in these contradictory messages to women. The model for good womanhood in the Catholic Church is a self-sacrificing mother who has infinite compassion and commitment to others (Tanyag 2017). But, the church admonishes, these characteristics should be directed to their families, and within their households, not in waged work. Out of this rhetoric comes disapproval of women who would leave the country to work elsewhere – even as they do so to support their families.

There is yet another contradiction here. For all the discourse about a gendered moral order that would keep women at home making sacrifices for their families, the state has not backed this rhetoric with the kind of support for families that might allow them to thrive or even survive. Government debt and SAPs have resulted in much less support for families, in poorer schools, less accessible health care, and a general hollowing out of welfare programs. Because of the central role they play in taking care of their families, women are particularly vulnerable to the state's withdrawal of support.

Philippine women are thus caught in a bind from which it is hard to find a winning path. As the Philippine economy and state are increasingly reliant on women's waged labor and remittances to keep the country running, it is nearly impossible for women to meet their families' needs and also fulfil some exaggerated notion of their role in upholding traditional patriarchal families. They are expected to marry men, to bear many children to populate the country, and to take care of their families and children.

Fathers face far fewer sanctions in this arrangement. They too migrate, often using the wages they earn to help support their families. But they are not vilified as women migrants are for abandoning their families, and they are less likely to be the targets of challenge, encouragement, or disparagement around their own fertility. It is true that if a family feels that a mother's income is needed for family support or survival, the father's ability to properly support his family is called into question. But because of social norms about proper gender roles, there are fewer expectations for men to step in and do housework or child care, even when their wives are working overseas. Men are less often the target of government and other sanctions for improper family situations.

At any rate, it is not families, but the Philippine state and its connection to global capitalism that are the source of these difficulties. The quagmire of debt and the constraints placed on the economy by outside forces make it impossible for families to survive without women's wages. The state does not provide enough services for children or families, forcing individuals to find their own solutions. Women are left to fend for themselves and their families without state support or traditional family networks.

In addition to the challenges that women face in supporting their families in the often dire circumstances they find themselves, they also face other obstacles in reaching their reproductive goals. The 1986 Constitution makes clear that women are the "wombs of the nation [and] are obliged to reproduce the population" (Parreñas 2003: 34). One provision asserts that the state will "protect" women and "enable them to realize their full potential in the service of the nation" (cited in Parreñas 2003). As evidence of this "support," and bolstered by Catholic Church ideology, abortion is outlawed and access to contraception is restricted, even with the passage of the 2012 Responsible Parenthood and Reproductive Health Act, which gave women more access to contraceptive services. Access is constrained particularly for women who fall outside the idealized family structure. In recent decades, free or subsidized contraception has, like other public services, declined, leaving women dependent on finding private sources and funding for contraception (Guttmacher Institute 2010). For them to reach their "reproductive potential" as imagined by the state – and have more children – women would have to abandon their outside jobs, leaving their families unable to survive. Women have little "choice" in these circumstances, given the lack of support for their lives and needs, a lack that forces them into places and situations that may be only the best option out of a series of bad ones. Given the dire state of the Philippine economy and global economic inequalities, emigration to other countries may be the only choice that women have to provide for their families, often forcing them to postpone or forgo childbearing even as they work in domestic service in wealthy countries.

Women's lack of control of their reproduction – biological or social – thus comes not by direct fiat as we have seen in some countries, like China, where the state dictates how many and when women can bear children. But the forces of neoliberal restrictions combined with the gendered social norms coming out of the economic crisis in the Philippines is binding nevertheless. In these circumstances, women often have as little control over whether and how many children they have or when they have them as do women who live in other societies where the state is more explicit and more direct in its control of fertility, reproduction, and population.

Learning to Value Individualism in Egypt

In addition to its effect on economic policy, neoliberalism also influences ideology, as we see in Egypt's family planning program. As we saw in Chapter 3, the specific goals of the program were to reduce births and increase contraceptive use, with the aim of reducing the TFR – which stood at 3.9 in the early 1990s (Ali 2002: 33). But another goal of the program has had deeper implications: to convince women to take on characteristics of "modern" women, which would bring them into the neoliberal fold. In examining Egypt's family planning program, we see the power of a strategy to shape not only fertility levels but even how women come to think of themselves and their communities.

Egypt's family planning program of the 1980s was established as part of its structural adjustment program designed by the World Bank, the IMF, and the US government after Egypt sought loans from them following economic crisis. In addition to required changes in the economy – similar to those imposed on the Philippines – these foreign groups also recommended changes in its population stance. They argued that lower fertility rates would allow Egypt more rapid and efficient economic growth. Some of the economic changes that were required, such as reducing state subsidies and increasing the prices of goods or services, were partly designed to discourage women from having children. If services and basic needs were expensive, perhaps they would be more likely to accept and use contraception

(Ali 1996). In addition, they urged Egypt to redesign the family planning program itself – to make it more robust and targeted; the US – through USAID – became a central player.

Along with the specific demographic goal of reducing fertility, the program's foundations were strongly neoliberal, rooted in western notions of society and individualism. Pointing to their higher levels of fertility relative to educated urban women, the program particularly targeted rural and poor women (who – like Filipino women – were most affected by the SAPs). It sought to change the way women thought about themselves, to create "new selves" (Ali 2002: 139). Women were encouraged to see themselves as individualized, autonomous beings who can make good choices. In this model, good choices are those that contribute positively to the future of the nation – which entails fewer children and the reliable use of contraception. The program discouraged women from thinking of themselves as they had in the past, as interconnected with others around them, or viewing reproduction as part of and bound to the community or family. Instead, the program emphasized individual "rights" and "choice," and worked to get women to see themselves as independent in their thinking and decisions. The program thus focused not only on changing reproductive behavior, but also on modifying the very way women thought about themselves and their connections to family, community, and nation. In this way, "Egypt, as a modernizing state, would use the family planning program as a pedagogical project to manage its population" (Ali 2002: 5).

The goal was to get individuals to voluntarily seek out ways to accommodate to the state's goals of economic change and modernity and to "internalize and thus normalize market-oriented behavior" (Harvey 2005: 12). Individuals and their actions – not government interventions – would change Egypt for the better. The focus on women and reproduction was also significant. If mothers shape the ways their children come to see the world, then convincing women to strive to be modern, self-regulating individuals would go far in changing how entire communities come to understand their role in the new society. Thus, in their construction of the risks and problems of "too many children," these programs and their sponsors encourage women to "feel responsible for the social and economic problems facing the entire nation. In the name of individual choice they are guided into accepting contraception as part of being responsible citizens who may have to suffer 'minor health problems for the larger social good'" (Ali 2002: 54). It is an appeal to individual actors – often the most disempowered – to solve systemic problems of equity and equality, echoing what we saw among Palestinian women (Chapter 5), as they struggled to find a place in "modern" Israeli society.

The power of neoliberalism to influence the Global South – even beyond the economic power we saw in the Philippines – is readily apparent in these processes in Egypt. Here, it is neoliberal ideology that is doing the work. Kamran Ali, an anthropologist studying and working alongside local health workers, labels their work a "form of conversion, a conversion into modern sensibilities of self-consciousness and of agency" (2002: 83). USAID, a long-time funder of Egypt's family planning program, includes in its goals the training of health and education officers "in behavior change methodologies; participants are applying this expertise in engagements with the Egyptian public" (USAID 2021). Ali writes about this practice of behavior change: "We believed that they [women] were not choosing as individuals, not taking responsibility for their own improvement, and therefore, they were hindered by 'tradition' ... We were critically unaware ... that the constitution of their individuality was embedded in a multiplicity of social and communitarian relationships" (2002: 83). What got ignored in this approach to family planning – and what accounted for much of the resistance to the program – was how women saw motherhood and children, and the ways that modern contraception threatened their sense of themselves (Bier 2010). In her study of poor urban women in Egypt, Marcia Inhorn (1996) argues that, for some women, motherhood is their most important role; for them, to be a woman is to be a mother. Motherhood gives them power, love, and an identity; children bind them to their family and community in important ways and provide companionship and shape women's daily routines. Anything that threatens these women's role as mothers is dangerous because it can destabilize their access to vital social capital. That version of Egyptian women's understanding of motherhood is erased in the western, neoliberal version of modernity.

Nevertheless, the Egyptian state, supported and pressured by outside institutions, continued to work toward changing women's ways of being as they came to adopt modern contraceptives. In this process, the Egyptian state used the family planning program as a way to mold its population into a western, neoliberal version of modern citizenry. Such an approach presumes that a smaller population guarantees a wealthier population and that individual reproductive rationality automatically leads to economic gains at the family and national level. If women could be convinced to think like "modern" women through their interaction with the family planning program, they would then come to see themselves as choosing family planning and smaller families voluntarily, through their own choice, and the state could avoid having to impose heavy-handed measures to reach its goals. This perspective supports Foucault's argument (1991) about how the modern state controls its population – not through coercive means, but through influencing the populace to take on self-management, becoming self-regulating citizens and, on their own, support state goals.

> Whereas [in the past] social reformers had discussed women as objects of population policy, new policy planners, public figures, and the press began to talk of gendered national subjects for whom the use of birth control constituted the performance of the duties of citizenship. Women were recognized as having an important role to play in determining their own, and more importantly, the nation's reproductive destinies. (Bier 2010: 414)

In Egypt's family planning program we see neoliberalism in action, as "culturally neutral and seemingly universal concepts of free choice and autonomy … become indicators for women's emancipation from more 'traditional' sets of constraints" (Ali 2002: 84). In many ways, these ideological tenets of neoliberalism have been at least as powerful as its economic mandates.

Cairo ICPD, and Feminist Perspectives

The example of Egypt allows us to see how neoliberalism has caused major shifts in family planning and reproductive health programs in recent decades. Further evidence of this shift comes from two important UN conferences: the first, the ICPD held in 1994 in Cairo, focused on population; the second, the Fourth World Conference on Women held in Beijing in 1995, focused on women. These two conferences marked important watershed moments in a shift from population programs that had often been coercive to programs focused on reproductive health and rights. Feminists dominated these conferences, their agendas, and their Programs of Action (PoA). At Cairo, they were adamant that family planning programs needed to change. The Cairo PoA called for a focus not on population targets but on expanding reproductive health for women. It argued that all individuals have "the right ... to make decisions concerning reproduction free of discrimination, coercion and violence as expressed in human rights documents" (UNFPA 2014 [1994]). The PoA also argued that these reproductive rights must be embedded in "mutually respectful and equitable gender relations." This shift, which pivoted to centering on women – not on counting numbers of births – as the focus of more expansive reproductive health programs, was seen as a milestone in the global population program.

> [Cairo was] a clear denunciation of the demographic, target-driven programmes that have reflected the population policies of so many countries ... condemning incentive and disincentive schemes as well as targets and quotas. In these ways, the Cairo Programme codifies the expansive vision of reproductive health and rights for which women's health movements have campaigned and provided models throughout the past decade. (Petchesky 1995: 154)

Indeed, this shift led to many positive outcomes, particularly in the ways that this stance allowed women more control over reproduction in some circumstances. Notably, the PoA was endorsed by most governments across the world, and in many places, feminists and health workers used the Cairo platform – and their government's promise to adhere to it – to push for more and better reproductive health services in their countries, services not reduced to contraception or sterilization alone (WGNRR 2004: 7).

But even as the Cairo ICPD was being celebrated by many as a new and better way forward, and even though many argued that Cairo reflected a sea change in how contraception was delivered, in the shift from coercion to rights, programs hewed to a neoliberal model. In achieving the "Cairo consensus" – an agreement across NGOs, governments, and organizations such as the World Bank – much of the original political, liberating energy was lost to the new language and goals of neoliberalism. No longer relying on coercion or suggesting that the best way to change fertility rates is to round up women for sterilization, today's rhetoric is more likely to focus on choice and empowerment. But here, the emphasis is on how women's empowerment is a better pathway to lower fertility, not necessarily an end in itself. As we saw in both the Philippines and Egypt, this rhetoric and approach feed into a neoliberal assumption that the best way to effect change is to put the responsibility for it on women, without giving them or their families much in the way of social services. The focus is on individuals, and the larger social structures and vast inequalities that shape the lives of those individuals are never attended to and rarely acknowledged. Thus, programs encourage a woman to make the "right" choices, as if the right decision will mean her success and well-being, suggesting that if she is unable to achieve good health or economic success, it must be that she made the wrong choice. As we have seen, these new emphases on choice came as neoliberal and structural adjustment policies were cutting back or eliminating many publicly financed health programs; the remaining reproductive health services, which were increasingly privatized, often narrowed women's choices in the new era. As we argued in Chapter 1, "choice" is only available to those who have options; emphasizing "choice" is another way of focusing on individuals rather than the context in which those individuals act. Without attention to the wider context in which women seek reproductive health services, the language at Cairo was not effective. For women to have the right to decide about when and whether to have children, they need resources.

In the decades after Cairo, scholars and activists have sought to analyze why so many of the goals set at the conference were not implemented, despite the energy and commitment shown at the time. Some argue that there was not enough political will on the part of governments (Potts 1996; Finkle and McIntosh 1996). Others point to the resistance to the platform by religious and conservative groups (Puri and McLellan 1996; Hempel 1996). One of the most important reasons was the ways in which neoliberal and structural adjustment and austerity programs, in place before Cairo and continuing long afterward, had hollowed out health services and closed down access to reproductive and other health programs across the world; the demands of deregulation and market liberalization had also resulted in lower wages, the weakening of worker protections, and growing inequality. Because Cairo did not address or challenge the prevailing and deepening neoliberal climate and its effects on women's lives, any enactment of the resultant goals had to take place in environments deeply unfriendly to good health and reproductive care.

Consequently, family planning programs in most places did not expand to include the more inclusive reproductive health services that were central to Cairo's goal (Kane 1996; Sexton and Nair 2010: 36). In most countries subject to structural adjustment and austerity measures, health care has been privatized and families struggle to pay for health care out of pocket; health care expenditures often cause financial disaster for families or, even worse, people are not able to get any health care at all. Women of reproductive age are particularly harmed in this environment. "Many women have little or no access to reproductive health services, or even any decent health services at all, because they are not provided or because they are not affordable" (Sexton and Nair 2010: 36).

We can trace these influences in the "safe motherhood" programs, strongly promoted at Cairo. Feminist activists worked to expand these programs, hoping that it would mean better and more health care for women at all stages of their lives. But the form these programs took after Cairo is often not distinguishable from what came before. Programs often focused on reducing "reproductive risk." Key to that risk reduction is reducing fertility; after all, if a woman does not get pregnant, she faces little reproductive risk. More than 60 percent of the funds allocated to reproductive health go to family planning and reducing fertility (WGNRR 2014: 22). Thus rather than an expansion of available health services, many of the post-Cairo programs resemble old wine in new bottles, with programs continuing to focus on women changing their behavior and reducing fertility to achieve individual and societal success.

India provides a good example of what Cairo has achieved and missed. As we discussed in Chapter 2, the Indian state has long supported a family planning program, often using coercive methods to "convince" women (and sometimes men) to undergo sterilization or use a long-acting hormonal method such as Depo-Provera. After agreeing to the Cairo program goals, the Indian state vowed to change its ways. Certainly, much of its rhetoric changed. The program underwent a name change, from the Family Welfare Programme to the Reproductive and Child Health Programme (RCH), to signal its intention to move away from family planning targets and shift to providing comprehensive services to women. Incentives – to those accepting contraceptives or to local health workers – were dismantled. Following the kinds of suggestions made in the PoA in Cairo, India vowed to offer a "cafeteria approach," with women able to choose if and what kind of contraceptive method they wanted to use. And the state promised that it would be "women-centered," rather than population-focused.

While there may have been good intentions on the part of some in the Indian government to make these changes, in practice, India's population program has continued many of its old ways. One scholar activist declared that "India's population policies [have been] untouched by the Cairo rhetoric" (Rao 2005: 21). The reasons for this are several. First and foremost, many leaders in India continued to believe that population – its growth, size, and quality – had been holding India back from economic stability, development, and success. This meant that, as much as officials wanted to provide other reproductive health services, family planning remained the core of the program and was where most of the funding and efforts continued to be focused. Another factor was that states were given more control over implementing the new population goals, and some states (including Andhra Pradesh, Rajasthan, and Uttar Pradesh) continued policies that were coercive. The governments of these states and others punished those who had more than two children and rewarded those who agreed to sterilization, through such incentives or punishments as restrictions on hiring, tax punishments, or allocation of land or housing (WGNRR 2004: 28). While India no longer has national population "targets," there are now state-level "Expected Levels of Achievement" (Wilson 2018: 119). In 2012, Human Rights Watch investigated India's program and found that:

> In much of the country, authorities aggressively pursue targets, especially for female sterilization, by threatening health workers with salary cuts or dismissals. As a result, some health workers pressure women to undergo sterilization without providing sufficient information, either about possible complications, its irreversibility, or safer sex practices after the procedure. (HRW 2012)

"Health workers who miss sterilization targets ... risk losing their jobs in many parts of the country," said one of the investigators.

In addition, foreign governments and NGOs continued to encourage and to fund incentives and disincentives (Hartmann 2011). Perhaps most telling has been the influence from India's neoliberal approach to health, including reproductive health. The government has increasingly encouraged private and corporate involvement in its population policies and programs, positioning women as clients and consumers rather than rights-bearing citizens.

> By invoking the language of neo-liberalism, the state legitimizes the development of a "marketplace" of population policy. Thereby, the state could justify the emphasis on efficiency, opening up options that were not previously acceptable such as encouraging private providers in the production, marketing, and sales of family welfare services and products and cutting down services and subsidies. In principle, all of this was rationalized as being for the benefit of the "client/consumer." (Simon-Kumar 2010: 148)

These changes have resulted in a decline in government-funded health services and more reliance on paid-for private services, making poorer citizens even more vulnerable. Increasingly reliant on private market approaches to health, women are encouraged to find their own way to creating a family and better reproductive health more generally, health that is increasingly out of reach of India's poor. The larger context of poverty and increasing class inequality, gender inequality, and religious discrimination are routinely ignored or seen as solved through the effort of individual women. Now that women are given more "choices" (through the market), they are expected to make responsible decisions and thereby reap the benefits of good behavior.

And so, Cairo, hailed by some to be leading edge of better health for women, did not meet its goals. By aligning with institutions that operated under neoliberal ideologies, feminist organizations were unable to achieve their political, liberating aims. In its focus on rights, choice, and empowerment,

> [the ICPD failed to address how a woman can] avail herself of this right if she lacks the financial resources to pay for reproductive health services or the transport to get to them; if she is illiterate or given no information in a language she understands; if her workplace is contaminated with pollutants that have an adverse effect on pregnancy; or if she is harassed by parents, a husband or in-laws who will abuse or beat her if they find out she used birth control. (Petchesky, quoted in WGNRR 2004: 14)

The Cairo and, especially, the Beijing conferences were also important in the ways that spotlighted the role of NGOs in the area of reproduction and women's health. Both conferences welcomed NGOs as strong players in these areas, reflecting how, as the state has moved away from many services and programs it once provided, NGOs and corporations have stepped in. Many NGO programs might be considered an alternative to state action, providing services for free or at a lower cost than those offered by private businesses. But while their independence from the state is sometimes assumed or even desired, many of them work in conjunction, or even partnership, with national and local governments.

Sometimes hailed as indicators of vibrant civil society involvement, the politics of NGOs vary from right-wing conservative to deeply progressive (Bernal and Grewal 2014). Many NGOs focus on issues of gender and women; those that focus on women's health are now the most common type of feminist NGO (Murphy 2012: 6), which speaks to the gaps that the thinning of government programs left in the area of reproductive health.

> Neoliberalization fosters feminist NGOs on two levels: first, the withdrawal of state and public resources from welfare sectors creates a gap that NGOs seek to fill, taking on public roles from private positions and second, those spaces of state withdrawal were often already sites of women's paid and unpaid labor and feminist struggles for resources and services. (Bernal and Grewal 2014: 10)

In at least this way, NGOs are deeply connected to the state and its actions and non-actions. NGOs are also not wholly different from the state in their discourses and ideologies (Kamat 2004). As Victoria Bernal and Inderpal Grewal also note: "The NGO form produces and converts what is outside the state into a legible form within a governmentality that parallels official state power. In this way the NGO form, somewhat paradoxically, derives power from working with the biopolitical logics of the state" (2014: 8). Even gender-focused programs have been coopted by neoliberal notions, focusing less on dismantling the larger structures of inequality and more on encouraging the "empowerment" of individual women as the best way forward (Chant 2008, 2016b; Eisenstein 2005, 2009; Fraser 2009; Murphy 2012; Hickel and Khan 2012). And many NGOs are also structured around inequalities between North and South, with northern feminists more likely to hold positions of power, have better access to funding, and have more say in the direction of the organization than feminists from the Global South (Desai 2007). We will see in the next section that many of them are imbued with neoliberal ideology, with quite a few drawing from neoliberal discourse in their policies and planning in ways that can "serve unwittingly as the hand-maiden of corporate globalization" (Desai 2007: 798).

The Girl Effect as Smart Economics

We turn to one such program, a public/private partnership focused on girls. The Girl Effect was founded by the Nike Corporation in 2004 and in 2015 became an NGO. Nike still supports the organization, but the program gets funding and support from other corporations and campaigns, including UNICEF, corporations like telephone companies and Facebook, and other NGOs. While we focus our discussion here on The Girl Effect, we note that it is one of many such organizations that target girls as a way to reduce poverty across the world. Other programs are run by other NGOs or international organizations. USAID has two such programs. Let Girls Learn was initiated in 2015 by Michelle and Barack Obama, focusing on getting and keeping girls in school in poorer countries. DREAMS (Determined, Resilient, Empowered, AIDS-free, Mentored and Safe), a public/private partnership launched in 2015, focuses on HIV and AIDS among young women in sub-Saharan Africa. The Adolescent Girls Initiative was a World Bank public/private partnership that ran from 2008 to 2015, which promoted girls' move from school to employment in several Global South countries. From 2012 to 2018, Because I Am a Girl, launched by Plan International, worked for girls' rights through programs focused on health and education; it had government (USAID), multilateral (World Bank), and corporate partners (Citibank; JP Morgan; Comedy Central TV).

Nike's The Girl Effect, as the first and one of the largest of these programs, has had an enormous impact on development discourse and policy; a focus on girls as the solution to poverty and other ills is now part of nearly every global development organization. The Girl Effect operates in countries throughout the world, and strives to connect the lives of girls in both poor and rich countries. The website makes its case: "Because when a girl unlocks her power to make different choices that change her life, it inspires others to do so too. She starts a ripple effect that impacts her family, her community, her country. That's the Girl Effect." Increasing education for girls is, by nearly all standards, an important goal, and such a goal is laudable. It is the underlying reasons for promoting girls' education and empowerment that warrant attention; whatever good outcomes these programs achieve, a central goal is to bring young women into global capitalism.

Investing in girls – in their education, jobs training and entrepreneurship, health and reproduction – has come to be seen as the most effective means to propel a country's economic development (Moeller 2018). Economist Lawrence Summers makes clear the economic value and labor market benefits: "educating girls quite possibly yields a higher rate of return than any other investment available in the developing world" (quoted in Murphy 2017). Through these programs, girls and women will be empowered, able to make their own choices and find their way forward into a productive life and away from traditional constraints. Indeed, a major theme running through most girl-targeted programs and rhetoric is the need for girls to break free from "cultural" beliefs and practices that have kept them back all along. Just as we saw was the case in US involvement in the Egyptian family planning program, this discourse reflects the presumption that the West is best, and that women in the Global South will do better – and help their communities and nations – if they start thinking and acting like westerners.

The underlying argument is that investing in these programs, focused on girls and young women, will pay off in higher rates of economic growth and greater societal and community stability. As The Girl Effect argues in one video, "An educated girl will stay healthy, save money, build a business, empower her community, lift her country, and save the world." The alternative path is disaster: "When a girl turns 12 and lives in poverty, the future is out of her control" – she will be married by 14, pregnant by 15, she may have to sell her body to support her family, and will then be at risk for contracting and spreading HIV. In this scenario, the future of the world rests on the shoulders of girls.

The pathway to such success is through global capitalism, entrepreneurship, and consumption. The Girl Effect's promotional materials make it clear that a major goal of the program is to bring girls and young women into the global market economy. Indeed, while there are many reasons that increasing education opportunities would benefit girls, The Girl Effect's focus on education is directed toward a specific aim: following neoliberal logic, education is the way to teach young women how to become proper consumers and thus helps to embed them in the market economy. For example, in 2011, a subsidiary program of The Girl Effect named Girl Hub began a program in Rwanda, focused on girls aged from 10 to 12. It worked to expand education opportunities for the 600 girls in the program, but not simply for the sake of education. Rather, it saw as most important the development of "entrepreneurial and business skills, as well as access to financial capital [with] enterprise training and micro-finance products tailored to adolescent girls" (Boyd 2016: 155). Education modules would include information "about savings and lending, mobile phone banking, and imparting employable skills" (Boyd 2016: 156). These skills, the program argued, would give girls the skills to change their lives, and to "shift the social norms that hold girls back, and drive better investments that directly benefit girls" (GirlHub 2014).

Whatever benefits girls receive from such training, the larger payoff will be to the economy, a process often labeled "smart economics." As another Girl Effect video puts it, after we invest in a girl and get her successfully connected to the market, we can expect a series of positive events:

> Let's put her in a school uniform and see her get a loan to buy a cow and use the profits from the milk to feed her family ... Soon the village is thriving. Healthier babies. Peace. Lower HIV. Food. Education. Commerce. Sanitation. Stability. Which means the economy of the entire country improves and the whole world is better off. ... Invest in a girl and she will do the rest.

The argument is that doing so will be good for girls, for their communities, and for nations, and also, perhaps most importantly, for market profits. In another Girl Effect video, a 17-year-old Bangladeshi woman demonstrates just such drive and success: through a loan, she bought a young cow. The cow has grown and she now brings in a monthly income from the sale of its milk and from selling vegetables. She uses that income to help her family, including paying her younger brother's school fees, and to "save for her future." As if to underscore the message of this story and this program, the woman's name is "Sanchita," which in Bengali means "abundance."

The Girl Effect programs have a reproduction component to them as well. While lower fertility is not usually in the headlines of The Girl Effect goals, that goal is present implicitly throughout. Still connected to the presumption that lower fertility is necessary for economic growth, that such a program might mean fewer children born is one of the predicted positive outcomes. The argument for programs focused on girls is that if girls choose this "better" pathway to success, they will delay marriage and childbearing and that will mean lower fertility for the girls themselves and the community as a whole, long a goal of fertility control programs targeted at the global South (Connelly 2009). Targeting girls in adolescence is viewed as particularly critical for any future impact because it is at this time, as they reach sexual and reproductive maturity, that their lives can take different pathways. The presumed connection between education, marriage, and childbearing is made explicit in another of The Girl Effect videos: "A girl with 7 years of education marries 4 years later and has 2.2 fewer children." The Sanchita video mentioned above begins with a reminder that 51 percent of girls in Bangladesh are married before they are 17, in order to contrast Sanchita's situation with such a fate. Thus, "The Girl Effect can be seen as confirming the continued preoccupation with fertility coupled with the current emphasis on empowerment and rights" (Koffman and Gill 2013: 105). As the Melinda and Bill Gates Foundation argues: "We must see women's sexual and reproductive health not just as a personal issue, but also as a political one that is central to women's empowerment, gender equality, and achieving development goals" (Gates Foundation 2022). Here, then, is another way in which girls have a responsibility to solve a country's economic woes, through control of their fertility.

The Girl Effect and other programs that are built on this "smart economics" model do not envision greater gender equality or increased resources going to girls and women simply because that is more just. Neoliberal rhetoric and ideology are at the basis of these programs; not only are they the products of private corporations such as Nike and Goldman Sachs, but they focus on the choices, opportunities, and work of individuals as the solutions to economic growth and the reduction of poverty. That corporations are underwriting these programs – in concert with governments and NGOs – follows the intimate connections that have been established among them. Whether or not women or girls are better off themselves, these programs are based on a belief that the market is the solution to the world's problems (A. Roberts 2015). Rather than putting attention and efforts toward structural issues such as poverty, SAPs, postcolonial economic relationships, growing inequality, or labor exploitation, these programs focus on individual effort and the ways in which market connections are the solution to poverty, gender inequality and all else that is found wanting in the world.

> The girl effect project shifts attention away from global structural violence as it casts blame for underdevelopment on local forms of personhood and kinship, which it judges from the standpoint of Western ontology. Women and girls are made to bear the responsibility for bootstrapping themselves out of poverty that is caused in part by the very institutions that purport to save them. (Hickel 2014: 1356)

Conclusions

The examples in this chapter epitomize the neoliberal turn in development policy generally, and the ways in which such a turn affects women's lives and their reproduction. In this neoliberal age, the state's role in reproduction is often organized, directed, and complemented by outside forces, including the World Bank, the IMF, and foreign governments. Reproduction is less likely to be controlled by means of heavy-handed state laws, nor even necessarily by any laws at all. Many programs do not even focus explicitly on lower fertility, even as fertility control is a central goal. Rather, these programs, constructed on neoliberal philosophies and approaches, work to shape population, reproduction, and women's lives through more subtle influence on norms, values, and behavior such as: what makes a modern woman, family, or country; individual responsibility; gender norms; and how a proper woman takes care of family members and their future by making correct investments. They encourage the "right" choices and argue that these individual choices will change women's lives, their communities, and their nations.

In these ways, control of reproduction is no longer linked to a single state's policies but is deeply embedded in forces and processes that have spread across the world. By linking women's "empowerment" with reproduction, states may argue that family planning programs are about gender equality and giving women control of their bodies.

The irony here is important to acknowledge. Indeed, the power to access contraception, to secure reproductive health services, and to get an education is necessary if women are to be able to control their own lives. But the neoliberal principles that are embedded in these recent reproductive health and education programs mean that little attention is paid to the overall gender, class, racial, and national inequities that are at the core of gender inequality and the challenges women face in controlling their own reproduction. Instead, as Nancy Fraser has put it, "the dream of women's emancipation is harnessed to the engine of capitalist accumulation" (2009: 110–11).

7
The Global Interconnections of *Reproscapes*

Today's world is highly interconnected. That means that things, people, ideas, money, and media circulate and connect across borders. Along the way, new things and ideas are made, or foreign things become embedded in new contexts. In this chapter, we explore what those global interconnections mean for reproduction and its control.

Our perspective on global circulation draws from Arjun Appadurai's arguments that the world is far from homogenized or uniform. Things, ideas, and people move across borders not in a predictable center–periphery direction but in ways that are disjunctive and often contentious, contradictory, and overlapping. "At least as rapidly as forces from various metropolises are brought into new societies they tend to become indigenized" (Appadurai 1996: 32). Appadurai labels various types of these transfers "scapes": *mediascapes* draw attention to the movement of and through media, while *technoscapes* are transfers of technology. Particularly relevant to our focus here are three other of Appadurai's scapes: *ethnoscapes*, which name the movement of people (tourists, refugees, migrants) across borders, and *ideoscapes*, the ideologies, theories, and other ideas that move across the globe. In addition, *financescapes* follow the economic links and travels across the world. Appadurai argues in favor of understanding the enormous flux and multidirection of these flows and movements so that pinning anything down as having a starting point or finishing point is difficult.

We build on Appadurai's framework to examine reproduction in this global age. First, we would suggest adding at least two "scapes" to his five. A sixth – a *bioscape* – would describe how biology and biological forms also move across borders. These include organs, such as kidneys, that have been traced traveling from poorer to richer countries. Such a scape could include other forms too; after the world's experience with the Covid-19 pandemic, we know that viruses also cross borders with ease. Marcia Inhorn and Pankaj Shrivastav have argued for thinking about a seventh scape, which is particularly relevant to our work here: "*reproscape*," which incorporates Appadurai's other scapes. They write of "a new world order characterized not only by circulating reproductive technologies (technoscapes) but also by circulating reproductive actors (ethnoscapes) and their body parts (bioscapes), leading to a large-scale global industry (financescapes) in which images (mediascapes) and ideas (ideoscapes)" play a role. They point out that "the global 'reproscape' … is an uneven terrain, in that some individuals, some communities, and some nations have achieved greater access to the fruits of reproductive globalization than others" (Inhorn and Shrivastav 2010: 69S).

Indeed, a second addition to Appadurai's framework comes from Inhorn and Shrivastav's last point. While Appadurai is right to point out the multidirectional and chaotic nature of these flows, we must note the asymmetrical relations of power that are also at work in the movement of people, ideas, and things. Recognizing the different positions and power of states, communities, and individuals in contemporary global circulation underscores how some parts of the world have "a greater weight [in] flows of capital, especially financial capital, and to a lesser extent the landscapes of centralized political power" (Heyman and Campbell 2009: 132). Thus, the landscape through which these scapes move is not flat, but subject to forces that ease or restrict movement, often because of geopolitics and global inequality and what Gillian Hart calls the specificities of the "interrelations of objects, events, places and identities" (2006: 996). For example, we saw in earlier chapters how Filipina lives and reproduction options have been shaped both within the Philippines by structural readjustment programs instigated by the US, and in the diaspora by inequalities between the Philippines and, for example, Singapore.

Keeping those ideas and frameworks in mind, in this chapter we trace some further ways that different places across the globe are connected – whether that be a development program originating in the West or the kind of indigenization of an ideology that might have traveled from another place. These examples illustrate how reproductive politics are part of global circulatory patterns of people, money, power, and ideologies. We discuss several reproductive processes and programs that have nodes of influence – and resistance – across boundaries of nation, community, gender, and race. Each of these processes is part of the globalization of reproduction and how it involves the movement of people, ideas, money, and power across the world. Our examples provide further support for Inhorn and Shrivastav's argument that reproscapes combine many of the scapes first identified by Appadurai. As we will see, when different dimensions, such as finance and ideology, combine, their influence on reproduction can be especially potent.

The Influence of the Global North

The Global North has had a major impact on most aspects of life in many parts of the Global South. While some of that power derives from the historical experience of colonialism, neo-imperialist processes such as those we saw operating in the Philippines have sustained these Global North/South disparities and dynamics, and serve as a basis of contemporary state-to-state relationships. Who has power and how they use it becomes clear in the power of the US to shape reproductive policies and practices across the world. For the past many decades, the US has been the major player in the field of global population and reproduction. It has been the largest donor to population and family planning programs, funding such things as contraceptive development, program implementation, and the salaries of local health officials. That combination of ideology (ideoscape) and funding (financescape) results in US and western dominance in many areas of reproduction.

Knowing a population through data

Since 1984, the US government – through its development arm, USAID – has underwritten the world's largest data-gathering organization focused on population and health. The Demographic and Health Surveys (DHS) program has conducted surveys in more than 90 countries in the Global South; thus, the surveys cover countries like Tanzania and India, but not Switzerland or Canada. The surveys collect data on fertility, child mortality, nutrition, contraceptive use, gender violence, and many other topics that a government might feel are relevant to understanding and controlling population (Chatterjee and Riley 2018). US involvement in this data-collection project is important for several reasons.

For one, US perspectives and ideologies are infused throughout the projects and surveys. The organization of these surveys, the topics they cover, and the people they include in their samples are all part of a neoliberal, developmentalist, approach. Such data and the knowledge it produces are at the heart of population surveillance, and allow a state to police women's bodies and reproduction (Foucault 1978, 1991). We can see these issues in DHS involvement in India. DHS fielded its first survey there in 1993, and has done four more national survey rounds since. The data gathered have yielded significant information, as DHS and India's National Family Welfare Program explains:

> The main objective of the survey has been to provide policymakers and programme administrators with a comprehensive snapshot of the demographic and health status of households, women, and children. This information will assist them in monitoring progress towards the achievement of population, health, and nutrition goals, identifying problem areas, and planning and implementing strategies to improve existing programmes. (IIPS 2000: 21)

Thus, the survey serves as "surveillance of women for the purpose of planning and managing the population" (Chatterjee and Riley 2018: 43).

In a sample of questions from the DHS shown in Figure 7.1, we can see the kinds of data that are collected. In Section A, women are asked about their current use of contraceptives. If unable to produce the name of The Pill or condom brand, interviewers are instructed to ask them to show the package. In Section B, the respondents are asked about their plans for future pregnancy. Here, interviewers are told to match the women's answers with what they earlier reported; if they report they don't want to get pregnant, interviewers ask them why, in that case, they are not using contraception. These data will provide authorities with what they need to develop or strengthen family planning programs. But, as James Scott argues, even as authorities attempt to collect data in order to know and plan the

A

303 Are you or your partner currently doing something or using any method to delay or avoid getting pregnant?
YES
NO.

304 Which method are you using?
RECORD ALL MENTIONED.

FEMALE STERILIZATION
MALE STERILIZATION
IUD
INJECTABLES
IMPLANTS
PILL
CONDOM
FEMALE CONDOM
EMERGENCY CONTRACEPTION
STANDARD DAYS METHOD
LACTATIONAL AMENORRHEA METHOD
RHYTHM METHOD
WITHDRAWAL
OTHER MODERN METHOD
OTHER TRADITIONAL METHOD

305 What is the brand name of the pills you are using?

____

DON'T KNOW

Interviewer Instructions: IF DON'T KNOW THE BRAND, ASK TO SEE THE PACKAGE

306 What is the brand name of the condoms you are using?

____

DON'T KNOW

Interviewer Instructions: IF DON'T KNOW THE BRAND, ASK TO SEE THE PACKAGE

B

804 Now I have some questions about the future. Would you like to have (a/another) child, or would you prefer not to have any (more) children?
HAVE (A/ANOTHER) CHILD
NO MORE/NONE
SAYS SHE CAN'T GET PREGNANT
UNDECIDED/DON'T KNOW .

805 How long would you like to wait from now before the birth of (a/another) child?
___MONTHS
___YEARS
SOON/NOW
SAYS SHE CAN'T GET PREGNANT
AFTER MARRIAGE
OTHER
DON'T KNOW

* * * * *

Interviewer instructions: CHECK 303: USING A CONTRACEPTIVE METHOD? If not currently using, ask:

810 You have said that you do not want (a/another) child soon. Can you tell me why you are not using a method to prevent pregnancy?

FERTILITY-RELATED REASONS
NOT HAVING SEX
INFREQUENT SEX
MENOPAUSAL/HYSTERECTOMY
CAN'T GET PREGNANT
NOT MENSTRUATED SINCE LAST BIRTH
BREASTFEEDING
UP TO GOD/FATALISTIC

OPPOSITION TO USE
RESPONDENT OPPOSED
HUSBAND/PARTNER OPPOSED
OTHERS OPPOSED .
RELIGIOUS PROHIBITION

LACK OF KNOWLEDGE
KNOWS NO METHOD
KNOWS NO SOURCE

METHOD-RELATED REASONS
SIDE EFFECTS/HEALTH CONCERNS
LACK OF ACCESS/TOO FAR
COSTS TOO MUCH
PREFERRED METHOD NOT AVAILABLE
NO METHOD AVAILABLE
INCONVENIENT TO USE
INTERFERES WITH BODY'S NORMAL PROCESSES

Any other reason?

Do you think you will use a contraceptive method to delay or avoid pregnancy at any time in the future?
YES
NO
DON'T KNOW

Figure 7.1. Sample questions from the DHS program in India

population using neat categories (wants another child; does not want another child), these seemingly regular categories only paper over the "chaotic, disorderly, constantly changing social reality beneath" (Scott 1999: 81) – a social reality where women have contradictory feelings about more children, or where it may be another family member who gets the final say about whether she has more children, or where the social environment around her prevents her from achieving her reproductive goals. Questions are rarely asked about these messy processes. In the end,

> The aspiration to such ... order alerts us to the fact that modern statecraft is largely a project of internal colonization, often glossed, as it is in imperial rhetoric, as a "civilizing mission." The builders of the modern nation-state do not merely describe, observe, and map; they strive to shape a people and landscape that will fit their techniques of observation. (Scott 1999: 82)

Importantly, such surveillance is focused on individual women. DHS (like most demographic data collection) focuses on the individual, reflecting a neoliberal ideology that it is individuals' decisions that are most important. This approach reflects assumptions that

> the key to understanding fertility and effecting fertility change is to ask individual women about their beliefs and behavior, making it clear that reproduction and overpopulation (and the problems stemming from these, such as poverty and backwardness) are problems of individual women, not of something larger than individuals (e.g., poverty, resource distribution, or social inequality). The solutions, then, to the management of the population and the population problem are also individually based; explicit here is the conviction that the solutions of global and national ills are in the hands of individual actors. (Chatterjee and Riley 2018: 47)

In language that mirrors that promoted by Cairo's ICPD, the assumption throughout these surveys is that individual women "choose" among a variety of options. What goes missing is the context – and the constraints on choice – in which any individual decision is made. While we can learn a great deal about how a poor woman uses contraception in a state in India, we do not learn about what led to the enormous and pervasive income inequality across the country, the continuing influence of India's colonial past, or how government investment in certain aspects of population control through family planning programs have led to coercive practices in some Indian states. Our attention remains focused on individual women, their choices and decisions, and how those lead to better or worse lives. Following a neoliberal ideological trail, we look to women to improve their lives and find success. Hidden and erased are the larger forces that are at the root of individual reproductive outcomes.

Perhaps as important as what kind of information is collected in DHS surveys is the power such data have. The DHS program and the data it provides are highly respected and widely used – by scholars, program administrators, and government officials. The data provide evidence for many things: how many children women want or have; whether or not family planning programs are welcoming; how effective programs are in lowering child mortality rates; whether women are subject to violence in their homes. Categories – even identities – are made up through such data. As one scholar reminds us, surveys construct people as

> objects of scientific inquiry. Sometimes to control them, as prostitutes, sometimes to help them, as potential suicides. Sometimes to organise and help, but at the same time keep ourselves safe, as the poor or the homeless. Sometimes to change them for their own good and the good of the public, as the obese. Sometimes just to admire, to understand, to encourage and perhaps even to emulate, as (sometimes) geniuses. (Hacking 2006; see also Porter 1995)

In the process, the data are "making up people" (Hacking 2006) and we come to understand individuals and groups through how they are categorized in the data. The DHS data show that some women come to be seen as part of a group with an "unmet need" for contraception. Or, perhaps, a woman can be identified as having "traditional" ideas, if survey data suggest she seems to be resistant to modern contraception. Especially for countries where there is little reliable data available, a lot of what we know about many poor countries comes from these surveys; it is through these data that the public comes to know the society, further constructing population, fertility, and associated issues as regulated through the bodies and choices of individual women. It is difficult to underestimate the power these data have; because of the authority and respect they have garnered across the world, their influence is immeasurable (Halfon 2007: 128). The implicit assumptions and ideologies – and what is missing from these surveys – get forgotten in the wonder of all this new knowledge.

Aid to countries to plan families

We can also see the role of the US as we look at the history of population control in specific countries; again, US power in financescapes combines with American ideology (ideoscapes) to influence reproductive practices in many places. We saw in earlier chapters the outsized role the US played in India's population policies. That role began in the 1950s and has continued through the present, though it has taken different forms. The US has provided considerable funding to India for family planning, mostly through USAID, and sometimes less directly through USAID funding of US foundations, such as the Ford or Rockefeller Foundations that work in India. Sometimes acting as "foreign advisors," US officials coach Indian officials about how best to deliver services and have, at times, been supportive of the program using incentives and disincentives to further demographic aims (Connelly 2006). Throughout, the US has pushed state programs that prioritize population control over the provision of welfare services. In the early years, this rhetoric came from the widespread belief that only when population was "under control" and fertility was low would any country be able to begin to achieve its economic goals. More recently, we can see the influence of western neoliberal ideology at work in India with the state's emphasis on the market as providing women with the choice they need to control their fertility (WGNRR 2004: 28).

As the largest funder of population programs in the world today, the US has played similar roles in many countries. In 2000, for example, USAID provided funding for a mass sterilization campaign in Peru that targeted indigenous Quechua women, in which 200,000 women were sterilized, most against their will (Ewig 2006). USAID did not help to carry out the sterilizations themselves, but it sanctioned the campaign through its funding of the violence the Peru government committed on women (Hartmann 2011).

US influence also includes the economic impacts we saw in the Philippines, where structural adjustment policies, market deregulation, and austerity programs have decimated the economy, undermined the financial and social security of families, and sent Filipinos as migrants to other countries. But influence can be just as powerful when it takes the form of new ideology, as we saw in the US's role in Egypt's family planning program and its goal to convince women to think like modern women.

In addition to the US government's direct role in family programs across the world, often funneled through USAID, the US regularly partners with other governments and organizations such as the World Bank, the International Planned Parenthood Foundation, the WHO, and other UN organizations to construct global population policy. These organizations are often transnational or international in their operations, but the US plays a major role in most of them, because of the funding that comes from the US government and because American ideas and values often shape their policies and programs. In contrast to the US role, many smaller countries are often affected by the programs that are run and funded by these organizations, but they generally have little say in their development.

In 2012, for example, the London Family Planning Summit convened to set an agenda on family planning across the world. Attending were many NGOs and government organizations, including the British Government, USAID, the Bill and Melinda Gates Foundation, and other international organizations. Over the course of the London summit, these groups designed and announced a far-reaching global family planning strategy. Its goal was to launch "a groundbreaking effort to make affordable, lifesaving contraceptives, information, services, and supplies available to an additional 120 million girls and women in the world's poorest countries by 2020" (London Summit on Family Planning 2012). Providing contraceptive access to those who have limited access is a laudable goal, and its intention "to put increased access to contraception for women in the developing world emphatically back on the global health and development agenda" was celebrated by many (Cohen 2012). Others raised concerns, however. Human Rights Watch pointed out that, while the organizers insisted the new programs would promote "voluntary" compliance, achieving these goals would likely rely on coercion (Wilson 2018: 95); adopting numerical targets went against the agreements made at the ICPD in Cairo in 1994, a decision made because of how numerical targets – and pressures on local health workers to achieve those targets – often lead to coercive methods. But alongside that debate, what is also notable is how a small group of powerful people gathered in London to set up a program that would affect millions of women, women who had very little voice at this summit but whose lives would most likely be affected by the decisions made there. As a result of the London Summit, for example, the Indian government has teamed with the Bill and Melinda Gates Foundation, the Path Foundation (a US-based NGO), Pfizer, and the US government to invest in and pressure women to use Depo-Provera, with the bodies of poor, Dalit, and Muslim women a particular target (Wilson 2018).

The influence of global capitalism, the partnerships across state and nonstate entities, and their control of the global markets can thus be traced right back to reproductive health programs and to individual women's access to reproductive health services. We might expect, after Cairo and the consensus that women's empowerment is an important goal, that women would be offered as much choice as possible as they decide on their reproductive plans. But, as we argued in Chapter 6, gender equality and women's empowerment were not seen as ends in themselves, but as means to a different end – both lower fertility and a deeper entanglement of women within the global market. Reflecting those goals, contraceptive development and distribution is clearly meant to meet those instrumental ends, rather than giving women control over their reproduction. The London Summit's emphasis on long-acting and irreversible contraception – such as Depo-Provera, Norplant, and sterilization – reflects how much of the investment of time and money in contraception has gone into developing and promoting the kinds of contraception that can remove control from women and make it easier for programs and their staff to intervene in reproduction. Those that are under the user's control, such as diaphragms and condoms, are seen as less promising in family planning programs, and are often not even available to clients. There is evidence that women in poorer countries, or in poorer communities in places like the United States, are much more likely to experience pressure to accept long-acting contraceptive methods such as Norplant or Depo-Provera than methods such as condoms or diaphragms (Holt et al. 2020; Yirgu et al. 2020). In Ethiopia, a woman explained how she was unable to choose a contraceptive at the government clinic: "I refused when they offered me the one that is inserted in the arm [Norplant]. I refused two or three times and it is difficult when they don't agree with your interest. So now I am using the method from a private facility, paying for the service" (cited in Yirgu et al. 2020). Staff members argue that long-acting methods are easier for clients to use and will be more effective in preventing pregnancy. But many clients, like this woman, see a loss of reproductive control in the pressure to accept such methods.

The global gag rule

As often as it indirectly influences reproduction across the world in the ways seen above, the US regularly asserts its power in direct ways as well. An example of such an impact on reproduction is the "global gag rule" (GGR), a policy that reflects a conservative, ideological aspect of US family policy and aid. The policy was first put into effect by the United States in 1985 after the UN ICPD in Mexico City, which is why it is sometimes also referred to as the Mexico City policy. In order to receive or continue to receive funding from the US for development purposes, all international NGOs providing family planning services had to agree to stop performing or promoting abortions. The US restricted not only the use of its own funds but, in addition, what groups could do with their own, non-US, funding. Thus, not only has this rule been employed to prevent US funds from being used for abortions, but the US has applied its economic power to export its own reproductive politics and policies and impose them on other countries. Because the US provides a substantial amount of the funding for economic development in many poorer countries, this rule has enormous consequences (HRW 2017). Since it was first implemented, the policy has been rescinded and reinstated depending on the political leanings of each US president's administration. Every Republican administration has put it into play and every Democrat administration has rescinded it. In 2017, the Trump administration went even further than had previous Republican administrations by expanding it to include in its restrictions *all* health organizations receiving US government funding, not just those involved in family planning. Thus, programs that provide services such as malaria treatment, HIV care, or child health care cannot also provide services for or mention abortion – even if no US funds are used for those abortion services. Thus, nearly US$9.5 billion of health assistance was subject to these restrictions (Ushie et al. 2020). In addition, arguing that it supports coercive abortion in China, the Trump administration pulled US funding for UNFPA, another major funder of contraception and maternal health services in poorer countries.

In addition to the explicit impacts the GGR has had, the language of the policy is vague in how extreme any enforcement will be, creating even more uncertainty (Filipovic 2017). If a health worker mentions abortion as one of several options for a pregnant woman, does that constitute promotion and endanger the entire health program? In order to complete her assessment, can a clinician ask an ailing patient if she has undergone a home abortion? These kinds of questions – and the lack of answers – severely constrain health care providers. In some places, concern grew that the US would cut off all development funds to any country where abortion was legal. In addition, the inconsistency of the US policy – which had the potential to be reversed or implemented every four years with each new US presidency – meant that organizations scrambled to find reliable funding from year to year (Ushie et al. 2020).

The effect of the GGR on women's lives and health was often immediate. Women were unable to find safe abortions, and resorted to unsafe methods to end pregnancies. Unsafe abortions are the cause of a significant portion of maternal mortality in poor countries; in Kenya, estimates suggest that a third of maternal mortality is due to unsafe abortion (Center for Reproductive Rights 2010: 25). In a country like Kenya, where 55 percent of foreign aid for all health programs and 95 percent of the foreign aid it receives for reproductive health services comes from the US government, these rules threatened the entire system of health provision for women and others too (Ushie et al. 2020).

Other countries have also been strongly affected. Madagascar relies heavily on foreign sources of funding for its health programs (72 percent), and receives a substantial portion of that funding from the US government. Notably, Madagascar is a country that has strict rules against abortion. In spite of the country's restrictions, women still seek abortions, and often end up having to choose unsafe options: it is estimated that nearly 12 percent of maternal deaths in 2015 were due to complications following a self-induced abortion. Madagascar has worked toward reducing those numbers, especially by expanding contraception access and provisions, particularly to rural, young, and poor populations. But even though Madagascar has abortion restrictions that are stricter than those listed in the GGR, enactment of the rule has affected a wide range of services in that country. Most notably, researchers found that the GGR and the funding lost from UNFPA severely impacted contraceptive services and delivery. Because of the restrictions placed on local clinics and the reduced funding and staffing, some had to close down and women lost access to contraception. Madagascar's experience speaks to the irony of such a mandate: in its efforts to reduce the number of abortions, its effect was a decrease in contraceptive use and an increase in unintended pregnancies (Ravaoarisoa et al. 2020).

Evidence like that from Madagascar and across the world around the GGR shows that efforts to block services for abortion or its aftermath do not necessarily decrease the numbers of women who seek abortion. Rather, its effects are often likely to increase the number of women who become severely ill or die from abortion. In addition, health workers were fearful of providing women support or aid, even after a botched abortion, worried that it would jeopardize the entire health program. Organizations "are placed in the difficult position of losing vital funds that support a range of health services they provide, or accepting the funds but undermining their patients' well-being by not being able to provide the full range of lawful sexual and reproductive health services and information" (Center for Reproductive Rights 2018). It is not only abortion services that are constrained; also affected are contraceptive and HIV services, breast and cervical cancer screening, and services for gender-based violence victims. Women's health suffers when access to health care, which has always been insufficient, is further restricted, as both providers and patients try to navigate the rules the US has put into place. And the GGR has impacts beyond services directed at women. A wide range of programs are affected, from HIV/AIDS programs to child health services to programs addressing other infectious disease. And all these effects come in places where providing health care has been a challenge to begin with. In addition, as one group that monitors the effects of this rule have pointed out, "the burden of implementing and monitoring the requirements of the policy bears heavily on organizations that have to cut programs, restructure, retrench staff, and closely monitor compliance. The policy is fracturing important partnerships and coalitions and limiting civil society's ability to work effectively and hold their governments accountable" (International Women's Heath Coalition: iwhc.org).

Joe Biden rescinded the GGR during the early days of his administration in 2021, and many are now calling for something that might permanently remove this kind of constraint imposed on other countries. The heavy-handedness and inconsistencies of the GGR demonstrate how a powerful country like the US can easily set the agenda for reproductive policies across the world. An editorial in *The Lancet*, a top British medical journal, pointed to the harm that the GGR has done to women across the world:

> That the global gag rule might ultimately prove to increase the number of abortions by reducing access to modern contraception is not just an unfortunate irony. Rather, it reveals the way in which the policy has little to do with fostering health and everything to do with politics. Abortion is the rallying cry that unites conservative attempts to control and coerce women. By targeting funding for abortion, the global gag rule weaponises US global health funding against sexual and reproductive health and rights more broadly, with the most severe consequences affecting the most vulnerable. Two years on from its reinstatement, evidence shows that for care to be effective it must be holistic, comprehensive, and patient centred. There can be no right to health without the right to access safe abortion. (*The Lancet* 2019: 2329)

The Spreading Influence of Neoliberalism

The US and other powerful countries also engage in less direct but no less powerful moves that influence reproductive politics across the world. We get some hint from meetings like the 2012 Family Planning Summit in London of the connections among the world's powers in supporting and promoting a neoliberal agenda and we have seen how countries have been constrained and harmed by the neoliberal and structural adjustment policies enforced by the US, the World Bank, and other global entities. But even beyond the direct power that the US exerts in areas such as the GGR, and even without the financial strings that are sometimes attached, the power it has through ideological influence is significant. We see the extent of western influence when we trace neoliberalism's impact well beyond those places where the US, or even the West, has a direct role. Here, we see how neoliberalist capitalism has become globalized. Even countries – like the two we discuss here, Mongolia and China – that do not have close connections to the US and that have strived for independence from the West, or have asserted that it does not follow a capitalist model, have accommodated to the power of neoliberalism across the world.

The story of how neoliberalist policies affected mothers in Mongolia is told by Craig Janes and Oyuntsetseg Chuluundorj in their article provocatively titled "Free markets and dead mothers." Mongolia, a country with an economy dependent on pastoralism, had been under the influence of the Soviet Union until 1990. After independence, the country's leaders enacted neoliberal market reforms in an effort to boost economic development; these reforms included trade liberalization, privatization of state-owned enterprises, and a reduction in government services. This marked a radical change from the preceding decades. Although there were many problems under the Soviet system, it was also true that economic inputs into the health care system allowed most in Mongolia to have access to basic health care. The post-independence reforms dismantled the support of both health care and other parts of the economy. The "impact of neoliberal macroeconomic reform – particularly through privatization and government disinvestment in public goods – on the traditional cooperative structures essential to effective pastoral production in the Mongolian environment [was] particularly evident"; these changes led to what many called "social chaos and economic collapse" (Janes and Chuluundorj 2004: 234). "The transition to a market-oriented economy has been accompanied by a decline in the average standard of living, a dramatic increase in poverty, greater economic insecurity and a rise in inequality in the distribution of income and productive assets" (Keith Griffin et al., cited in Janes and Chuluundorj 2004: 235). Government de-investment in services such as schools, health care, public health, and infrastructure had a devastating impact, particularly on the most vulnerable. The government also stepped back from regulating access to and use of lands, destabilizing the livelihoods of most rural herders. No longer provided government protection, herders became subject to the shocks of weather, animal diseases, over-grazed land, and market unpredictability. "It is clear that the socialist ethic of social solidarity and justice, where all individuals were provided access to essential services and buffered from the inherent risks of pastoralism in a harsh environment, has been replaced by an ethic of market justice, where services and benefits accrue only to those judged deserving by virtue of economic success" (Janes and Chuluundorj 2004: 240). Where there once was a system of interhousehold cooperation, the new system pitted household against household, raising the risk for all of them, as they fought for a piece of the shrinking pie.

Women were especially affected by these changes. Health care, especially in rural areas, became either nonexistent or of poor quality. Here again, we see women acting as "shock-absorbers" for the family's economic struggles. Women, who are involved in the subsistence economy of their families, will forgo their own needs – food or health needs – to take care of the family. What is noticeably missing in this new economy is the support there once was for laboring and delivering women. In the previous era, pregnant women in rural areas had access to special services that were specifically designed to mitigate the risks of living at a distance from health centers. A woman would travel to a "waiting home" toward the end of her pregnancy to await childbirth, and be able to rely on supportive maternal services – all supplied by the government. While she was away, she could rely on her neighbors to help with her work at home. Now that the government has eliminated those centers and services, and interfamily cooperation is lessened, pregnant women are at higher risk of birth complications. They are less willing to leave their home and work, and are less likely to find or afford good maternal care. Maternal mortality reflects these increased risks, with higher maternal mortality rates than before 1990, and with an increasing correlation between MMR and income: poorer women without private resources are most likely to be harmed. This research underscores how "events, processes, and factors occurring across the social scale 'get into' the body" (Krieger 1994) and the ways that neoliberalism often affects women's health and reproductive outcomes both directly, in the provision or lack of services, and through the larger effects of how neoliberal policies increase the risk of households generally, forcing individuals to incur those risks without government support.

We can see neoliberalist ideology in China as well. Despite the vows of Chinese leaders to forge their own kind of economic development, as China moves more fully into global capitalism, it has built its economy and population on foundations found in many other, very different nations. In Chapter 2, we saw how China's population control program targeted women as it pushed to bring its fertility and population growth rates to a level the state found more desirable. Since China has dismantled its more draconian population program, women and their reproductive behavior remain a focus of the state. Now increasingly focused on population *quality* rather than *quantity*, the programs and the state still hold women as responsible for China's success. We can see nods to neoliberalism in how the state has argued that China needs "high-quality" individuals – well educated and skilled – to help China push to the top of the global marketplace (Greenhalgh 2010b). This shift has entailed a new role for women. In the past, women and their bodies were surveilled, monitored, and controlled to ensure that they followed state rules on who could bear children, how many, and when. In recent years:

> state imposition of its norms on parents have been accompanied, and even replaced by, enthusiastic self-regulation by parents emphasizing individual imperatives to raise their children according to the new popular norms on health and education. Indeed, the quality project has become a major site for the creation of the sorts of self-regulating, "autonomous," neo-liberal subjects desired and assumed by both the marketizing quasi-capitalist economy and the slimmed down neo-liberalizing state. (Greenhalgh 2010a: 319)

Here, we see echoes of the values and ideology being pushed in Egypt's family planning program. The state is still concerned with reproduction, and sees women as central to its goals, but its attention is focused less on limiting births and is now also watching childrearing, promoting "good" mothers as those who do what they should to raise "high-quality" children. By making good choices, and engaging productively in the consumer market to buy opportunities and objects that help their children succeed, women continue to be in the state's sights as important to economic development. The Chinese state's version of modernity here may be somewhat different from that of western powers, and Appadurai's argument about how things become indigenized once they cross borders may be a useful way to consider China's pathway. At the same time, China's adoption of a market economy with neoliberalist guideposts make clear the weight of western ideology in global affairs.

Stratified Reproduction

State to state connections – through the scapes that Appadurai (1996) has outlined – shape how ideology, money, power, images, and much else travel around the world. Here we turn to stratified reproduction to examine how these connections and exchanges connect the global economy to women, their bodies, and their role in reproduction, in ways that Inhorn's retroscapes capture well.

Stratified reproduction identifies the way that social, and even biological, reproduction is unevenly distributed across populations. It refers to how "the hierarchical organization of reproductive health, fecundity, birth experiences, and child rearing ... supports and rewards the maternity of some women, while despising or outlawing the mother-work of others" (Rapp 2001: 469). When we focus on reproduction as a process that extends beyond a single woman's body, we can trace how the distribution of different elements of reproduction – from conception to birth to raising children – follows lines of social inequality. Thus, the "stratified" of stratified reproduction brings focus to inequalities based on class, race/ethnicity, nationality, or other social inequalities; in that way, reproduction parallels such social institutions and resources as education. As we saw in Chapter 5, part of what shapes reproductive outcomes are ideological issues that involve "who defines the body of the nation into which the next generation is recruited?" (Ginsberg and Rapp 1995: 3) and thus are embedded in norms, values, and actions about who should or should not bear children, who is recruited, charged, or restricted from raising kids. In addition, stratified reproduction underscores how global capitalism has led to the commodification of nearly everything – from goods and services to women's labor. It is not just bodies, but parts of bodies (kidneys, gametes, embryos) that also move through the global landscape.

While we have focused on biological reproduction for much of this volume, here, we expand our definition of reproduction to include both biological and social aspects of reproduction, and include those activities that are often referred to as "reproductive labor." In addition to pregnancy and childbirth, those also include the processes and work that involve reproducing families, the economy, and communities – activities such as child care, housework, education, and any other work that involves care and socialization of children and the support of the labor force. This work is valuable to any society or family, even though much of it is unpaid and unacknowledged.

Examining how reproduction is stratified brings to the analysis many of the key forces influencing reproduction and other social processes today, particularly the rise in technology, to address issues of infertility and parenting; the increasing globalization of everyone and everything; the ways that commodification and commercialization have become a part of nearly all aspects of social life; and the growing inequalities within and across societies. These have combined to make stratification around reproduction common and widespread, with connections spanning the world, and with many people involved in these processes along the way. Those with more resources are able to engage in what some have called "reproductive tourism," traveling to those parts of their own country or to other countries that will allow them to become a parent (Bergmann 2011) – by using technologies there to get pregnant, to buy sperm or eggs, hire a surrogate, or adopt a child. "Reproductive tourism" does not capture the costs and obstacles in this process (Inhorn and Patrizio 2009), but it does reflect the movement of people and body bits that move across borders with relative ease.

Stratified reproduction includes many processes including surrogacy, adoption, assisted reproductive technologies (ARTs), and child care practices. Here, we examine three interventions around pregnancy – ARTs, sperm and egg donation, and surrogacy – before examining adoption practices. In the final section we take up how inequalities, race, the market, and the state combine to shape the international division of the kinds of reproductive labor that takes place after children are born.

ART

When a woman is not able to conceive or carry a pregnancy to term, she and her partner may choose to pursue other pathways. Fertility challenges arise for many reasons. In heterosexual couples, one or both may have physical, hormonal, or other issues that prevent conception, pregnancy, or birth. Same-sex couples who wish to have children must find an alternative way to their goal. In some cases, couples choose not to go through pregnancy but still want to become parents. In any of these cases and others, there are an increasing number of options; assisted reproductive technologies and surrogacy are two of the most widely used. ART includes procedures focused on making it possible for a woman to become pregnant, often by manipulating sperm or eggs in the process. Such procedures include interuterine insemination, when sperm fertilizes an egg inside a woman's uterus; and in vitro fertilization (IVF) or intracytoplasmic sperm injection (ISI), in which an egg is fertilized by sperm outside the body, and later implanted into the uterus. These procedures and others give couples more options for pregnancy. For those who have struggled with infertility, successful ART allows couples to have children, often children who are biologically related.

But ARTs are unevenly available to couples throughout the world and within societies. In some places, the technology to perform these procedures is not available. In other societies, they are available only to some groups. In the European Union, most countries impose age limits on access. Some EU countries, including Italy, Poland, Turkey, and Switzerland, permit only married, heterosexual couples to access any fertility technology (EurekAlert! 2020). But the major factor in access in most places is cost. A single cycle of IVF, one of the most commonly used ARTs, costs about $20,000 in the US. For most couples, many rounds of IVF are necessary before achieving pregnancy. Some countries (including France, Sweden, Denmark, and the Netherlands) do provide some funding for these treatments, but most do not. In the US, there is no public funding for IVF and most couples cannot rely on health insurance to cover such expenses, so must pay out of their own pockets, making this procedure prohibitive or impossible. Importantly, less well-off people, who are more likely to have infertility issues because they are in poorer health, have lack of access to health care, suffer from exposure to harmful substances in low-paying jobs, and often live in communities that are environmentally polluted (Bell 2014), are also least likely to be able to undergo infertility treatment.

Trade in sperm and eggs

While some IVF and ISI procedures use couples' own sperm and eggs, there is also a widespread circulation of "donor" sperm and eggs across the world. These gametes – and related "body bits" – have been heavily commodified. This is the case particularly in the US, which is unusual for how little regulation there is around any form of ART. While IVF and ISI already carve a division between those who can and those who cannot afford such treatments, egg and sperm donations further follow divisions of class, race, and nationality and the demands of the market. Those that provide (usually through sale) eggs or sperm are more likely to be less well-off, less educated, and from poorer communities or societies than those who use (or buy) gametes.

> Despite popular protests to the contrary, and despite the heartfelt sentiments of parents and providers, there is a flourishing market for

> both children and their component parts. Eggs are being sold; sperm is being sold; wombs and genes and orphans are being sold; and many individuals are profiting handsomely in the process. (Spar 2006: xv)

Sperm is donated by – collected from – men and held in "sperm banks," a term that appropriately highlights the significant profits that accrue to these businesses. Relative to other technologies, sperm donation, storage, retrieval, and insemination are often cheaper and easier to access and use than other technologies. Even so, the commodification of sperm means that donors are paid under $100 and customers pay fees between $700 and $3,000 to buy that sperm, making it inaccessible to poorer individuals or couples who do not have such resources – again, the very people who are most likely to have infertility difficulties (Bell 2014). Those who are able and wanting to purchase sperm can usually choose among a wide range of donor characteristics, from race and educational level to height and BMI and even personality traits (Riley 2018). That parents are choosing their children based on assumptions that link race and characteristics such as athletic or intellectual ability suggests further problems: these processes of selling and buying gametes are often replicating "a biological version of race and inequality" (Riley 2018: 128; see also Roberts 2009).

Eggs too are bought and sold, and these processes are more complicated than sperm transfers for several reasons. Because of the difficulties and dangers involved, egg donation is outlawed in many countries, including Germany, Norway, Switzerland, and Turkey, although here again, there is little regulation of these procedures in the US. A woman who wants to "donate" her eggs must undergo procedures that can be harmful to her body: she takes hormones that stimulate egg production and then undergoes minor surgery for retrieval of those eggs. But, as Rene Almeling points out, egg and sperm donations are further differentiated by how gendered expectations – that lead to assumptions about women being more likely to "donate" eggs and men to "provide" sperm – also shape these processes (2011: 78ff.). As part of an attempt to keep the logics of market and family separate and to bolster what might be considered more acceptable gendered motivations (Almeling 2011: 116; Zelizer 1995, 2005), women who sell their eggs are more likely than sperm donors to be described as "donating" out of selflessness and a desire to help others. But donation does not accurately describe this process;

on average women are paid $4,200 to undergo such procedures, and those looking for "elite" donors pay much more, as they seek women who are attractive, white, athletic, and well educated. The market is fully involved in egg transfers; reliance on a self-regulating market in eggs has created a large gulf between those women who sell their eggs for the cash it provides, and other women who are able to procure the means to achieve a sought-after pregnancy.

Surrogacy

Surrogacy is another way used by some couples and individuals to create a family. There are many surrogacy configurations. It may be that a woman carries to term a pregnancy that started through donated sperm and egg, or the pregnancy may come from her own egg combined with either donated or the future father's sperm. Many see surrogacy as particularly vulnerable to exploitation of poorer women, a process that allows for "more intimate exploitation of inequality" (Singh 2014: 826). Surrogacy can also lead to emotional and political contest, as the early (1985) story of "Baby M" makes clear (Chesler 1992). In that case, a couple, the Sterns, contracted with a woman, Mary Beth Whitehead, to be their surrogate. For $10,000, Whitehead would carry a baby to term, a baby conceived through artificial insemination using Bill Stern's sperm and Whitehead's egg. But just after birth Mary Beth Whitehead changed her mind and decided to keep the baby. The case captured the public's attention, and brought many of the difficult issues of surrogacy to light. Whose baby did Mary Beth Whitehead have? She claimed it was hers, because it was her egg and her pregnancy. But the Sterns argued that Bill Stern was the father of the baby and they had a legal contract with Whitehead. There was a difficult legal battle between the Whiteheads and the Sterns, a fight that entailed arguments about how one determines parentage, but also brought issues of class difference into it. The Sterns were both medical doctors, and the Whiteheads were working class, and some argued that class should be a factor in determining whose house Baby M should grow up in. Two years after the child's birth, Bill Stern was awarded sole custody, with the court stating it was in the best interests of the child; Mary Beth Whitehead was granted visitation rights. Such potential entanglements and possible exploitation have led many countries, including Germany, Spain, Portugal, and France and many others, to heavily regulate these relationships. But again, surrogacy is mostly unregulated in the US, although rules do vary from state to state.

The recent history of surrogacy in India provides a lesson in how not only intra-country but global inequalities can be involved in these processes. Beginning in the early 2000s, India gained popularity as a site for transnational commercial gestational surrogacy, a practice that involved foreigners hiring Indian women to gestate and bear their child. In gestational surrogacy, the surrogate has no genetic connection to the fetus, but the pregnancy is created with gametes from either the hiring parents or from donated or purchased gametes from another source. The practice was controversial from the beginning, with many arguing that it was an extreme version of the exploitation of poorer local women by couples from richer countries. Foreign couples and individuals interested in surrogacy often rely on agencies created for these kinds of transnational transactions. These agencies screen potential surrogates, with many requiring that women must be married, have had children already, and obtain their husband's permission. Assessment of their health, nutritional, and mental status are all part of the screening. Once surrogates are chosen and become pregnant, they often live in special "homes" during pregnancy, allowing for closer regulation of their nutrition and even their social lives (Pande 2009). Women in India "choose" to become surrogates for the financial benefit they receive; many surrogates have used the money earned to pay for their children's education or to buy a house, or to build savings for their future (Singh 2018).

One American woman who hired an Indian woman as a surrogate argued that both she and the surrogate benefited from the transaction, an argument that is solidly built on the assumption that choice is available to all. She quotes the director of the institute through which she hired the surrogate: "At one end of this world, there is one woman who desperately needs a baby and cannot have her own child. And at the other end, there is a woman who badly wants to help her own family. If these two women want to help each other, why not allow that? They're helping one another to have a new life in this world." This American woman received "the gift of motherhood," while her surrogate chose this path to create "an opportunity to help her own growing business and to better care for their children." In the end, the American woman asserted: "I'm proud that India's surrogacy laws allowed us to help change her life for the better as she changed ours. Surrogacy was her choice, and mine" (Arieff 2012).

In spite of such arguments about "choice" and opportunities by those who hired surrogates, or those who ran businesses linking surrogates and those seeking to hire them, there was growing alarm about the practice and the techno-medical surveillance and control that it entailed. Concern arose about the physical and emotional risks that surrogates faced, about the large gulf in class and nationality between surrogates and those who hire them. Even in institutions where surrogate mothers receive the best care during pregnancy, surrogacy is risky and can harm women, depleting their own nutritional resources, interfering with family and community relationships, and raising questions about who controls their body – especially so for those who are poor and often undernourished to begin with and whose poverty may be the reason they decide to become surrogates. Some raised concerns about whether the practice of "wombs for rent" was a national embarrassment for India. Holly Singh points out a telling irony here: "Women and their wombs that are seen as dangerous when used for their own family's expansion become a source of value when engaged for surrogate pregnancy" (Singh 2018: 112).

The growing outrage in India about foreigners hiring Indian women to produce babies finally led the Indian government to ban this practice in 2015, at least for foreigners. Surrogacy continues in India today, but is limited to Indians hiring other Indians to produce their children. Under the new regulations, reproduction is still stratified, but now it is only class difference, not difference in nationality, that shapes surrogacy practices. As Singh (2014: 826) argues, inequalities continue to shape reproduction in India, and the inequality and exploitation in reproduction mirrors that found in other transactions. "The rhetoric around gestational surrogacy regularly adopts a language that comes from a long history in which wealthier (even middle-class) citizens regularly employ the labor of poorer Indians – to wash floors, to drive their cars, to care for their children." In this process, "many interested Indian parties to surrogacy will view the women who gestate and give birth to genetically unrelated babies as just 'labor' – a naturalized category of people who can be hired and let go at will, for whose well-being employers bear minimal responsibility, and who can be easily exchanged for others eager to take their place" (Singh 2014: 826).

India is now considering banning commercial surrogacy altogether and reactions to that possibility are mixed. Some argue that it will stop one path of exploitation of poor women in India. Others argue that the ban is not about exploitation but rather the government trying to dictate what kinds of families and family relationships are acceptable; the government, they argue, is really focused on preventing same-sex couples from creating families. From the women engaged in the practice itself come other concerns that they will lose a source of income vastly larger than anything they can earn at available jobs. One 34-year-old surrogate mother from a small town in Gujarat argued: "If they stop commercial surrogacy, it is not good for poor people like me … It is one way for us to make a better life. If we work day and night, we cannot save this kind of money." Now in her second surrogacy, she hopes to save money for her daughter's wedding (Bagri 2021). Some surrogates argue, as Singh did, that surrogacy is similar to other working situations, many of which are also exploitive of the lesser power of employees. This argument underscores how far the market has moved into the area of reproduction. One surrogate described her situation as: "I am simply giving my womb on rent" (Bagri 2021).

When India closed its doors to the transnational surrogacy business, those seeking surrogates looked elsewhere. Mexico, where some states permit foreigners to hire women to act as surrogates, became a new and growing site for this market (Burnett 2017). Concerns have grown about the need for regulation, for protection of surrogates, and around legal and moral complications about how to decide parenthood in contested cases. The recent war in Ukraine made visible the surrogacy industry that has been operating there for many years. As surrogates try to find a safe place or safe passage out of the country, trying to survive, help their families, and protect their pregnancy, it is apparent how "the interests of the surrogate and the interests of the parents don't always align. War just makes it that much more stark … Nothing crystallizes the 'her body, my baby' conundrum of surrogacy quite like a war" (Motluk 2021). The complicated questions that can arise in commercial surrogacy have led to it becoming banned in more and more countries across the world.

While reproductive technology has allowed some couples and individuals to have a child when they otherwise could not, we also need to put these technologies into the wider context. "Stratified reproduction is intertwined with other social institutions; the state, family, the economy, schooling and other social institutions help to shape reproductive practices across the world, and help define who has the children they want, how easy it is to raise them, and how and to whom reproductive labor is bought and sold" (Riley 2018: 121). It is important to understand how reproduction is not merely enhanced but controlled in these circumstances, and by forces well outside the individual. This technology has become more necessary partly because of the larger context in which people are attempting family-making, what Laura Briggs (2010) calls "structural infertility":

> Reprotech is addressing structural infertility and a considerable increase in difficulty getting pregnant caused by the fact that, on the whole, many middle-class women are being forced by family-unfriendly workplaces and educational institutions to delay childbearing until their thirties and beyond ... It's a not particularly effective, often hugely expensive Band-Aid on a considerable loss of reproductive choice in the last forty years. (2010: 373)

Women across all class and education strata often have to deal with such structural infertility; labor force demands can cripple women's attempts to create families and decide when and how many children they want. But given their difficult access of even the hope of a remedy for such infertility, these burdens and constraints are borne even more often and more deeply by the poor and marginalized.

Dorothy Roberts argues for further critical perspectives on what is happening around and through reproductive technologies. She points to how reproduction is classed and raced, and the ways poor and rich women are treated differently around issues of fertility.

> While welfare reform laws aim to deter women receiving public assistance from having even one additional healthy baby, largely unregulated fertility clinics regularly implant privileged women with multiple embryos, knowing the high risk multiple births pose for premature delivery and low birth weight. The public begrudges poor mothers a meager increase in benefits for one more child, but celebrates the birth of high-tech septuplets that require a fortune in publicly supported hospital care. (2005: 1344)

In a similar way, some welcome surrogacy in places like India, even as they work to keep poor women from having "too many" children.

In addition, the concerns and regulations around processes like surrogacy or egg selling/donation are often about more than worries for the health and safety of those involved in the process. As often, rules about these practices are attempts to shape the form that reproduction takes: which women in what kind of families have children. The ideological issues are sometimes as important as the physical ones presented in these new and different forms of family-making. In these clashes too, of course, some have more power than others to shape family-making processes.

Transnational adoption and the Hague Convention

Transnational adoption has become another way that families are created in the Global North, and another process in which those higher in stratification systems of class, race, and nationality have distinct advantages over those lower in these hierarchies. Transnational adoptions are nearly always about the movement of children from poorer countries to richer countries. While not all such adoptions are exploitative, many are, and all of them rest on the inequities found across the world and within countries themselves that make it difficult for poor mothers to find ways to raise their own children. In addition to the actual movement of children, we can see the global axes of power in the regulations around these adoptions as well, with states in the Global South often under pressure by wealthier countries to follow their initiatives and restrictions. International agreements about how such adoption should proceed reflect western ideologies and family practices, often at the expense of families and practices in poor countries. The Hague Convention on the Protection of Children and Cooperation in Respect of Intercountry Adoption of 1993 ("the Hague Convention") was meant to safeguard the safety, rights, and cultural identity of children (and their biological parents) across the world (*The Economist* 2016). It seeks to identify and regulate what constitutes proper or not-proper adoptions. But the Hague Convention was developed on the basis of American-based family ideologies, which we have seen are often deeply rooted in a belief in the market. Other societies are not organized in the same way, but are still obligated to follow Hague conventions, often to the detriment of their own citizens. For example, while the Hague Convention purports to protect the rights of those placing their children for adoption, its version of "rights" differs from that of many other countries. In the US, the state does not recognize poverty as structural violence, and sees the costs of bearing and raising a child as the responsibility of the parents. But in other countries, those costs are borne or supported by society, through taxes and welfare programs, often considered a right for any citizen. Because the US does not recognize these rights, it does not consider severe poverty that forces a mother to give up her child as a violation of her rights, as other societies would. Rather, an American interpretation would be that she has "chosen" a "rational" and positive solution to her unhappy plight.

In addition, the weight of the Hague Convention is such that it has made it more difficult for mothers in some countries to find solutions to temporary hardship. In Brazil, for example, when facing difficult times, a mother would sometimes place her children in a nearby institution on a temporary basis. Both mother and institution understood that she would return to take her children back once her financial situation had stabilized, and, meanwhile, her children would be given shelter and care (Fonseca et al. 2015). But because the Hague Convention insists on "clean break" adoptions – complete severance between biological mother and child – children who are in these institutions on a temporary basis are now being placed for international adoption, often without their mother's consent (Fonseca 2002). The Brazilian state faced international pressure to adhere to certain standards, and to provide more children for international adoption. As a consequence of that international pressure and the foreign standards in place, poor Brazilian women have been left with little support. "From their point of view, they had left their children in the care of the institution in the same spirit they would have resorted to a grandmother ... In the birth mother's confrontation with state authorities, the clash of different rationalities was glaringly evident" (Fonseca 2002: 402).

Reproduction, through processes like ART, the buying and selling of gametes, surrogacy, and adoption, is now stratified across borders, as women and families in some situations rely on the labor and bodies of others as they form and organize their own families. In the process, some people are able to have, bear, and raise children when it might previously have been impossible to do so, opening up new ways to form families. But at the same time, the globalization of reproduction, especially as it is built on a foundation of inequality, means that providers and receivers of these new opportunities are differently positioned – class, race, poverty, nationality, and gender all shape the distribution of these new global reproductive processes and opportunities.

The Global Care Chain

We see further stratification in reproduction when we consider the global care chain – the ways that care of children, the elderly, and the ill – links individuals, communities, and countries across the world. In this process, neoliberal economics in both the Global North and South link poorer and richer countries.

In Chapter 6, we discussed how the Philippines has been caught up in policies associated with neoliberalism and by SAPs based on those ideologies, resulting in many Filipinos seeking work outside the country. Those "push factors" out of the Philippines have been matched by "pull factors" into countries in the Global North where inequality and financial insecurity also play large roles and have created the need for the labor of Filipinos and others from the Global South.

Industrial nations increasingly look to migrants from poorer countries to provide care labor, for example in the form of nursing, home health aids, elder care, and child care. In the past, it was primarily wealthy households that employed outsiders to perform such reproductive labor, including child care or housework. Now, in the industrial north, patterns of family and reproductive work have shifted. Declining wages, increasing debt, higher student loans, and other economic changes have left more families facing financial precariousness (Cooper 2014). As jobs become increasingly unstable and financial risk rises even for middle-class families in industrialized societies, more women are entering the labor force to shore up family incomes. In such an environment, women's work is sometimes less a choice than an imperative, often undertaken to keep the family afloat in such difficult times.

But with both parents working at full-time jobs, more and more families are struggling to find ways to do the care work that daily life requires. Because so many services have been privatized under the neoliberal economy, families have a hard time finding or affording the support they need to cope with demands of home and work. Services such as child care, maternity or family leave, elder care, or options for flexible or remote work are scarce and expensive. Many jobs do not provide even the basic "benefits," such as health insurance, sick leave, or vacation or personal/family time. Notably, the United States lags considerably behind other industrialized countries in such support of workers or families. In the US, couples on average spend about a quarter of their yearly income on child care costs, a number that rises to 57 percent for single parents (Howard 2018). In other countries, the state underwrites welfare programs by providing substantial workers' pensions, health, maternity, and family allowances, housing assistance, sick-child days, paid parental leave, and free or inexpensive child care. In contrast to the US, couples in Denmark on average spend about 10 percent of their income on child care (Howard 2018). Not only does that mean more financial help for Danish families, but provision of these programs also gives families a buffer against the difficulties of the family/work crunch. Because the US government provides very few of these kinds of supports, "families are left to craft private solutions when paid work and child rearing create competing demands on their resources" (Gornick and Meyers 2003: 42). While some women find employment that offers certain benefits, low-paid work is unlikely to provide such support, leaving families struggling to find a way to cope. The stresses fall particularly hard on women, who continue to do more of the household and child care labor in industrialized countries (Parreñas 2015: 39). If a child is sick, it is generally mothers who stay home from work, leaving them at risk of losing their jobs.

The absence of support for families means they have to find their own solutions to staying intact and achieving success. Immigrants' lower salaries means that employing women from other parts of the world becomes one of the few solutions both available and affordable for the provision of care labor; increasingly, families and individuals rely on "off-shoring," hiring outsiders at low wages to make up for the family labor that women themselves used to provide. The global care chain thus connects the needs and demands of women in industrialized countries with those of women in the Global South. In the United States, migrants from many places, including Caribbean countries, the Philippines, and Mexico, provide extensive labor in areas of nursing, child care, elder care, and housework. Women from places like Sri Lanka work in Middle Eastern countries (Gamburd 2000); Indonesian women work in Hong Kong (Constable 2007); Bolivians travel to Spain to provide care labor (Leon 2010). Most of these cases involve poorer women migrating to richer countries and providing the reproductive labor that allows middle-class women in the Global North to work in the labor force. In other circumstances, the labor gap is filled by immigrant women of color already residing in the industrialized north (Glenn 1986; Ibarra 2012). Much of this labor force is female. They provide child care and elder care, and are employed as nurses and teachers. Rhacel Parreñas argues:

> The incorporation of Filipina domestic workers into the labor market constitutes a hierarchical and codependent relation with their mostly white female employers. They free their female employers of housework, allowing them to avoid demanding a fairer division of labor with their partners and at the same time enabling them to participate in the labor force. (2015: 39)

The global care chain stretches even further. When women from places like the Philippines[17] or the Caribbean work in the households of other women who are further up the care chain, their own children, still at home, are then taken care of by women who are further *down* the care chain. Some Filipino women can use out-migration to escape the poverty and gender inequality in their own country, but in their absence, other women, often more marginalized than those migrant women, will take up provision of child and elder care, household work, and other reproductive labor, thereby leaving their own families short of the attention and care *they* need.

In this way, the "global care chain" (Hochschild 2000) connects women and families across the world through the commodification of reproductive care. The buying and selling of these kinds of services are not new, as households have long employed servants and nannies to provide reproductive labor. Under slavery, it was slaves whose reproductive labor was bought and sold. But the chain is more global than it was in the past, and the lives of everyone along that chain have been influenced by a neoliberal global economy. Whatever the challenges faced by women in richer countries – including the less wealthy – they still have more resources than others, and are able to hire women from the Global South to do the care work they once provided. Those migrants in turn hire other women even poorer than they are. This "care chain" process leads to further inequality because women at the top of the chain, who are able to hire outside help, can continue to work outside the home and are thus able to keep stable, better-paying jobs; those at the bottom are left without support as they struggle to juggle family and work demands.

This reproductive division of labor across borders comes from a combination of a neoliberal economy in which reproductive activities have been commodified, gender inequality in both sending and receiving countries, and racialized economic inequality throughout the world. Here again, we see how globalization and the market economy shape reproduction in particular ways. In many ways, reproduction is not all that different from goods, where the market is assumed and trusted to reign supreme – and effectively so. "If globalization is a story of manufacturing moving outside the United States to lower its cost, it is equally a story of relying on the offshoring of reproduction, to lower the cost of *reproductive* labor" (Briggs 2017: 80).

Thus, adding retroscapes to Appadurai's (1996) list of scapes helps us to trace the ways that bodies and body bits migrate or are bought, sold, rented, used, or rejected across the global landscape. That process is abetted through the West's prominent role in financescapes, technoscapes, and ideoscapes. The combination ties the world together in a system of inequality and control of reproduction.

Neoliberal capitalism has made the commodification of these processes and corporeal bodies seem natural, expected, and profitable. But this landscape is neither equal nor flat. Even as these processes give some women and their families new ways to survive or thrive, and provide new pathways to parenthood and making families, it comes at a cost to many others. As neoliberalism takes hold, and state support of families or individuals is disappearing, the new reproductive technologies that appear on the horizon, and the new sources of available labor that can be used to shore up families, come about because others are providing them, often in very intimate, bodily ways. As some women are able to "choose" among options, we can easily lose sight of what influences those choices and of how control of reproduction lies beyond the scope of individuals. It is economic, political, and social structures that shape choice, by enabling some, prohibiting others, and making some simply unimaginable. And all these processes have become deeply commodified as they spread across the world. These "choices" are unsatisfactory private solutions to a public problem.

Tied to the commodification of bodies, body processes, and body-use is the power of ideologies and how they move through the world. What the few examples in this chapter highlight is how those ideologies combine with other forces – financescapes, mediascapes, technoscapes, and ethnoscapes – in commanding ways to shape reproduction, and women's lives everywhere. These connections and inequalities are behind the way in which: a group of mostly westerners in London has the power to enact a global family planning program; the US government and its affiliates are central to data collection in, and demographic knowledge of, most poor countries; and even countries more distant from the global centers of power find themselves following western pathways of neoliberalism. These examples underscore how reproductive processes across the world are connected, how their contours and borders are shaped by the inequalities – both material and ideological – that shape all world processes.

8
Looking Ahead

The Promise of Resistance

Throughout this volume, we have seen example after example of the ways that social actors – states, corporations, NGOs, religious institutions, family members, male partners – have worked to seize and keep control over reproduction. Being able to do this grants power over a process that is central to all social, political, and economic communities. Some of those efforts have been violent, as were many actions that were part of China's birth planning policies, or Ceausescu's brutal pronatalist polices. But we have seen that intervention in reproduction does not have to be violent or coercive, or even direct, for it to have influence. In Nordic countries today, government support for child care and parental leave from paid labor also helps to shape reproductive outcomes. One important similarity in all these instances of reproduction is how most actions – on the part of states, religions, families, or NGOs – are directed at women. It is women's bodies that bear children, and, most often, it is women who raise those children. And it is women who have long borne the brunt of efforts to control reproduction. In this volume, we have focused on the forces beyond individual women, examining how social institutions and ideology are involved in the processes of reproductive control. But these larger forces have direct and powerful impacts at the individual level, on a daily basis – making it possible, difficult, harder, or impossible for women to reach their own reproductive goals. And we have also seen that those efforts to control reproduction are part of the discrimination, violence, and inequality that women face in their everyday lives. Controlling reproduction brings with it control of women.

Women and their allies, however, have not been silent or passive in the face of these struggles. Across the world, in small and large communities, in the face of subtle or coercive policies that seek to limit their ability to control their reproduction, women have pushed back. They have done this work as individuals, in small groups, and in national protests. They have worked through organizations such as NGOs that have sought to give them leverage in reproduction and other areas of their lives. Local and national leaders have taken up these issues, working to get reproduction on the agendas of community forums, city councils, state legislatures, or national court dockets.

Thus, while efforts to control reproduction have often had sharp teeth and a long reach, those teeth and that reach are regularly blunted, silenced, avoided. That women have evaded that control speaks to several aspects of reproduction that are always important to keep in mind. Reproduction reflects the messiness of bodies (Fausto-Sterling 2000). "Women are somehow more biological, more corporeal, and more natural than men" (Grosz 1994: 14), and women's reproducing bodies may be especially messy and difficult to control. However states or other actors might want to corral these processes through laws and restrictions, they are not so easily contained through these actions.

The unruliness of reproducing bodies in thwarting control is clearly a factor. But so too is the willingness, readiness, and sometimes desperation that women bring to blunting the teeth of policies that would keep them from their reproductive goals. Women resist, and they often resist effectively. As we argued in an earlier chapter, a good example comes from China. In the midst of a sometimes brutal effort by the government to control women's fertility, thousands and thousands of women evaded the law, and had an "out-of-plan" birth – a birth that was strictly forbidden by state law. Every single "extra" birth is evidence of how – even in the face of danger and at great risk to themselves – women resisted and found success in that resistance. Resistance is also found in quiet ways, producing "hidden transcripts" (Scott 1990), and sometimes hiding in plain sight. Sometimes this resistance to expectations around reproduction actually fits well within the larger hegemonic structures. Thus, as we saw, although women in patriarchal China are expected to produce sons for their husbands' families, they themselves want sons (and daughters) because a woman's "uterine family" (Wolf 1972) will provide love and support in the sometimes alien environment of their husband's family.

In some instances, women can get caught in competing versions of reproductive control, as we saw in an indigenous village in Mexico, where women and men disagreed about whether women needed to produce many children to resist the Mexican state's attempt to control indigenous populations. Just as reproduction is messy, so too is the resistance to control it. In Japan, we have seen that women have resisted pressures to marry, finding more satisfaction outside the prescribed roles of family and motherhood. In Ireland, when abortion was illegal, women traveled to England to access a termination; such resistance was carried out by women as individuals, and nearly all of it was – by necessity and by the surrounding shame around abortion – kept private. But it is also significant that the need and desire for legal abortion eventually manifested in large, very public demonstrations, leading to Ireland's passing of laws in 2018 supporting the legalization of abortion.

Women's resistance – the courage to take on the kinds of forces that are thrown at reproduction – speaks to how important controlling reproduction is to individual women, how it can mean financial and sometimes physical survival, success, or failure. Or, as we saw with the importance of motherhood in Egypt, how that control is connected to their very identity. Being able to have however many children she wants, and into the kind of family structure she wants, can be just as important to a woman as being able to prevent an unwanted pregnancy. Alexis Pauline Gumbs, a queer American Black feminist theorist, sees resistance in some childbearing, arguing:

> Mothering, especially the mothering of children in oppressed groups ... is a crucial and dangerous thing to do. Those of us who nurture the lives of those children who are not supposed to exist, who are not supposed to grow up, who are revolutionary in their very beings are doing some of the most subversive work in the world. (Gumbs 2016: 20)

That importance of reproduction to individual women is partly the reason that "choice" has taken on such an outsized role in reproductive politics. But as we have seen, while choice is desirable, it is too narrow a concept to cover all the forces that are aligned to influence – to seize control over – reproduction. Choice is given so much weight – has become hegemonic – because it aligns with a neoliberal ideology that puts responsibility for individual success – and failure – on the shoulders of individuals, despite the fact that it is the market and the state's presence and absence that are often at the root of whether individual women are able to reach their economic, social, or reproductive goals. "Smart economics" and its focus on women might be touted as being good for women but what it is really good for is global capitalism. Only if we recognize how the language of choice mirrors the very forces that keep women from achieving reproductive justice will women – all women, not only those with resources – be able to control their reproduction. Sistersong and other organizations are now focused on expanding efforts to push back against those forces. The potential power of such broad resistance is evident when we watch a place like Poland, where women's efforts to resist the state's increasing control of reproduction have come to include efforts to wrest control from the state in other areas of civil life as well.

The examples we have presented throughout this volume make clear that resistance comes – must come – in different forms in different places. What might work in a rural village in China is not what Palestinian women in Israel can use. Some resistance comes in large public demonstrations like those in Ireland to support legalization of abortion. But in some places, where such public, organized opposition is particularly dangerous, we must look for the resistance that comes in small, easily missed actions of individual women, or their families. These include Chinese women secretly removing government-implanted IUDs; or the journeys that some women have undertaken to find contraceptive or abortion services that are unavailable in their communities; or how poor women in North Carolina feign mental illness so that they might be allowed to undergo a desired sterilization; or how some couples in India are defying accusations of "love jihad" and marrying spouses of a different religion.

We must always acknowledge and take seriously the ways that social entities like the state, the Church, or community or family members have often sought to control women and their reproducing bodies. That control has been refracted and intensified through the racism that exists across the world, so that it is women in marginalized communities – poor, African American, or Native American women in the US; Uyghers in China; Palestinians in Israel; Muslims in India – who are often the target of regimes. But we also need to recognize that, even in the most difficult of circumstances, women and their allies have found ways – although often under great risk and with great cost – to resist.

What Does the Future Hold? Insights from Feminist Speculative Fiction

As we look to the future and think about the possibilities around reproduction, its importance, including how it is contested by many constituencies, is key. We have seen that states recognize reproduction as central to their own ability to shape the size, racial, and gender composition of their populations, to how well countries can balance their needs and resources, to their position in the world. Communities know reproduction is vital to their survival. Families see reproduction as a way to continue a family line, as the way to provide support for parents in old age. Individuals see in reproduction the promise of love and community and, in its control, the challenges to their bodily autonomy. Organizations confronting racism or discrimination know that reproduction is part of the oppressions they face. How these different claims to reproductive control play out depends on many factors, and makes it hard to predict future events.

Throughout this volume, we have drawn from the work of researchers and activists as they explored and analyzed reproductive experiences and possibilities. As we consider the future, we now turn to authors who have explored some of these same issues, critiquing the current situation or wondering about the future, but in this case through speculative fiction. It is not difficult to understand why feminist science fiction has so often focused on the exploration of reproduction, gender hierarchies, and other themes that are central to this book. As a genre that can imagine nearly any future and watch it play out, if only on a book's pages, this fiction has interested many who are worried about where the current situation might lead or have been interested in a changed gender or reproductive landscape. Margaret Atwood defines speculative fiction as "literature that deals with possibilities in a society which have not yet been enacted but are latent" (Masterclass staff 2021).

In these novels, authors consider "what if?" What if things today go to a further extreme? What if the things that are not working in today's society were "fixed"? What would the world look like? In this final chapter, we discuss several feminist dystopian/speculative fiction novels that present different scenarios around reproduction. We will see many themes in these works that resonate with events and processes that have occurred throughout the world and that we have documented in this volume. But in these fictitious versions of reproductive crises or imaginings, authors imagine otherwise: they find ways to underscore the importance of reproduction; they react to or imagine what happens when reproduction is controlled by different social actors beyond women themselves; and they imagine gender or reproduction in an altogether different form from any we have seen. Notably, although the novels we discuss raise different aspects of the processes of reproduction, reproduction itself is at the center of each. As one novelist, Leni Zumas, explained about how she thought about such issues, "what would be a core or elemental restriction to put on or pressure to put on a group of characters? If they're women – that was the first thing I thought of – it is restricting their ability to make decisions about their own bodies" (HarperCollins 2018).

Part of the challenge this fiction has posed is to the field of science fiction itself. Until these and other women writers started to find recognition, the field was male-dominated, both in authorship and in the stories themselves. While the gender imbalance has changed over the past several decades, other representation has not seen as sizeable a shift. As we discuss further below, it is notable that feminist dystopian fiction continues to be dominated by North American/ European writers. Appadurai (1996) may point to the fluid nature of mediascapes as they move across borders, but here again, those connections are uneven and subject to inequalities and different access, with those in the Global North dominating the publishing, film, and theater arenas. Our choice of novels reflects these trends in the field of speculative fiction. All the writers we discuss here are women. And many of them write of societies that seem to most closely resemble a North American or European setting. Many of those writing about or from the West portray a white society, where racial history and tensions, or even questions about sexuality, do not enter the story. Even some who write about other societies – as Maggie Shen King does about China – are themselves living in the Global North. Writings from the Global South are more scarce because of the predominance of English in publishing across the world, because most of the big publishing houses are located in the West, and because of how difficult it is to break into that western-dominated world. It may also be that writers in the Global South are less interested in the topic of reproduction and focus on others instead, such as interethnic conflict, or economic issues. Later, we take up these issues again as we consider the future of feminist speculative fiction.

Two of the early pioneers in feminist dystopia fiction have imagined reproductive scenarios that challenge current-day assumptions and processes and who, by doing so, began to open the field to issues of gender and sexuality and reproduction itself, centering their imaginations around subjects that had previously received little notice. The difficulties of breaking into a male-dominated field shaped the early writings of Ursula Le Guin, who said of that work: "What I'd been doing as a writer was being a woman pretending to think like a man ... I had to rethink my entire approach to writing fiction ... it was important to think about privilege and power and domination, in terms of gender, which was something science fiction and fantasy had not done" (cited in Flood 2018). In a number of works, Le Guin explores new worlds of gender, challenging both conventional storylines in the field, and established gender norms in current-day societies as well.

Ursula Le Guin's "The matter of Seggri" (1994) is set on the planet of Seggri, a community of extreme gender segregation where females vastly outnumber males. At first glance it appears that women are burdened more heavily than men, doing much of the hard labor. But a later observer realizes the underlying social structure. In Seggri, women are in charge: only women are allowed an education, and women fill all key roles in society. Men are of little significance to the social organization: their real role is only in reproduction, in fathering children. Otherwise, they spend their lives playing games and partying, and provide sexual services to women. By flipping expected gender roles, norms, and privileges, Le Guin seems to be challenging her readers to see the absurdity of our current social organization, with women's role reduced to their reproductive capacity.

One of the best-known writers in the field of feminist dystopia is Margaret Atwood; her book *The Handmaid's Tale* can be seen as pathbreaking in how authors imagine and write about issues of reproduction. The novel was published in 1985, and in 2017 a serialized television version of the book gave the story even wider attention. Atwood tells the story of Offred, a woman who lives in the state of Gilead. Having overthrown the United States, the Republic of Gilead is a military dictatorship, purportedly built on Christian principles. It is a patriarchal state in which women are subjugated to men; they are not allowed to read, write, or own property or money, and are assigned various jobs that support the patriarchy. Some are "commanders' wives," others act as cooks and maids (the "Marthas"). Offred is part of another group, the "handmaids," chosen to bear children for the commanders. It is Offred's story about her role as child producer (a "two-legged womb") that offers the clearest vision of what a loss of women's reproductive control looks like. Under the watchful eye of her commander's wife (Serena Joy), Offred is forced to have sex with the commander on a regular basis, with the goal of pregnancy and childbirth. Because of environmental pollution, most women are infertile, and it is the responsibility of the handmaids – chosen for their fertility – to reproduce. Procreation is an important state goal, and all women are forced to contribute to it in any way they can, whether that is bearing a child or creating the façade of a proper family (the commanders' wives). Offred and other women do try to resist the state, but the tight control over all lives makes any resistance unlikely to succeed. Any deviance from the rules of Gilead is met with harsh punishment. Offred's friend Moira escaped the indoctrination center at which they were both being trained to be good handmaidens, and is consequently punished, forced to spend her days cleaning up toxic waste. Other resisters are killed outright, left hanging in public as a lesson to anyone else thinking of such acts.

Atwood has been interviewed widely about *The Handmaid's Tale*, giving readers insight into her intentions in writing it, and the ways that such fiction is often written in response to what is happening around an author. Atwood has explained that the world of Gilead is drawn from existing societies and events. She insists that "there's not a single detail in the book that does not have a corresponding reality, either in contemporary conditions or historical fact" (Vintage Books 2018). And while Atwood has mentioned the Romanian regime's population control program as important in her thinking, she also argues such ideology and actions can be found in many places.

For example, she has talked about how her visions were partly drawn from 1980s American politics:

> I started actually thinking about [the book] in 1981. What had just happened? Ronald Reagan had been elected, and the religious right was on the rise in those years, the early Eighties. The Seventies was a "fermentous" time, with second-wave feminism making a lot of gains – but not the adoption of the Equal Rights Amendment, which got nixed ... And then there was a backlash. There are always backlashes. In the Eighties, that is when people started saying things like "Women belong in the home." (Vintage Books 2018)

In another interview, as Atwood and the interviewer looked over her archives at the University of Toronto, the author explained her process and the events she drew from to create her fictional world:

> There was no Internet then, you couldn't just go online and put in a topic, so this is just stuff I came across when reading newspapers and magazines. I cut things out and put them in a box. I already knew what I was writing about and this was backup. In case someone said, "How did you make this up?" As I've said about a million times, I didn't make it up. This is the proof – everything in these boxes ... My intention was just to document what I was doing and had done. As somebody on Twitter put it, "How do you come up with this shit?" As if I invented it. (Penguin 2019)

She points to the kinds of things that were happening around her as she was writing. In Canada, one government official pointed to the country's very low fertility rate and "suggested that Canadians start with renewed vigour over the holidays to increase the country's population ... 'It ought to be public policy to encourage families to have more children,' said [Dave] Nickerson ... 'Might I suggest that we could all start with renewed vigour this Christmas.'" Pointing to another newspaper article in the archive, Atwood continues: "Which leads nicely into this one, I think: 'Artificial birth methods are attacked by some feminists fearing male control. There is concern that we are moving toward methods that are not always in the best interests of individual women,' says a sociologist. No kidding" (Penguin 2019).

With the rise of the Christian Right and the election of Donald Trump, Atwood's writing seemed even more prescient. Even before the most recent events that have made reproductive rights in the US less available than they have been for 50 years, Atwood has been watchful of how American society and others are moving to curtail women's freedoms and reproductive rights. She writes (2017):

> Is *The Handmaid's Tale* a prediction? That is [a] ... question I'm asked – increasingly, as forces within American society seize power and enact decrees that embody what they were saying they wanted to do, even back in 1984, when I was writing the novel. No, it isn't a prediction, because predicting the future isn't really possible: There are too many variables and unforeseen possibilities. Let's say it's an antiprediction: If this future can be described in detail, maybe it won't happen. But such wishful thinking cannot be depended on either.

The popularity of Atwood's book, along with the made-for-TV series based on it, has suggested the ways in which her ideas and concerns resonate with many people. During protests and gatherings that are focused on protecting women's reproductive rights – whether they have been organized about the appointment of anti-abortion judges to the Supreme Court, or states preventing women from undergoing abortion – some women don a uniform taken straight from the pages of *The Handmaid's Tale*. Their red capes and white, face-shielding bonnets seem to bring Atwood's warnings even closer, and seem to have become a symbol of what many fear: that, with *The Handmaid's Tale*, Atwood is predicting what is to come.

The world created by Hilary Jordan, in *When She Woke* (2011), also draws from some current reproductive politics. In this world, women's reproduction has become difficult because of a sexually transmitted infection that affects only women's fertility. The novel, which has clear parallels to Nathanial Hawthorne's *The Scarlet Letter* (1850), looks at a more contemporary source of stigma and punishment – the violating of laws of reproduction. In Jordan's world, the threat to human reproduction has combined with already-existing efforts to control women's reproduction. Jordan's fictional world has strong echoes of the present-day United States, with many of the scenes taking place in a Texas imagined in some near-future time. Readers are left pondering the similarities to what is happening or might happen soon in the US: a rise of the Christian Right; the line between church and state dissolved; overturn of Roe *v.* Wade, making all abortion illegal; and no access to any reproductive health services. In an interview about her book, Jordan speaks to these echoes: "Dystopian novels are by definition cautionary tales that use elements of the present to paint a grim portrait of the future. I wish *WSW* were 100 percent fiction but if it were, I wouldn't have felt compelled to write it" (Lawless 2012). In Jordan's novel, women who violate any of the reproductive laws are punished. The main character, Hannah, gets pregnant during an affair with a mega-church minister, and undergoes an illegal abortion. Abortion is seen as both a moral failing and as dangerous to a society in which too few babies are born. Hannah is apprehended, arrested, and consequently "chromed," her skin dyed a bright red for 16 years. Chromes are targets of harassment, hatred, and violence. During those years, an implant will prevent her from bearing a child. Another part of her punishment is incarceration, first in isolation and then at the Straight Path Center, where she spends her time learning how she should have been a proper mother to her aborted fetus.

Jordan seems to be arguing here that Hannah's situation – punishment for sex outside marriage, or for pursuing an abortion – is the outcome of state and religion combining to place reproduction under such strict, constant, and heavy control, and to deprive women of all bodily autonomy. The state and its allies seek to control how women lead their lives, with whom they partner, what happens in these sexual relationships, as well as their pregnancies, births, and even how they raise their kids. There are resistance groups, but they operate in great danger and are not always successful in aiding women who have been caught in the state's net or are trying to push back against state regulations. It is only after escaping to Canada that Hannah is safe from those who seek to punish her. The author explains that her novel is "a cautionary tale about where we might be headed if we don't change course" (Connecticut Style 2011), a warning that the fundamentalist Christian theocracy of this imagined Texas future is closer than we want to believe.

In *Before She Sleeps* (2018), Bina Shah also imagines a world where reproduction is in jeopardy. Shah, a Pakistan-based writer, brings a different perspective to this genre, beyond the mostly-white worlds of Atwood and Jordan, and has created a South Asian country ruled by patriarchy. As one reviewer points out, "the novel has obvious parallels with the world the author inhabits in Pakistan – where although women now play a greater part in politics and the economy, they are still subjected to high levels of domestic violence, for example" (Kramatschek 2019).

The novel takes place in Green City, a new settlement constructed after a nuclear war and climate catastrophe had wiped out much of the population. Women are even scarcer than men because the radiation fallout has led to high numbers of women dying of cervical cancer. The state sees women – and their reproductive capacity – as valuable to the future of the country, and puts in laws and regulations to protect them. "Protection" of women, however, often takes the form of control:

> Nobody dared disobey the new directives that kept Green City under control in the Emergency years ... Already half a generation had been lost to war, terror, and disease; women were now the endangered species. The Perpetuation Bureau acted fast; before they knew what had happened, the remaining women in Green City found themselves put on an eerie pedestal to bring an entire nation back to life. At least that's how it was presented to us; in reality, refusal to obey the new rules would result in an accusation of reluctance or revolt, a swift trial, and elimination. The Leaders did not mind sacrificing a few women in order to make the rest of us compliant. (Shah 2018: 35)

Like Ursula Le Guin in "The matter of Seggri," Shah is commenting on narrow roles that define women, here reduced to their reproductive contributions. Much of the ideology and many rules of the Green City society echo the maternalism at the center of some policies that we saw in places like Latin America – "mothers at the service to the state" (Molyneux 2007) – but taken to an extreme. In this world, women are valued strictly for their ability to reproduce, "too valuable" to do any work that might interfere with their reproductive production. As part of the protection they receive, women are restricted in their movements and required to wear a chador. Abortion and contraceptives are outlawed and the shortage of women is behind the expectation that each woman should marry two to four men. Significantly, in Shah's world, their "value" does not give women power, but instead is more justification for outside forces to control them.

The setting of the novel – somewhere in South Asia – is a key factor in the world Shah has created. In other writing, she has rejected the belief that Islam is the dominant force in women's lives, arguing that "the world's biggest religion is not Christianity, Islam or Judaism, but patriarchy" (Shah 2021); that viewpoint shapes her fictional society. There, Islam plays no role in shaping women's lives, but patriarchal norms and laws – including those regarding segregation/purdah and gender selection in addition to reproduction – produce powerful constraints that women must navigate. Even resistance is shaped by those forces: some women have withdrawn from regular society, live in a bunker underground, and only in that voluntary seclusion are they able to escape "the regime's repressive grip [and] find refuge" (Kramatschek 2019), an ironic twist to the practice of purdah in many societies. Reflecting again the ways in which these writers draw from the world around them, Shah commented about her thinking behind *Before She Sleeps*: "In patriarchy, women are always going to end up being the losers ... What's going on now in Saudi Arabia, Pakistan and Afghanistan is worse than what's happening in *The Handmaid's Tale*" (cited in Alter 2018).

Red Clocks (2018), by Leni Zumas, does not seem futuristic at all, and, because of that, may be one of the most alarming of these feminist dystopia novels. As a reviewer in *The Atlantic* writes: "The America in ... *Red Clocks* is so familiar as to be almost unremarkable" (Gilbert 2018). Indeed, it is how things change gradually without most people noticing that is an important message of the novel. Set in the US Pacific Northwest, Zumas tells a story of several women who get caught in the increasingly harsh control of women and their bodies in the not-very-future. In this setting, women seem to lead independent lives: they go to school, work in the labor force, live by themselves or with others in families. But at the same time, they are not allowed control of their own reproduction. One of the themes throughout the novel mirrors what we see in societies across the world: the processes of reproduction, parenthood, family, and gender are messy. Answers are not always easy or clear, or even consistent. The characters in the novel struggle to find ways through their own questions and contradictions around these issues. In this story, after the quiet passing of the Personhood Amendment to the US Constitution, abortion is not only banned but criminalized; anyone having or involved in an abortion will be charged with murder. That same law has made IVF illegal, because fertilized eggs are now protected as future children. Another recently passed law, "Every Child Needs Two," is the basis for new restrictions that allow child adoption only by married heterosexual couples. Under these rules, one of the main characters (Ro), who is single and desperately wants a child, is left with no options for creating a family. Another, a teen who is pregnant and seeking an abortion, runs into the "Pink Wall," the law that prevents those seeking abortion from fleeing to Canada. Most importantly, perhaps, it is not just the biological processes of birth that are targeted, but the structures – families, not-families, individuals – that are also under increasing regulation by the state, as reproduction comes to be allowed only in family structures that the state deems proper. Tellingly, in *Red Clocks*, as in *When She Wakes*, it is the alignment of religion – evangelical Christianity – with the state that underlies the reproductive politics found in this fictional society, echoing the ways the state and church have partnered in places like Poland to restrict women's reproduction.

Reading this novel at a time when the US is tightening rules around reproduction makes this novel particularly poignant. In Zumas's – barely fictionalized – world, Ro recounts how she – who was once active in the feminist movement – saw headlines that suggested that these changes and rules were coming, but she could not imagine losing the reproductive choices that she had long had. Those headlines seemed a scare tactic to her at the time, and she was not motivated to respond as she might have been in the past. Now, women are caught in a tightening net over their reproduction. Zumas wrote her book in 2018, but the fictional abortion law of *Red Clocks* is hauntingly similar to that passed by the state of Texas in 2021, which criminalizes abortion and allows regular citizens to enforce the law.

Since the publication of her book, Zumas has talked explicitly about the "death by a 1,000 cuts" that reproductive access is experiencing. She points out that we "can get lulled into complacency" (HarperCollins 2018); her story is an argument for paying attention and pushing back against even the most gradual of efforts to shut down women's control of reproduction. As one reviewer writes:

> There's no mass epidemic of infertility in *Red Clocks*, no impending threat to the existence of humankind. Male politicians simply take away women's rights because they don't think women should have them … *Red Clocks* is plausible because men's opinions on abortion and assault and female bodily autonomy have always counted more than women's. (Gilbert 2018)

This kind of fictional tale underscores the ways that much reproductive control today is done not in the brutal ways that the Ceausescu regime implemented its policies, but through small and often unnoticed processes.

Maggie Shen King also writes close to current realities in her novel *An Excess Male* (2017). Taking place in China in the near future, the novel imagines the aftermath of state intervention in reproduction. The premise of the book – that a population policy that limits couples to one child in a society where son preference is very strong will wreak demographic havoc – comes fairly close to what China is facing even today. The book may be a more extreme version of current reality, but not by too much. In the book, as in Chinese society, there is an excess number of men, and therefore a large percentage of the male population has little chance of finding a spouse. Wei-guo, the main character, represents such men, at the bottom of the social hierarchy and unable to have a good marriage. In this new society, polyandry is encouraged, and women regularly have two or three husbands. But, as in Bina Shah's book, the scarcity of women does not mean that women have power or more control over their reproduction or lives. Those at the top of the hierarchy – rich, powerful men who are able to have a single wife to themselves – make the rules and keep the people in line. Women are confined to their homes; their responsibility is to be good mothers, be good wives to all their husbands, and produce children. The entire population is under constant electronic surveillance, a detail in the novel that also mirrors the current situation in China today. Wei-guo hopes to be able to join the family of May-ling, as a "third-level" husband. The depictions of May-ling and her family give the reader a glimpse into the authoritarian, sexist, and homophobic society they live in: one husband is gay, and, if found out, he will lose his rights as a father. Another husband is neuro-atypical, and for that reason is vulnerable to being disposed of by the state. Wei-guo, as an excess male, is also considered disposable.

As do others of these dystopian writers, King is taking pages from a current society to imagine what the future might look like, with a warning about state intervention in reproduction and its effect on social structure and stability. In this case, King's version of a future does not veer too far away from what many currently predict might happen in China, where many have warned of "unintended consequences" of the Beijing regime's draconian population policies, its tight surveillance of citizens, and its policies to weed out what the state deems as undesirable groups, such as political dissidents, queer people, or the Uyghurs in Xinjiang. Combined with continuing gender imbalances, with class, gender, and urban/rural inequalities, and with an authoritarian government, China may face just such social (dis)organization, laws, and violence as depicted in King's book.

Sheri Tepper's *The Gate to Women's Country* (1988) is also about leaders' attempts to shape a society through reproduction, but here women are in charge. Believing that it is men who are to blame for the nuclear war that wiped out most human settlements, the leaders of Women's Country work to change the future. Men and women live separately, with women inside the town walls and men in warriors' camps outside the walls. Men seem to have a privileged life relative to women, at least at first glance. In the garrisons, they play games and seem to have few responsibilities. The organizational structure of Women's Country resembles that of Le Guin's world in "The matter of Seggri." But in Tepper's world, the entire set-up is a ruse for something else. Few are aware that, behind the scenes, the women leaders are actually managing a selective breeding program. Tepper goes further than Le Guin: in her world, women are secretly working to breed out the violent tendencies of men that wreaked havoc on the world when they were in charge. Women leaders are using secret sterilization and targeted breeding to create humans who are not violent and who have qualities that will allow the surviving humans to live better, less dangerous, lives. Most men are not allowed to breed; this role is reserved only for men who have proven themselves to be not violent. And women's reproduction is also secretly controlled, so that only those women who have desirable traits are allowed to produce children.

Within the novel, Tepper finds ways to remind readers of what Women's Country is resisting. In his travels, one of the male characters (Chernon) finds another community, the Holylanders. That community is a Christian fundamentalist patriarchy where women are brutally enslaved to their husbands. Violence is pervasive, including toward children, who face severe physical punishment for infractions of rules. Chernon sees this community as a good alternative to Women's Country and tries to bring that vision into the garrison. But the plan of the Women's Country leaders prevails and the Holylanders exist only on the very outskirts of the central core of society.

In Women's Country, those in charge are intervening in reproduction, but for a different purpose than, say, the Chinese state is today. Like China's leaders, perhaps, the leaders of Women's Country are convinced they can manufacture a better society. But in this feminist-imagined future, it is not a particular group of people who are targeted, but violence they are seeking to eliminate. What is similar between states like that of China and the leaders of Women's Country is how, in both cases, reproduction is key to achieving future goals, whether that is a modern country capable of competing in the global economy or a future without violence. In both, those in charge see control of reproduction as the pathway to a desired future. Are we to judge one as better than the other, or is it the case that intervention is still intervention?

In some feminist speculative fiction, reproduction is important, but the imagined future is centered not on human reproduction but on reproduction between species. Octavia Butler uses cross-species reproduction to explore new worlds and familiar issues such as race, gender, colonialism, and exploitation in *Dawn* (and in the other books in her Xenogenesis Trilogy, *Adulthood Rites* and *Imago*). *Dawn* (1987) is the story of Lilith Ayapo, who survives a nuclear war that destroys nearly all earthly life. She is abducted by the Oankali, an alien species, who have put her into a sleep state for more than 200 years. When she awakens, she is aboard a giant Oankali ship orbiting earth and learns that the Oankali expect her to lead the repopulation of the planet, a plan that calls for mating between humans and Oankali. The Oankali see this as a trade: their involvement in this reproduction will allow the earth and humans a renewed future, but Oankali will also benefit, as they are gene-traders, searching the universe for partners with whom they can breed to improve their own race.

In her work, Butler, an African American feminist, explores the complexities of race and gender partly by juxtaposing familiar and unfamiliar scenarios and actions. *Dawn* challenges human readers to consider something as alien to their current social organization as extra-species reproduction. But other aspects of the novel will be familiar to many of Butler's readers: Lilith is a Black woman, and faces all the sexism and racism that we might expect when she tries to take charge of a group of humans. The gender system includes some familiar constructions (Lilith and the other humans are gendered as male or female) but the Oankali system, with its three genders and unfamiliar family configurations, provides readers the space to question their own systems and assumptions, including a human-centric view of the world around us.

Oankali control humans in a way that is reminiscent of colonial encounters that seem, at times, very familiar. Lilith is told by her Oankali minders that only with her consent will she undergo mating with an Oankali partner. But what does consent mean when someone has no say in their being held by a dominant group?

> Under the guise of kindness, the Oankali have taken complete control over the humans: they keep the remaining humans captive on their ship, put them to sleep if they become too difficult to control, keep them in isolation until they are within an inch of [losing] their sanity. Butler complicates the traditional dystopian victimization narrative by portraying the Oankali as – in a certain sense – more peaceful and "civilized" than the humans they are subjugating. (Tracey 2017)

Oankali thinking and action echo the historical experience of Native Americans and the ways whites purportedly "helped" them become more civilized and successful by subjecting them to "Americanization" and by "civilizing" and controlling their reproduction. Later, in a process that seems eerily similar to the placement of Native American children in white foster homes, "construct" (*hapa*) Oankali children are sold to well-off human couples.

But Butler does not seem to want to present clear or consistent answers or solutions to these issues. As one critic noted of her work,

> Dominance and submission, masters and slaves characterize the future as well as the past; rape is a constant danger in even sympathetic social relations ... Resolution, if and when it comes, is hard ... Her futures are populated with recognizably raced subjects and textured by histories that cannot be left behind. (Kilgore and Samantrai 2010: 354)

In *Dawn*, Butler seems most successful in raising questions about family, women, gender, and reproduction and the role of power and control around their structure and functions. Readers are left with a dizzying sense of the complexities of and connections among these issues – which may be the most accurate reflection of current reality and the messiness of bodies and reproduction.

Whether depicting a scenario that seems easily possible, as in *Red Clocks*, or something that is much further from our expectations, as in *Dawn*, all these novels see reproduction as central to social life. *The Children of Men* (1992), by P.D. James, was an early novel in this genre, one whose main lesson to readers seemed to be that reproduction is vital to our social organization and lives. Written in 1992, it is the story of the United Kingdom of 2021, when no child has been born for 20 years. It is not clear what caused this catastrophe, but it is clearly that: a disaster. Perhaps drawing from recent evidence that sperm counts are declining, but never really making explicit the cause of the worldwide sterility crisis, this story focuses on the way that, with no promise of a future, society loses its purpose. Without youth, without new births, it is impossible to staff and run a society in any ordinary way. Shortages of food, services, and labor are rampant. In this system, foreign workers are brought in to provide basic manual labor at low wages, and are then sent back to their own countries once they reach 60 years old and are no longer useful. With no young people, the society struggles to find ways to care for the elderly; they are encouraged to kill themselves when they get to the age of 60. A society that can no longer rely on regular reproduction loses its very essence, the glue that keeps society intact, and has to resort to practices and actions that would have been considered immoral, illegal, or impossible in the past.

"By extrapolating from things that are happening now and projecting into the future" (Lai 2004: 172), speculative fiction adds an important voice to discussions about reproduction and gender. We are now seeing this genre spreading beyond its earlier boundaries with the emergence of new figures and imaginings in who is writing, what topics are being covered, and where the work is being published and read. These writers are introducing new ways to consider gender, sexuality, and reproduction, further challenging how we assess and make sense of these issues. The availability of the internet for making public, for accessing and learning about, new work, means that some of the gatekeeping of publishing companies (primarily in the West) is less of an obstacle. We have seen the ways in which "a writer's unique social and historic embodiment" (Kilgore and Samantrai 2010: 355) influences her writing: Le Guin and Atwood helped to open speculative fiction to critical perspectives on the gender front; as an Asian American born in Taiwan, King looked beyond the West, to China, as Shah focused on Pakistan. Positionality is important in these processes, as we saw in how the Sistersong movement arose out of Black women's experience to challenge a white-centric version of reproductive politics. It is partly because Butler wrote from her position as a Black American woman that so much of her work "is fundamentally engaged with survival and adaptation strategies in hostile environments [and that] these strategies entail the understanding and assimilation of otherness, in both the physical and personal spheres" (Ferreira 2010: 401). All these writers contributed new voices and perspectives to how we imagine the world. The newest writers in these genres challenge issues of diversity and positionality even further. Many identify as being at the margins or intersections of various communities – Asian American, Latinx, queer, hapa, trans, non-binary (Johnson 2018; LeRoy 2019; Goodwin 2020). They are expanding the field, with imagined societies and lives that include and cross genders, sexualities, races, ethnicities, nationalities, species, and "repronormality" altogether (Denbow 2015: 174).

Not all these new writers consider reproduction – or human–human reproduction – to be central to society. And in centering their imagined worlds differently from the one we currently live in, with some refusing to put reproduction at the center, some of these new writers might be addressing one of the most threatening challenges to our current societies: when reproduction is *not* at the center. In James's novel, reproduction is impossible for most people, a situation that has led to societal disaster. But *voluntary* non-procreation might be even more alien and threatening to our current setting.[18] Voluntary or deliberate decisions not to procreate question reproduction, gender, family, and other social institutions on which most societies are built. If controlling women and controlling gender often operate together, then a non-procreative path – for women, for humans in general – challenges the very essence of social organization.

Final Thoughts

It should not be a surprise that feminists make up a significant portion of speculative fiction writers. As we try to understand the present, wrestle with a potential future where women's lives are more constrained than we were raised to think they would be by now, where reproduction is increasingly controlled, speculative fiction gives us new worlds. Sometimes they take our fears to new ends, underscoring the direction we are headed. Sometimes they help us to imagine a better world, one where there is no need for a #MeToo movement, where women are not raped as an act of war, where women have access to the resources they need to make their own decisions about reproduction, where neither race nor poverty plays a central role in who controls reproduction. About having and raising a child, or perhaps not having a child.

As we have seen in just these few works under discussion here:

> Some of these novels imagine preposterous scenarios ... But some aren't preposterous at all, and that's where it gets more alarming. Writers

> including ... Leni Zumas, and Bina Shah are warning readers of what could happen in a near-future world, with sperm counts mysteriously plummeting, global temperatures and STD rates rising, and a pivotal anti-abortion vote poised to tip the balance of the Supreme Court. Dystopian fiction isn't soothing anymore. It's too close for comfort. (Gilbert 2018)

Other fiction shatters altogether the connections between today's reproductive systems and what might be possible in the future – imagining worlds of extra-species reproduction or no reproduction at all.

It is not only in fiction that feminists have tried to disentangle the connections between gender inequality and reproduction. In 1970, radical feminist Shulamith Firestone made waves when she published *The Dialectic of Sex*; her ideas went beyond most fictional accounts of an imagined future. Firestone was 22 when she published the book, and was living at a time when "women held almost no major elected positions, nearly every prestigious profession was a male preserve, homemaking was women's highest calling, abortion was virtually illegal, and rape was a stigma to be borne in silence" (Faludi 2013). In her controversial book – a "case for feminist revolution" – Firestone imagined a better future for women. She argued that because reproduction was at the center of women's oppression, the only way to achieve gender equality was to break the connection between gender and biological reproduction.[19] Going beyond Marx's call for workers to seize the means of production to throw off their class oppression, Firestone argued that the "sexual class system" predates any class system and called for women to "seize the means of reproduction." She envisioned new technology that would remove pregnancy from women's – or anyone's – bodies. When fetuses were gestated in artificial wombs, women would be freed from "the tyranny of reproduction." Here, she underscores the way that charting a non-procreative future can be a form of resistance, a pathway championed by Jennifer Denbow (2015) nearly 50 years later. Denbow sees a refusal to procreate – through voluntary sterilization or abortion – as a form of resistance to the state's control of reproduction.

But for Firestone, she envisioned something more. She saw the separation of women from reproduction as the way to women's liberation. She argued that by removing the connection between women's lives and reproduction, the entire social structure would have to change; everything from the economy to schools to religion to sexual relations would undergo radical shifts. She proposed new ways to raise children, relieving women of the oppression that comes with women's role in childrearing: instead of in biological heterosexual nuclear families, children would be raised in collective extended households, and be better for that arrangement. Firestone's book created an uproar among feminists and others, some seeing her writing as preposterous and the stuff of science fiction. Others saw her ideas and claims, pointing to reproduction as the source of women's oppression, as nothing short of brilliant. Kate Millett, author of *Sexual Politics* and another important feminist of the time, said of Firestone: "I was taking on the obvious male chauvinists. Shulie was taking on the whole ball of wax. What she was doing was much more dangerous" (cited in Faludi 2013). While other feminists were more moderate in their demands, looking for acceptance of women into mainstream society or equal pay with men, feminists like Firestone "wanted to reconceive public life and private life entirely" (Faludi 2013). Now, more than 50 years later, Shulamith Firestone seems less radical than she did then. Fetuses are not growing in artificial wombs, but we have vastly more advanced reproductive technology available than we did in 1970. And Firestone's belief in the importance of reproduction as central to women's position and oppression does not seem very radical at all. In her imagining of how "to create a paradise on earth anew" (1970: 242), Firestone shares space with feminist speculative fiction authors. As Adrienne Maree Brown (2015) has argued "All social justice work is science fiction. We are imagining a world free of injustice, a world that doesn't yet exist."

Gilbert notes the way so much of feminist speculative fiction highlights "the paradox of female fertility." The ability to reproduce is both a lifeline and a life sentence. As Moira Weigel (2017) wrote in a review of Hulu's TV adaptation of *The Handmaid's Tale*, "The one thing that gives you value in society is the very thing for which you are hated." Another researcher has pointed to what these efforts to control reproduction mean for women in general:

> Many controversies over reproductive rights originate in society's efforts to use women's childbearing function as a justification for depriving them of rights or burdening them with duties. It is important

> to remember that these restrictions are not imposed only on women who are actual or potential mothers. They are imposed on all women. (Baer xxiv, cited in Faucheaux 2014)

Perhaps Shulamith Firestone was right: reproduction is at the center of it all.

Notes

1 While we often think of a male-dominated system as a patriarchy, the formal definition is more specific; it defines a family system in which the eldest male holds the most power. In such a system, men hold more power than women.
2 https://www.nps.gov/articles/sojourner-truth.htm.
3 Throughout this volume, we use "Global North" and "Global South" to distinguish groups of countries based vaguely on their location but the term is more explicitly used to signal differences in income level and level of industrialization, and often connects to the history of colonialism.
4 The TFR is often used as an easy measure of the average number of births a woman has in her lifetime. The formal definition indicates its calculation: the average number of births a woman would have by age 50 assuming the current age-specific fertility rates.
5 Rubin and many other feminist writers have developed theories about why women are subordinate to men. And while obviously important, we are not able to address that key underlying issue.
6 To illustrate this effect, we can imagine two societies in which each couple has only one child. In one, everyone marries at age 20; in 100 years, each family would have produced five children. In the second society, if everyone marries at age 25, each family will have four children in 100 years. In a large population like China's, such a difference in length of generation results in huge differences in the numbers of births.
7 See https://data.worldbank.org/indicator/SP.DYN.TFRT.IN?locations=CN. Replacement fertility is the TFR needed in a population from one generation to the next, estimated to be 2.1 (one child to replace each parent, with a slight adjustment for mortality).
8 MMR measures the risk of death to women during and immediately after pregnancy. It is calculated by the number of maternal deaths in a year per 100,000 live births in that year.
9 We must note that this is one of the few instances where surveillance

and coercion were focused on men rather than on women. Scholars have pointed to how this targeting was partly connected to the ways that the constructions and control of masculinity are part of state power and how the targeting of lower-class men for sterilization reflected those ideologies and practices (Scott 2014).

10 Social institutions are the basic building blocks of any society, constituting the apparatus of social life, organized around norms and values, and contributing to the integration of individuals into the society.

11 Important to note here is that, at the time, Southern and Eastern Europeans were not considered "white," and their inclusion in the restriction group reflected that racial construction.

12 Difficulty in health access is compounded by the lack of universal health care in the US. The US remains the only high-income country in the world that does not guarantee universal health care, a situation that is connected to how racism has shaped and continues to shape health outcomes in the country (Downs 2015; Interlandi 2019).

13 Eugenics is a theory and practice based on a belief that mental illness, disabilities, intelligence, and even undesirable behavior were genetic. To improve population quality, eugenicists believed that those with undesirable traits should be prevented from reproducing. The theory was popular in the US during the first half of the twentieth century. It has now been discredited, especially after Hitler's policies relied on eugenic theories to justify exterminating 11 million people – Jews, Jehovah's Witnesses, homosexuals, mentally disabled, and others – in their efforts to create a "master race." In the US, eugenics was used to justify sterilization of those with mental illness or genetic disabilities, but also those who were poor or nonwhite.

14 Settler colonialism is a particular type of colonialization where settlers invade a territory with the goal of claiming and occupying the land for themselves. The process often leads to the elimination of the original inhabitants through warfare, genocide, assimilation, or removal from the land. Canada, the US, Australia, South Africa, amongst others, are settler colonial societies.

15 It is important to note that those population numbers, particularly those from Palestinian communities, have been unreliable, but that unreliability does not undermine how both sides see reproduction as important to survival and land claims.

16 Arab women in Jordan have a TFR of 2.69 compared to those in Palestine's 3.49; while the TFR of Jews in Israel is 3.17, the TFR of Jews in the US and Britain is only 1.5 (Kaufman 2021).

17 The International Labor Organization and the Philippine government estimate that, of the 11 million domestic workers worldwide, one in four is from the Philippines (Redfern 2021).

18 An example of this threat comes from contemporary China, where young people are chafing under a state that surveils and regulates nearly

all aspects of their lives. Some see a refusal to bear more children, as the state implores, as one of their only means of resisting an increasingly oppressive state. "As ordinary people who're not entitled to individual dignity, our reproductive organs will be our last resort," wrote one person on the platform Weibo (Yuan 2022).

19 There are serious blind spots in Firestone's analysis, particularly regarding race – an institution that she mostly ignores. In her push to imagine how to overturn the present sexist system, she misses the ways that race – and colonialism, even most aspects of compulsory heterosexuality – are part of that system. For commentary on these aspects of Firestone, see Davis 1981: 180ff.; Lewis 2021.

References

Aderet, Ofer. 2019. "For the first time in Israel's history, Jewish fertility rate surpasses that of Arabs." *Haaretz*. December 31. https://www.haaretz.com/israel-news/.premium-in-first-for-israel-jewish-fertility-rate-surpasses-that-of-arabs-1.8343039.

Ali, Kamran. 1996. "The politics of family planning in Egypt." *Anthropology Today* 12 (5): 14–20.

Ali, Kamran. 2002. *Planning the Family in Egypt: New Bodies, New Selves*. University of Texas Press.

Aljazeera. 2021. "Chile takes first steps towards decriminalizing abortion." September 28. https://www.aljazeera.com/news/2021/9/28/chile-takes-first-step-towards-decriminalising-abortion.

Almeling, Rene. 2011. *Sex Cells: The Medical Market for Eggs and Sperm*. University of California Press.

Almeling, Rene. 2015. "Reproduction." *Annual Review of Sociology* 41: 423–442.

Alok, S.K. 1992. *Family Welfare Planning: The Indian Experience*. South Asia Books.

Alter, Alexandra. 2018. "How feminist dystopian fiction is channeling women's anger and anxiety." *New York Times*, October 8. https://www.nytimes.com/2018/10/08/books/feminist-dystopian-fiction-margaret-atwood-women-metoo.html.

Alvarez Minte, Gabriela. 2020. "Resistance to sexual and reproductive rights: Maternalism and conservatism." In A. Ramm and J. Gideon, eds., *Motherhood, Social Policies and Women's Activism in Latin America*. Palgrave Macmillan, pp. 123–144.

Anderson, Benedict. 1991. *Imagined Communities: Reflections on the Origin and Spread of Nationalism*. Verso.

Apolitical.com. 2018. "Norway's 'daddy-quota' means 90% of fathers take parental leave." September 17. https://apolitical.co/en/solution_article/norways-daddy-quota-means-90-of-fathers-take-parental-leave.

Appadurai, Arjun. 1996. "Disjuncture and difference in the global cultural economy." In *Modernity at Large*. University of Minnesota, pp. 27–47.

Arieff, Adrienne. 2012. "Motherlode: Having twins with a surrogate – in India." *New York Times*, March 19.

Arnold, Fred. 1975. *The Value of Children*. Vol. 1: *Introduction and Comparative Analysis*. East-West Center Publications.

Arreola, Cristina. 2019. "Abortion rights are under attack. In *Red Clocks*, Leni Zumas writes about what comes next." *Bustle*, May 13. https://www.bustle.com/p/in-red-clocks-leni-zumas-imagines-what-happens-when-reproductive-rights-are-taken-away-entirely-17868008.

Atwood, Margaret. 1985. *The Handmaid's Tale*. McClelland and Stewart.

Atwood, Margaret. 2017. "What *The Handmaid's Tale* means in the age of Trump." *New York Times* Op-Ed, March 10. https://www.nytimes.com/2017/03/10/books/review/margaret-atwood-handmaids-tale-age-of-trump.html.

Bagri, Neha Thirani. 2021. "A controversial ban on commercial surrogacy in India could leave women with even fewer choices." *Time Magazine*, June 30. https://time.com/6075971/commercial-surrogacy-ban-india/.

Bakhru, Tanya S. 2019. "Introduction: Thinking transnationally: Reproductive justice in a globalized era." In T. Bakhru, ed., *Reproductive Justice and Sexual Rights*. Routledge, pp. 3–12.

Balk, Deborah. 1994. "Individual and community aspects of women's status and fertility in rural Bangladesh." *Population Studies* 48: 21–45.

Barham, Tania, et al. 2021. "Thirty-five years later: Long-term effects of the Matlab maternal and child health/family planning program on older women's well-being." *Proceedings of the National Academy of Science (PNAS)* 118 (28): e2101160118.

Basu, Alaka. 2020. "Make no mistake, a population control policy will target the marginalized." *The Wire*, February 13. https://thewire.in/rights/india-population-control-policy.

Beauvoir, Simone de. 1979. *The Second Sex*. Vintage.

Bell, Ann. 2014. *Misconception: Social Class and Infertility in America*. Rutgers University Press.

Benson, Janie, Kathryn Andersen, and Ghazaleh Samandari. 2011. "Reductions in abortion-related mortality following policy reform: Evidence from Romania, South Africa and Bangladesh." *Reproductive Health* 8 (39). http://www.reproductive-health-journal.com/content/8/1/39.

Bergmann, Sven. 2011. "Fertility tourism: Circumventive routes that enable access to reproductive technologies and substances." *Signs* 36 (2): 280–289.

Bernal, Victoria, and Inderpal Grewal. 2014. "The NGO form: Feminist struggles, states, and neoliberalism." In V. Bernal and I. Grewal, eds., *Theorizing NGOs: States, Feminisms, and Neoliberalism*. Duke University Press, pp. 1–18.

Bernstein, Elizabeth, and Janet Jakobsen. 2010. "Sex, secularism and religious influence in US politics." *Third World Quarterly* 31 (6): 1023–1039.

Bhatia, Rajani, et al. 2020. "A feminist exploration of 'populationism': Engaging contemporary forms of population control." *Gender, Place, and Culture* 27 (3): 333–350.

Bier, Laura. 2010. "'The family is a factory': Gender, citizenship, and the regulation of reproduction in Postwar Egypt." *Feminist Studies* 36 (2): 404–432.

Biswas, Amit, et al. 2017. "Women's autonomy and control to exercise reproductive rights: A sociological study from rural Bangladesh." *Sage Open* (April–June): 1–10.

Blackwood, Evelyn. 2000. *Webs of Power: Women, Kin, and Community in a Sumatran Village*. Rowman & Littlefield.

Blake, Judith. 1994. "Fertility control and the problem of voluntarism." *Population and Development Review* 20 (1): 167–177.

Bloomberg. 2021. "China's data collectors discover they missed 11.6 million children born in the 2000s." *Forbes*, November 23. https://fortune.com/2021/11/23/china-population-data-births-undercount-statistics-census-one-child-policy/.

Borchorst, Anette. 2006. "The public–private split rearticulated: The abolishment of the Danish daddy leave." in A. Ellingsseter and A. Leira, eds., *Politicising Parenthood in Scandinavia: Gender Relations in Welfare States*. Policy Press, pp. 101–120.

Boston Women's Health Book Collective. 1984. *The (New) Our Bodies Ourselves*. Simon and Schuster.

Boyd, Ginger Ging-Dwan. 2016. "The girl effect: A neoliberal instrumentalization of gender equality." *Consilience: The Journal of Sustainable Development* 15 (1): 146–180.

Bridges, Khiara. 2011. *Reproducing Race: An Ethnography of Pregnancy as a Site of Racialization*. University of California Press.

Briggs, Laura. 2002. *Reproducing Empire: Race, Sex, Science and US Imperialism in Puerto Rico*. University of California Press.

Briggs, Laura. 2010. "Reproductive technology: Of labor and markets." *Feminist Studies* 36 (2): 359–374.

Briggs, Laura. 2017. *How All Politics Became Reproductive Politics*. University of California Press.

Brown, Adrienne Maree. 2015. "Introduction." In A.M. Brown and W. Imarisha, eds., *Octavia's Brood: Stories from Social Justice Movements*. AK Press.

Browner, Carole H. 1986. "The politics of reproduction in a Mexican village." *Signs* 11 (4): 710–724.

Bryant, Allison S., Ayaba Worjoloh, Aaron B. Caughey, and A. Eugene Washington. 2010. "Racial/ethnic disparities in obstetric outcomes and care: Prevalence and determinants." *American Journal of Obstetrics and Gynecology* 202 (4): 335–343.

Bulatao, Rodolpho. 1975. *The Value of Children*. Vol. 2: *Philippines*. East-West Center Publications.

Bumiller, Elizabeth. 1990. *May You Be the Mother of a Hundred Sons*. Fawcett Columbine.

Burnett, V. 2017. "As Mexican state limits surrogacy, global system is further strained." *New York Times*, March 23. https://www.nytimes.com/2017/03/23/world/americas/as-mexican-state-limits-surrogacy-global-system-is-further-strained.html?_.

Burrell, Darci. 1995. "The Norplant solution: Norplant and the control of African American motherhood." *UCLA Women's Law Journal* 5 (2): 401–444.

Butler, Octavia. 1987. *Dawn*. Grand Central Publishing.

Caldwell, John C. 1976. "Toward a restatement of demographic transition theory." *Population and Development Review* 2 (3/4): 321–366.

Caldwell, John, and Peter McDonald. 1982. "Influence of maternal education on infant and child mortality: Levels and causes." *Health Policy and Education*. 2 (3–4): 251–267.

Calkin, Sydney. 2015. "Feminism interrupted? Gender and development in the era of 'Smart economics.'" *Progress in Development Studies* 15 (4): 295–307.

Camarota, Steven, and Karen Zeigler. 2021. "Fertility among immigrants and native-born Americans: Difference between the foreign-born and the native-born continues to narrow." Center for Immigration Studies, Backgrounder Report. https://cis.org/Report/Fertility-Among-Immigrants-and-NativeBorn-Americans.

Carpenter, Zoe. 2019. "Las Comadres is fighting to make abortion safe in Ecuador – even while it's illegal." *The Nation*, May 7. https://www.thenation.com/article/world/abortion-activism-prosecutions-ecuador/.

Center for Reproductive Rights. 2010. *In Harm's Way: The Impact of Kenya's Restrictive Abortion Law*. http://reproductiverights.org/sites/crr.civicactions.net/files/documents/InHarmsWay_2010.pdf.

Center for Reproductive Rights. 2018. "Fact Sheet: The global gag rule and human rights." January 10. https://reproductiverights.org/fact-sheet-the-global-gag-rule-and-human-rights/.

Chant, Sylvia. 2008. "The 'feminisation of poverty' and the 'feminisation' of anti-poverty programmes: Room for revision?" *Journal of Development Studies* 44 (2): 165–197.

Chant, Sylvia. 2016b. "Women, girls, and world poverty: Empowerment, equality, or essentialism?" *International Development Planning Review* 38 (1): 1–24.

Chasnoff, Ira, et al. 1990. "The prevalence of illicit drug or alcohol use during pregnancy and discrepancies in mandatory reporting in Pinellas County, FL." *New England Journal of Medicine* 322: 1202–1205.

Chatterjee, Nilanjana, and Nancy E. Riley. 2001. "Planning an Indian modernity: The gendered politics of fertility control." *Signs* 26 (3): 811–845.

Chatterjee, Nilanjana, and Nancy E. Riley. 2018. "Women, biopower, and the making of demographic knowledge: India's Demographic and Health Survey." In N.E. Riley and J. Brunson, eds., *International Handbook on Gender and Demographic Processes*. Springer, pp. 37–54.

Cheang, Ko Lyn. 2021. "When pregnancy is a crime." *Yale Daily News* 143 (June 16). https://yaledailynews.com/blog/2021/06/16/when-pregnancy-is-a-crime/.

Chesler, Phyllis. 1992. *Sacred Bond: Legacy of Baby M*. Random House.

Clark, Rodney, and Norman B. Anderson. 1999. "Racism as a stressor for African Americans." *American Psychologist* 54 (10): 805–816.

CNN. 2010. "What 'The Pill' did." May 7. http://www.cnn.com/2010/OPINION/05/06/pogrebin.pill.roundup/index.html.

Coale, Ansley, and Edgar Hoover. 1958. *Population and Economic Development in Low-Income Countries*. Princeton University Press.

Cohen, David, and Carole Joffe. 2020. *Obstacle Course: The Everyday Struggle to Get an Abortion in America*. University of California Press.

Cohen, Susan. 2012. "London summit puts family planning on the agenda, offers new lease on life for millions of women and girls." *Guttmacher Policy Review* 15 (3): 20–24.

Collins, James W., Richard J. David, Arden Handler, Stephen Wall, and Steven Andes. 2004. "Very low birthweight in African American infants: The role of maternal exposure to interpersonal racial discrimination." *American Journal of Public Health* 94 (12): 2132–2138.

Connecticut Style. 2011. "When she woke: Interview with Hillary Jordan" Connecticut 8. https://www.youtube.com/watch?v=7wZU02pkmXU.

Connelly, Matthew. 2006. "Population control in India: Prologue to the Emergency Period." *Population and Development Review* 32 (4): 629–667.

Connelly, Matthew. 2009. *Fatal Misconception: The Struggle to Control World Population*. Harvard University Press.

Constable, Nicole. 2007. *Maid to Order in Hong Kong: Stories of Migrant Workers*, 2nd ed. Cornell University Press.

Cooper, Marianne. 2014. *Cut Adrift: Families in Insecure Times*. University of California Press.

Cornwall, Andrea, Jasmine Gideon, and Kalpana Wilson. 2008. "Introduction: Reclaiming feminism. Gender and neoliberalism." *IDS Bulletin* 39 (6): 1–9.

Cutler Blayne, and Sean Greene. 1987. "Singapore's designer genes." *Consumer Markets Abroad* 6 (8): 8–11.

Davis, Angela. 1981. *Women, Race and Class*. Random House.

Davis, Kingsley. 1944. "Demographic fact and policy in India." *Milbank Memorial Fund Quarterly* 22 (3): 256–278.

Dejong, David H. 2007. "'Unless they are kept alive': Federal Indian schools and student health, 1878–1918." *American Indian Quarterly* 31 (2): 256–282.

Denbow, Jennifer. 2015. *Governed Through Choice: Autonomy, Technology, and the Politics of Reproduction*. New York University Press.

Desai, Manisha. 2007. "The messy relationship between feminisms and globalizations." *Gender and Society* 21 (6): 797–803.
di Leonardo, Micaela. 1987. "The female world of cards and holidays: Women, families, and the work of kinship." *Signs* 12 (3): 440–453.
Dommermuth, Lars, Bryndl Hohmann-Marriott, and Trude Lappegard. 2017. "Gender equality in the family and childbearing." *Journal of Family Issues* 38 (18): 1803–1824.
Downs, Jim. 2015. *Sick from Freedom: African American Suffering during the Civil War and Reconstruction*. Oxford University Press.
Eckner, Constantin. 2018. "Germany's heated asylum debate has dark parallels to events 30 years ago." *The Conversation*, September 14. https://theconversation.com/germanys-heated-asylum-debate-has-dark-parallels-to-events-30-years-ago-102693.
The Economist. 2016. "Babies without borders." August 6. https://www.economist.com/news/leaders/21703369-hundreds-thousands-children-languish-orphanages-adopting-them-should-be-made.
Edin, Kathryn, and Maria Kefalas. 2007. *Promises I Can Keep*. University of California Press.
Ehrlich, Paul. 1968. *The Population Bomb*. Ballantine Books.
Eisenstein, Hester. 2005. "A dangerous liaison? Feminism and corporate globalization." *Science and Society* 69 (3): 487–518.
Eisenstein, Hester. 2009. *Feminism Seduced: How Global Elites Used Women's Labor and Ideas to Exploit the World*. Paradigm.
Emecheta, Buchi. 1980. *The Joys of Motherhood*. George Braziller.
Escobar, Arturo. 1988. "Power and visibility: Development and the invention and management of the Third World." *Cultural Anthropology* 3 (4): 428–443.
EurekAlert! 2020. "Europe moves towards complete statutory regulation of ART." European Society of Human Reproduction and Embryology. https://www.eurekalert.org/news-releases/895168.
Ewig, Christina. 2006. "Hijacking global feminism: Feminists, the Catholic Church and the family planning debacle in Peru." *Feminist Studies* 32 (3): 633–670.
Faitelson, Yakov. 2009. "The politics of Palestinian demography." *Middle East Forum* 16 (2): 51–59.
Faludi, Susan. 2013. "Death of a revolutionary." *The New Yorker*, April 8.
Faucheux, Amandine. 2014. "'Nolite te bastardes carborundorum': Reproduction and resistance in Octavia Butler, Margaret Atwood, and the Alien Series." University of New Mexico Master's Thesis. https://digitalrepository.unm.edu/fll_etds/68.
Fausto-Sterling, Anne. 2000. *Sexing the Body: Gender Politics and the Construction of Sexuality*. Basic Books.
Fei Xiaotong. 1992. *From the Soil: The Foundations of Chinese Society*. University of California Press.
Ferreira, Maria Aline. 2010. "Symbiotic bodies and evolutionary tropes in the work of Octavia Butler." *Science Fiction Studies* 37 (3): 401–415.

Filipovic, Jill. 2017. "The global gag rule: American's deadly export." *Foreign Policy*, March 20. http://foreignpolicy.com/2017/03/20/the-global-gag-rule-americas-deadly-export-trump-africa-women-reproductive-rights/.

Finkle, Jason L., and Alison McIntosh. 1996. "Cairo revisited: Some thoughts on the implications of the ICPD." *Health Transition Review* 6 (1) : 110–113.

Firestone, Shulamith. 1970. *The Dialectic of Sex: A Case for Feminist Revolution*. Bantam Books.

Flavin, Jeanne. 2009. *Our Bodies, Our Crimes: The Policing of Women's Reproduction in America*. New York University Press.

Fletcher, Ruth. 2005. "Reproducing Irishness: Race, gender, and abortion law." *Canadian Journal of Women and the Law* 17 (2): 365–404.

Flood, Alison. 2018. "Ursula K. Le Guin film reveals her struggle to write women into fantasy." *Guardian*, May 30. https://www.theguardian.com/books/2018/may/30/ursula-k-le-guin-documentary-reveals-author.

Fonseca, Claudia. 2002. "Inequality near and far: Adoption as seen from the Brazilian favelas." *Law and Society Review* 36 (2): 397–432.

Fonseca, Claudia, Diana Marre, and B. San Román. 2015. "Child circulation in a globalized era: Anthropological reflections." In R.L. Ballard et al., eds., *The Intercountry Adoption Debate: Dialogues Across Disciplines*. Cambridge Scholars Publishing, pp. 157–192.

Foucault, Michel. 1978. *History of Sexuality*, vol. 1. Random House.

Foucault, Michel. 1991. "Governmentality." In G. Burchell, C. Gordon, and P. Miller, eds., *The Foucault Effect: Studies in Governmentality*. Harvester Wheatsheaf, pp. 87–104.

Foucault, Michel. 2004. *"Security, Territory, Population": Lectures at the Collège de France 1977–1978*. Palgrave Macmillan.

Fraser, Nancy. 2009. "Feminism, capitalism and the cunning of history." *New Left Review* 56 (March–April): 97–117.

Frayer, Lauren. 2021. "In India, boy meets girl, proposes – and gets accused of jihad." NPR, October 10. https://www.npr.org/2021/10/10/1041105988/india-muslim-hindu-interfaith-wedding-conversion.

Gal, Susan, and Gail Kligman. 2000. "Reproduction as politics." In *The Politics of Gender after Socialism*. Princeton University Press, pp. 15–36.

Gallop. 2021. "Abortion." https://news.gallup.com/poll/1576/abortion.aspx.

Gamburd, Michelle. 2000. *The Kitchen Spoon's Handle: Transnationalism and Sri Lanka's Migrant Housemaids*. Cornell University Press.

Gates Foundation. 2022. "Family planning." https://www.gatesfoundation.org/our-work/programs/global-development/family-planning.

GBD 2015 Maternal Mortality Collaborators. 2016. "Global, regional, and national levels of maternal mortality, 1990–2015: A systematic analysis for the Global Burden of Disease Study 2015." *The Lancet* 388: 1775–1812.

Gilbert, Sophie. 2018. "The remarkable rise of the feminist dystopic." *The*

Atlantic, March 18. https://www.theatlantic.com/entertainment/archive/2018/10/feminist-speculative-fiction-2018/571822/.
Ginsberg, Faye, and Rayna Rapp, eds. 1995. *Conceiving the New World Order*. University of California Press.
GirlHub. 2014. "GirlHub Global evaluation, research, and learning." https://www.itad.com/project/girl-hub-global-evaluation-research-and-learning/.
Glenn, Evelyn Nakano. 1986. *Issei, Nisei, Warbride: Three Generations of Japanese American Women in Domestic Service*. Temple University Press.
Glenn, Evelyn Nakano. 2015. "Settler colonialism as structure: A framework for comparative studies of US race and gender formation." *Sociology of Race and Ethnicity* 1 (1): 52–72.
Goldsmith Weil, Jael. 2020. "Constructing maternalism from paternalism: The case of state milk programs." in A. Ramm and J. Gideon, eds., *Motherhood, Social Policies and Women's Activism in Latin America*. Palgrave Macmillan, pp. 69–96.
Goodwin, Matthew. 2020. *Latinx Rising: An anthology of Latinx Science Fiction and Fantasy*. Ohio State University Press.
Gordon, Linda. 2007. *The Moral Property of Women: A History of Birth Control Politics in America*. University of Illinois Press.
Gornick, Janet, and Marcia Meyers. 2003. *Families that Work: Policies for Reconciling Parenthood and Employment*. Russell Sage Foundation.
Grant, Rebecca. 2019. "Meet Mississippi's fiercest advocate for reproductive justice." *The Nation* 308 (9): 13–15.
Green, David. 2017. "As population ages, Japan quietly turns to immigration." Migration Policy Institute, March 28. https://www.migrationpolicy.org/article/its-population-ages-japan-quietly-turns-immigration.
Greenhalgh, Susan. 1994. "Controlling births and bodies in village China." *American Ethnologist* 21 (1): 3–30.
Greenhalgh, Susan. 2010a. "China's population policies: Engendered biopolitcs, the one-child norm, and masculinization of child sex ratios." In M. Rao and S. Sexton, eds., *Markets and Malthus: Population, Gender, and Health in Neo-liberal Times*. Sage, pp. 299–337.
Greenhalgh, Susan. 2010b. *Cultivating Global Citizens: Population in the Rise of China*. Harvard University Press.
Greenhalgh, Susan, and Jiali Li. 1995. "Engendering reproductive policy and practice in peasant China: For a feminist demography of reproduction." *Signs* 20 (3): 601–641.
Grosz, Elizabeth. 1994. *Volatile Bodies: Towards a Corporeal Feminism*. Routledge.
Gumbs, Alexis Pauline. 2016. "M/other ourselves: A Black queer feminist genealogy for radical mothering." In A. Gumbs, C. Martens, and M. Williams, eds., *Revolutionary Mothering: Love on the Front Lines*. PM Press, pp. 19–32.
Gupte, Prajakta. 2017. "India: 'The Emergency' and the politics of mass sterilization." *Education about Asia* 22 (3): 40–44.

Guttmacher Institute. 2010. "Facts on barriers to contraception in the Philippines." Likhaan Center. https://www.guttmacher.org/fact-sheet/facts-barriers-contraceptive-use-philippines.

Guttmacher Institute. 2021. "State facts about abortion: Mississippi." https://www.guttmacher.org/fact-sheet/state-facts-about-abortion-mississippi#.

Hacking, Ian. 2006. "Making up people." *London Review of Books*, August 17.

Hacking, Ian. 2015 [1983]. "Biopower and the avalanche of printed numbers." In V.W. Cisney and N. Morar, eds., *Biopower: Foucault and Beyond*. University of Chicago Press, pp. 65–80.

Haile, Amaha, and Fikre Enqueselassie. 2006. "Influence of women's autonomy on couple's contraception use in Jimma town, Ethiopia." *Ethiopian Journal of Health Development* 20: 145–151.

Halfon, Saul. 2007. *The Cairo Consensus: Demographic Surveys, Women's Empowerment, and Regime Change in Population Policy*. Lexington Books.

HarperCollins. 2018. "In conversation with Leni Zumas about her new novel, *Red Clocks*." harpercollins.co.uk https://www.youtube.com/watch?v=GX3EfJlc1k4.

Hart, Gillian. 2006. "Denaturalizing dispossession: Critical ethnography in the age of resurgent imperialism." *Antipode* 38 (5): 977–1004.

Hartmann, Betsy. 2011. "The return of population control: Incentives, targets, and the backlash against Cairo." *DifferenTakes* 70 (Population and Development Program, Hampshire College).

Harvey, David. 2005. *A Brief History of Neoliberalism*. Oxford University Press.

Heinen, Jacqueline, and Stéphane Portet 2010. "Reproductive rights in Poland: When politicians fear the wrath of the Church." *Third World Quarterly* 31 (6): 1007–1021.

Heinz, Erin, and Louis Roth. 2019. "As many as I can afford: Ideal family size in contemporary Uganda." In T. Bakhru, ed., *Reproductive Justice and Sexual Rights*. Routledge, pp. 191–212.

Hempel, Margaret. 1996. "Reproductive health and rights: Origins of and challenges to the ICPD agenda." *Health Transition Review* 6 (1): 73–85.

Henley, Jon, and Kasia Strek. 2020. "'A backlash against a patriarchal culture': How Polish protests go beyond abortion rights." *Guardian*, November 6. https://www.theguardian.com/world/2020/nov/06/a-backlash-against-a-patriarchal-culture-how-polish-protests-go-beyond-abortion-rights.

Hernandez Castillo, R. Aida. 2010. "The emergence of indigenous feminism in Latin America." *Signs* 35 (3): 539–545.

Heyman, Josiah, and Howard Campbell. 2009. "The anthropology of global flows: A critical reading of Appadurai's 'Disjuncture and Difference in the Global Culture Economy'." *Anthropological Theory* 9 (2): 131–148.

Hickel, Jason. 2014. "The 'girl effect': Liberalism, empowerment and the contradictions of development." *Third World Quarterly* 35 (8): 1355–1373.

Hickel, Jason, and Arsalan Khan. 2012. "The culture of capitalism and the crisis of critique." *Anthropological Quarterly* 85 (1): 203–227.

The Hindu. 2021. "Fertility rates of Hindus and Muslims converging: study." September 21. https://www.thehindu.com/news/national/indias-religious-mix-has-been-stable-since-1951-says-pew-center-study/article36596965.ece.

Hinton, Carmen (dir.) 1984. *Small Happiness: Women of a Chinese Village*. Long Bow Group.

Hisanaga, Ryuichi. 2021. "Japan's births in 2020 lowest ever: Fewest marry since WWII's end." *Asahi Shimbun*, June 4. https://www.asahi.com/ajw/articles/14365588.

Hochschild, Arlie Russell. 2000. "Global care chains and emotional surplus value." In W. Hutton and A. Giddens, eds., *On the Edge: Living with Global Capitalism*. Jonathan Cape, pp. 130–146.

Holt, Kelsey, et al. 2020. "Beyond same-day long-acting reversible contraceptive access: A person-centered framework for advancing high-quality equitable contraceptive care." *Journal of Obstetrics and Gynecology* 222 (4), Supplement 878: 1–6.

Hord, Charlotte, Henry P. David, France Donnay, and Merrill Wolf. 1991. "Reproductive health in Romania: Reversing the Ceausescu legacy." *Studies in Family Planning* 22 (4): 231–240.

Howard, Jacqueline. 2018. "The costs of child care around the world." CNN, April 25. https://www.cnn.com/2018/04/25/health/child-care-parenting-explainer-intl/index.html.

HRW. 2012. "India: Target-driven sterilization harming women." Human Rights Watch. https://www.hrw.org/news/2012/07/12/india-target-driven-sterilization-harming-women#.

HRW. 2017. "Trump's Mexico City policy or 'global gag' rule." Human Rights Watch. https://www.hrw.org/news/2017/06/22/trumps-mexico-city-policy-or-global-gag-rule.

Huang, Priscilla. 2008. "Anchor babies, over-breeders, and the population bomb: The reemergence of nativism and population control in anti-immigration policies." *Harvard Law and Policy Review* 2 (2): 385–406.

Hughes, Cortney. 2011. "The 'amazing' fertility decline: Islam, economics, and reproductive decision making among working class Moroccan women." *Medical Anthropology Quarterly* 25 (4): 417–435.

Hughes Rinker, Cortney. 2013. "Responsible mothers, anxious women: Contraception and neoliberalism in Morocco." *The Arab Studies Journal* 21 (1): 101–125.

Hughes Rinker, Cortney. 2015. "Creating neoliberal citizens in Morocco: Reproductive health, development policy, and popular Islamic beliefs." *Medical Anthropology* 34 (3): 226–242.

Hurst, Daniel. 2017. "Japan racism survey reveals one in three foreigners experience discrimination." *Guardian*, March 31. https://www.theguardian.com/world/2017/mar/31/japan-racism-survey-reveals-one-in-three-foreigners-experience-discrimination.

Ibarra, Maria de la Luz. 2012. "My reward is not money: Deep alliances and end-of-life care among Mexicana workers and their wards." In E. Boris and R. Parreñas, eds., *Intimate Labors*. Stanford University Press, pp. 117–131.

IIPS and ORC Macro. 2000. *National Family Health Survey (NFHS-2), 1998–99: India*. Mumbai: International Institute for Population Sciences.

Immerwahr, Daniel. 2019. *How to Hide an Empire*. Farrar, Straus, Giroux.

Inagawa, Hidekazu. 2018. "Demographic policy." In Y. Funabashi, ed., *Japan's Population Implosion*. Palgrave Macmillan, pp. 97–114.

Inhorn, Marcia. 1996. *Infertility and Patriarchy: The Cultural Politics of Gender and Family Life in Egypt*. University of Pennsylvania Press.

Inhorn, Marcia C., and Pankaj Shrivastav. 2010. "Globalization and reproductive tourism in the United Arab Emirates." *Asia-Pacific Journal of Public Health* 22 (3): 68S–74S.

Inhorn, Marcia C., and Pasquale Patrizio. 2009. "Rethinking reproductive 'tourism' as reproductive 'exile'." *Fertility and Sterility* 92 (3): 904–906.

Interlandi, Jeneen. 2019. "Why doesn't the United States have universal health care? The answer has everything to do with race." *New York Times Magazine*, August 14.

Ishikawa, Yoshitaka, ed. 2015. *International Migrants in Japan; Contributions in an Era of Population Decline*. Trans-Pacific Press.

James, P.D. 1992. *The Children of Men*. Knopf.

Janes, Craig, and Oyuntsetseg Chuluundorj. 2004. "Free markets and dead mothers: The social ecology of maternal mortality in post-socialist Mongolia." *Medical Anthropology Quarterly* 18 (2): 230–257.

Jejeebhoy, Shireen J. 1995. Women's Education, Autonomy, and Reproductive Behaviour: Experience from Developing Countries. Clarendon Press.

Jencks, Christopher, and Kathryn Edin. 1985. "Do poor women have a right to bear children?" *American Prospect* 20: 43–52.

Johnson, Kay Ann. 2017. *China's Hidden Children: Abandonment, Adoption, and the Human Costs of the One Child Policy*. University of Chicago Press.

Johnson, Ross. 2018. "11 Works of Trans-Positive Science Fiction & Fantasy." B&N Reads. https://www.barnesandnoble.com/blog/sci-fi-fantasy/7-works-of-trans-positive-science-fiction-fantasy/.

Jordan, Hillary. 2011. *When She Woke*. Algonquin Books.

Joshi, Shareen, and T. Paul Schultz. 2013. "Family planning and women's and children's health: Long-term consequences of an outreach program in Matlab, Bangladesh." *Demography* 50: 149–180.

Jütte, Robert. 2008. *Contraception: A History*. Polity.

Kamat, Sangeeta. 2004. "The privatization of public interest: Theorizing

NGO discourse in a neoliberal era." *Review of International Political Economy* 11 (1): 155–176.

Kanaaneh, Rhoda Ann. 2002. *Birthing the Nation: Strategies of Palestinian Women in Israel.* University of California Press.

Kandiyoti, Deniz. 1988. "Bargaining with patriarchy." *Gender and Society* 2 (3): 274–290.

Kane, Penny. 1996. "Family planning reproductive health: The neglected factor." *Health Transition Review* 6 (1): 103–107.

Kaufman, Eric. 2021. "Israel's population time bomb." *Unherd*, May 21. https://unherd.com/2021/05/israels-population-time-bomb/.

Kazue, Suzuki. 1995. "Women rebuff the call for more babies." *Japan Quarterly* 42 (1): 14–20.

Khawaja, Noorulain. 2018. "The politics of demography in the Israeli-Palestinian conflict." *Journal of International Affairs*, April 27. https://jia.sipa.columbia.edu/online-articles/politics-demography-israeli-palestinian-conflict.

Kilgore, De Witt Douglas, and Ranu Samantrai. 2010. "A memorial to Octavia E. Butler." *Science Fiction Studies* 37 (3): 353–361.

Kim, Joon, Ernesto Sagas, and Karina Cespedes. 2018. "Genderacing immigrant subjects: 'Anchor babies' and the politics of birthright citizenship." *Social Identities* 24 (3): 312–326.

King, Maggie Shen. 2017. *An Excess Male.* Harper Voyager.

Kintz, Linda. 1994. "Motherly advice from the Christian Right: The construction of sacred gender." *Discourse* 17 (1): 49–76.

Kirk, Dudley. 2000 [1943]. "Dudley Kirk on population changes and prospective power relations after World War II: A view from 1943." *Population and Development Review* 26 (3): 583–596.

Kishor, Sunita. 1995. *Autonomy and Egyptian Women: Findings from the 1988 Egypt Demographic and Health Survey (Occasional Papers no. 2).* Macro International.

Kligman, Gail. 1992a. "Abortion and international adoption in post-Ceausescu Romania. *Feminist Studies* 18 (2): 405–419.

Kligman, Gail. 1992b. "When abortion is banned: The politics of reproduction in Ceausescu's Romania, and after." National Council for Soviet and East European Research. https://www.ucis.pitt.edu/nceeer/1992-805-14-Kligman.pdf.

Kligman, Gail. 1995. "Political demography: The banning of abortion in Ceausescu's Romania." In F. Ginsburg and R. Rapp, eds., *Conceiving the New World Order.* University of California Press, pp. 234–255.

Kligman, Gail. 1998. *The Politics of Duplicity: Controlling Reproduction in Ceausescu's Romania.* University of California Press.

Koffman, Ofa, and Rosalind Gill. 2013. "'The revolution will be led by a 12-year-old girl': Girl power and global biopolitics." *Feminist Review* 105: 83–102.

Kotch, Alex. 2019. "These corporations and public charities funded the state abortion bans." *American Prospect*, June 21. https://prospect.org/health/corporations-public-charities-funded-state-abortion-bans/.

Kramatschek, Claudia. 2019. "A bleak future scenario: Bina Shah's *Before She Sleeps*." *Quantara.de*, July 25. https://en.qantara.de/content/book-review-bina-shahs-before-she-sleeps-a-bleak-future-scenario.

Krause, Elizabeth. 2005. *A Crisis of Births: Population Politics and Family-Making in Italy*. Wadsworth.

Krause, Elizabeth. 2006. "Dangerous demographies: The scientific manufacture of fear." *Corner House* 36. http://works.bepress.com/elizabeth_krause/34/.

Krause, Elizabeth. 2012. "'They just happened': The curious case of the unplanned baby, Italian low fertility, and the 'end' of rationality." *Medical Anthropology Quarterly* 26 (3): 361–382.

Krause, Elizabeth. 2018. "Reproduction in retrospective, or, what's all the fuss over low fertility?" In N.E. Riley and J. Brunson, eds., *International Handbook on Gender and Demographic Processes*. Springer, pp. 73–82.

Krause, Elizabeth, and Silvia De Zordo. 2012. "Ethnography and biopolitics: Tracing 'rationalities' of reproduction across the North–South Divide." *Anthropology & Medicine* (19) 2: 137–151.

Krieger, Nancy. 1994. "Epidemiology and the web of causation: Has anyone seen the spider?" *Social Science and Medicine* 39: 887–903.

Lai, Larissa. 2004. "Future Asians: Migrant speculations, repressed histories, and cyborg hope." *West Coast Line* 38 (2): 168–175.

Lam, David. 2021. "Reduced fertility from better access to contraception may not improve women's health." *Proceedings of the National Academy of Sciences of the United States of America* 118: 29–31.

Lam, David, and S. Duryea. 1999. "Effects of schooling on fertility, labor supply, and investments in children, with evidence from Brazil." *Journal of Human Resources* 34: 160–192.

Lammi-Taskula, Johanna. 2006. "Nordic men on parental leave: Can the welfare state change gender relations?" in A.L. Ellingsaeter and A. Leira, eds., *Politicising Parenthood in Scandinavia: Gender Relations in Welfare States*. Policy Press, pp. 79–100.

The Lancet. 2019. "Editorial: The devastating impact of Trump's global gag rule." *The Lancet* 393 (15 June): 2359.

Lawless, Stephanie. 2012. "Scarlet skins and dystopian letters: Hillary Jordan in interview." *Three Monkeys Online*. https://www.threemonkeysonline.com/when-she-woke-hillary-jordan-interview/.

Lawrence, Jane. 2000. "The Indian health service and the sterilization of Native American women." *American Indian Quarterly*, 24 (3): 400–419.

Le Guin, Ursula. 1994. "The matter of Seggri." In B. Cholfin, ed., *Crank! #3*. Broken Mirrors Press.

Leon, Margarita. 2010. "Migration and care work in Spain: The domestic sector revisited." *Social Policy and Society*, 9 (3): 409–418.

LeRoy, E.J. 2019. "Sci-fi sim subs." *Submittable*, October 30. https://discover.submittable.com/blog/sci-fi-sim-subs/.

Lewis, Helen. 2019. "Why we should fear populists like Orbán and Erdoğan who want women to be baby machines." *New Statesman*, February 13. https://www.newstatesman.com/politics/feminism/2019/02/why-we-should-fear-populists-orb-n-and-erdogan-who-want-women-be-baby.

Lewis, Sophie. 2021. "Feminism: Reading Shulamith Firestone in the pandemic." *Nation* 313 (2): 28–30.

Lipka, Michael. 2020. "Half of Americans say Bible should influence US laws." Pew Research Center, April 13. https://www.pewresearch.org/fact-tank/2020/04/13/half-of-americans-say-bible-should-influence-u-s-laws-including-28-who-favor-it-over-the-will-of-the-people/.

London Summit on Family Planning. 2012. https://www.gov.uk/government/news/family-planning-london-summit-11-july-2012.

Luscombe, Belinda. 2021. "Contraceptive access may not be as life-changing for the world's poorest women as previously thought, according to a new study." *Time Magazine*, July 13. https://time.com/6078884/contraception-poor-women-study/.

Malthus, T.R. 1993 [1798]. *An Essay on the Principle of Population*, ed. and with an intro by G. Gilbert. Oxford University Press.

Mann, Charles. 2018. "The book that incited a worldwide fear of overpopulation." *Smithsonian Magazine*. https://www.smithsonianmag.com/innovation/book-incited-worldwide-fear-overpopulation-180967499/.

Marchesi, Milena. 2012. "Reproducing Italians: Contested biopolitics in the age of replacement anxiety." *Anthropology and Medicine* 19 (2): 171–188.

Masci, David. 2016. "Where major religious groups stand on abortion." Pew Research Center. https://www.pewresearch.org/fact-tank/2016/06/21/where-major-religious-groups-stand-on-abortion/.

Masci, David. 2018. "American religious groups vary widely in their views on abortion." Pew Research Center. https://www.pewresearch.org/fact-tank/2018/01/22/american-religious-groups-vary-widely-in-their-views-of-abortion/.

Mason, Karen O. 1986. "The status of women: Conceptual and methodological issues in demographic studies." *Sociological Forum* 1: 284–300.

Masterclass staff. 2021. "What is speculative fiction?" https://www.masterclass.com/articles/what-is-speculative-fiction-defining-and-understanding-the-different-genres-of-speculative-fiction#the-history-of-speculative-fiction.

Matynia, Elzbieta. 1994. "Women after communism: A bitter freedom." *Social Research* 61 (2): 351–377.

Metcalf, S. 2017. "Neoliberalism: The idea that swallowed the world." *Guardian*, August 18. https://www.theguardian.com/news/2017/aug/18/neoliberalism-the-idea-that-changed-the-world.

Meyer, Holly. 2021. "Religious abortion rights supporters fight for access."

ABC News, November 28. https://abcnews.go.com/US/wireStory/religious-abortion-rights-supporters-fight-access-81431484.

Miller, Claire Cain, and Margot Sanger-Katz. 2022. "What would the end of Roe mean?" *New York Times*, May 3. https://www.nytimes.com/2022/05/03/upshot/abortion-united-states-roe-wade.html.

Mills, C. Wright. 2000 [1959]. *The Sociological Imagination.* Oxford University Press.

Mills, Melinda, et al. 2008. "Gender equity and fertility intentions in Italy and the Netherlands." *Demographic Research* 18 (1): 1–26.

Mishtal, Joanna. 2015. *The Politics of Morality: The Church, the State, and Reproductive Rights in Postsocialist Poland.* University of Ohio Press.

Moeller, Kathryn. 2018. *The Gender Effect: Capitalism, Feminism and the Corporate Politics of Development.* University of California Press.

Molina, Natalia. 2006. *Fit to Be Citizens? Public Health and Race in Los Angeles, 1879–1939.* University of California Press.

Molina, Natalia. 2014. *How Race is Made in America.* University of California Press.

Molyneux, Maxine. 2007. "Change and continuity in social protection in Latin America: Mothers at the service to the state?" Gender and Development Program, Paper No. 1, May. UN Research Institute for Social Development. https://www.files.ethz.ch/isn/45959/001.pdf.

Monbiot, George. 2016. "Neoliberalism: The ideology at the root of all our problems." *Guardian*, April 15. https://www.theguardian.com/books/2016/apr/15/neoliberalism-ideology-problem-george-monbiot.

Morgan, Lynn M., and Elizabeth F. Roberts. 2012. "Reproductive governance in Latin America." *Anthropology and Medicine* 19 (2): 241–254.

Morgan, S. Philip, and Bhanu B. Niraula. 1995. "Gender inequality and fertility in two Nepali villages." *Population and Development Review* 21: 541–561.

Motluk, Alison. 2021. "Ukraine's surrogacy industry has put women in impossible positions." *The Atlantic*, March 1. https://www.theatlantic.com/health/archive/2022/03/russia-invasion-ukraine-surrogate-family/623327/.

Murphy, Michelle. 2012. *Seizing the Means of Reproduction: Entanglements of Feminism, Health, and Technoscience.* Duke University Press.

Murphy, Michelle. 2017. *The Economization of Life.* Duke University Press.

Mutambudzi, Miriam, John D. Meyer, Susan Reisine, and Nicholas Warren. 2017. "A review of recent literature on materialist and psychosocial models for racial and ethnic disparities in birth outcomes in the US, 2000–2014." *Ethnicity and Health* 22 (3): 311–332.

Myrskylä, Mikko, Hans-Peter Kohler, and Francesco Billari. 2011. "High development and fertility: Fertility at older reproductive ages and gender equality explain the positive link." MPIDR Working Paper 2011-017. https://repository.upenn.edu/psc_working_papers/30/.

Narayana, G., and John Kantner. 1992. *Doing the Needful: The Dilemma of India's Population Policy*. Westview.

Nash, Elizabeth, and Lauren Cross. 2021. "26 States are certain or likely to ban abortion without Roe." Guttmacher Institute Policy Analysis, October. https://www.guttmacher.org/article/2021/10/26-states-are-certain-or-likely-ban-abortion-without-roe-heres-which-ones-and-why.

Nelson, Jennifer. 2003. *Women of Color and the Reproductive Rights Movement*. New York University Press.

Ngai, Mae. 2004. *Impossible Subjects: Illegal Aliens and the Making of Modern America*. Princeton University Press.

Novak, Nicole, and Natalie Lira. 2018. "Forced sterilization programs in California once harmed thousands – particularly Latinas." *The Conversation*, March 22. https://theconversation.com/forced-sterilization-programs-in-california-once-harmed-thousands-particularly-latinas-92324.

Novak, Nicole, et al. 2018. "Disproportionate sterilization of Latinos under California's Eugenic Sterilization Program, 1920–1945." *American Journal of Public Health* 108 (5): 611–613.

Obermeyer, Carla. 1992. "Islam, women, and politics: The demography of Arab countries." *Population and Development Review* 18 (1): 33–60.

Obermeyer, Carla. 1994. "Religious doctrine, state ideology, and reproductive options in Islam." In G. Sen and R. Snow, eds., *Power and Decision: The Social Control of Reproduction*. Harvard University Press, pp. 59–75.

Palen, John. 1986. "Fertility and eugenics: Singapore's population policies." *Population Research and Policy Review* 5 (1): 3–14.

Pande, Amrita. 2009. "'It may be her eggs but it's my blood': Surrogates and everyday forms of kinship in India." *Qualitative Sociology* 32 (4): 379–404.

Pandey, Erica. 2022. "Poll: Majority of Americans disapprove of overturning Roe *v.* Wade." *Axios*, June 26. https://www.axios.com/2022/06/26/cbs-poll-americans-roe-v-wade-abortion-rights.

Parreñas, Rhacel. 2003. "At the cost of women: The family and the modernization-building project of the Philippines in globalization." *Interventions* 5 (1): 29–44.

Parreñas, Rhacel. 2005. *Children of Global Migration: Transnational Families and Gendered Woes*. Stanford University Press.

Parreñas, Rhacel. 2015. *Servants of Globalization: Migration and Domestic Work*, 2nd ed. Stanford University Press.

Pawlak, Justyna, and Alicja Ptak. 2021. "As Poland's church embraces politics, Catholics depart." *Reuters*, 3 February. https://www.reuters.com/article/us-poland-church-insight/as-polands-church-embraces-politics-catholics-depart-idUSKBN2A30SN.

Peffer, George Anthony. 1999. *If They Don't Bring Their Women Here: Chinese Female Immigration before Exclusion*. University of Illinois Press.

Penguin. 2019. Interview: "Margaret Atwood on the real-life events that inspired *The Handmaid's Tale* and *The Testaments*." https://www.penguin.co.uk/articles/2019/sep/margaret-atwood-handmaids-tale-testaments-real-life-inspiration.html.

Petchesky, Rosalind. 1995. "From population control to reproductive rights: Feminist fault lines." *Reproductive Health Matters* 3 (6): 152–161.

Pew Research Center. 2018. "Being Christian in Western Europe." Pew Research Center. https://www.pewforum.org/2018/05/29/being-christian-in-western-europe/.

Pineda-Ofreneo, Rosalinda. 1991. *The Philippines: Debt and Poverty*. Oxfam.

Porter, Theodore. 1995. *Trust in Numbers: The Pursuit of Objectivity in Science and Public Life*. Princeton University Press.

Potasse Megan, and Sanni Yaya. 2021. "Understanding perceived access barriers to contraception through an African feminist lens: A qualitative study in Uganda." *BMC Public Health* 21(1): 267–280.

Potts, Malcolm. 1996. "The crisis in international family planning." *Health Transition Review*, 6 (1): 114–119.

Power to Decide. 2019. "Access to birth control and contraceptive deserts." Fact Sheet. https://powertodecide.org/what-we-do/information/resource-library/access-birth-control-and-contraceptive-deserts.

PRRI Staff. 2020. "The 2020 Census of American religion." July 8. https://www.prri.org/research/2020-census-of-american-religion/.

Puri, Sunetra, and Alison McLellan.1996. "ICPD and family planning associations." *Health Transition Review* 6 (1): 95–97.

Purohit, Kunal. 2019. "The Islamophobia roots of population control efforts in India." *Al Jazeera*. https://www.aljazeera.com/features/2019/8/9/the-islamophobic-roots-of-population-control-efforts-in-india.

Ramm, Alejandra. 2020. "Latin America: A fertile ground for maternalism." In A. Ramm and J. Gideon, eds., *Motherhood, Social Policies and Women's Activism in Latin America*. Palgrave Macmillan, pp. 13–38.

Rao, Anupama. 2010. "India and global history." *History and Technology* 26 (1): 77–84.

Rao, Mohan. 2005. "India's population policies: Untouched by the Cairo rhetoric." *Development* 48 (4): 21–27.

Rao, Mohan, and Sarah Sexton, eds. 2010. *Markets and Malthus: Population, Gender and Health in Neoliberal Times*. Sage.

Rapp, Rayna. 2001. "Gender, body, biomedicine: How some feminist concerns dragged reproduction to the center of social theory." *Medical Anthropology Quarterly* 15 (4): 466–477.

Ravaoarisoa, Lantonirina, et al. 2020. "Slowing progress: The US global gag rule undermines access to contraception in Madagascar." *Sexual and Reproductive Health Matters* 28 (3): 39–53.

Razavi, Shahra, and Anne Jenichen. 2010. "The unhappy marriage of religion and politics: Problems and pitfalls for gender equality." *Third World Quarterly* 31 (6): 833–850.

Redfern, Corinne. 2021. "'I want to go home': Filipina domestic workers face exploitative conditions." *Guardian*, January 27. https://www.theguardian.com/world/2021/jan/27/domestic-workers-philippines-coronavirus-conditions.

Rich, Motoko. 2019. "Craving freedom, Japan's women opt out of marriage." *New York Times*, August 3. https://www.nytimes.com/2019/08/03/world/asia/japan-single-women-marriage.html.

Riley, Nancy E. 1998. "Research on gender in demography: Limitations and constraints." *Population Research and Development Review* 17: 521–538.

Riley, Nancy E. 2017a. "Good mothering in China: Effects of migration, low fertility, and birth constraints." In D. Poston, ed., *Low Fertility Regimes and Demographic and Societal Changes*. Springer, pp. 115–132.

Riley, Nancy E. 2017b. *Population in China*. Polity.

Riley, Nancy E. 2018. "Stratified reproduction." In N.E. Riley and J. Brunson, eds., *International Handbook on Gender and Demographic Processes*. Springer, pp. 117–138.

Riley, Nancy E., and Deborah DeGraff. 2018. "Measuring gender in the context of demographic change." In N.E. Riley and J. Brunson, eds., *International Handbook on Gender and Demographic Processes*. Springer, pp. 15–36.

Riley, Nancy E., and James McCarthy. 2003. *Demography in the Age of the Postmodern*. Cambridge University Press.

Roberts, Adrienne. 2015. "The political economy of 'transnational business feminism'." *International Feminist Journal of Politics* 17 (2): 209–231.

Roberts, Dorothy. 1997. "Unshackling black motherhood." *Michigan Law Review* 95 (4): 938–965.

Roberts, Dorothy. 1998a. *Killing the Black Body: Race, Reproduction, and the Meaning of Liberty*. Vintage.

Roberts, Dorothy. 1998b. "Punishing drug addicts who have babies: Women of color, equality, and the right of privacy." In R. Solinger, ed., *Abortion Wars: A Half Century of Struggle, 1950–2000*. University of California Press, pp. 124–155.

Roberts, Dorothy. 2002. *Shattered Bonds: The Color of Child Welfare*. Basic Books.

Roberts, Dorothy. 2005. "Privatization and punishment in the new age of reprogenetics." *Emory Law Journal* 54 (3):1343–1360.

Roberts, Dorothy. 2009. "Race, gender and genetic technologies: A new reproductive dystopia?" *Signs* 34 (4): 783–804.

Roberts, Dorothy E. 2012. "Prison, foster care, and the systemic punishment of Black mothers." *UCLA Law Review* 59 (6): 1474–1500.

Roberts, Dorothy. 2015. "Reproductive justice, not rights." *Dissent Magazine*. Fall. https://www.dissentmagazine.org/article/reproductive-justice-not-just-rights.

Roberts, Glenda. 2016. *Japan's Evolving Families: Voices from Young Urban Adults Navigating Change*. East-West Center Publications.

Rosenthal, Lisa, and Marci Lobel, 2011. "Explaining racial disparities in adverse birth outcomes: Unique sources of stress for Black American women." *Social Science and Medicine* 72: 977–983.

Ross, Loretta. 2016. "The color of choice: White supremacy and reproductive justice." In INCITE, ed., *Color of Violence*. Duke University Press, pp. 53–65.

Ross, Loretta, and Rickie Solinger. 2017. *Reproductive Justice: An Introduction*. University of California Press.

Rubin, Gayle. 1975. "The traffic in women: Notes on the 'political economy' of sex." in R. Reiter, ed., *Toward an Anthropology of Women*. Monthly Review Press, pp. 157–210.

Sabry, Mohamed. 2021. "Egypt's Dar al-Ifta pushes birth control to stem overpopulation." *Al-Monitor*, February 23. https://www.al-monitor.com/originals/2021/02/children-egypt-birthcontrol-religion-ifta-policy.html.

Saez, Macarena 2022. "Chile's new president-elect sets out a feminist government." Human Rights Watch, January 25. https://www.hrw.org/news/2022/01/25/chiles-new-president-elect-sets-out-feminist-government.

Salzman, Todd. 1998. "Rape camps as a means of ethnic cleansing: Religious, cultural, and ethical responses to rape victims in the former Yugoslavia." *Human Rights Quarterly* 20 (2): 348–378.

Sarcar, Aprajita. 2021. "TIF: Planning the family, planning the nation." *The India Forum*, May 7. https://www.theindiaforum.in/article/planning-family-planning-nation.

Scheper-Hughes, Nancy. 1993. *Death without Weeping: The Violence of Everyday Life in Brazil*. University of California Press.

Schneider, Jane, and Peter Schneider. 1996. *Festival of the Poor: Fertility Decline and the Ideology of Class*. University of Arizona Press.

Schoen, Johanna. 2005. *Choice and Coercion: Birth Control, Sterilization and Abortion in Public Health and Welfare*. University of North Carolina Press.

Schuler, Sidney Ruth, et al. 1995. "Bangladesh's family planning success story: A gender perspective." *International Family Planning Perspectives* 21 (4): 132–166.

Scott, Gemma. 2014. "Gender and power: Sterilisation under the Emergency in India, 1975–1977." *The Luminary* 5.

Scott, James. 1987. *Weapons of the Weak: Everyday Forms of Peasant Resistance*. Yale University Press.

Scott, James. 1990. *Domination and the Arts of Resistance: Hidden Transcripts*. Yale University Press.

Scott, James. 1999. *Seeing Like a State: How Certain Schemes to Improve the Human Condition have Failed*. Yale University Press.

Scott, Joan W. 1988. *Gender and the Politics of History*. Columbia University Press.

Scott, Joan W. 2010. "Gender: Still a useful category of analysis?" *Diogenes* 225: 7–14.

Sekhon, Joti. 1999. "*Gender & Nation*, Nira Yuval-Davis (book review)." *Contemporary Justice Review* 2 (2): 225–229.

Semuels, Alana. 2017. "The mystery of why Japanese people are having so few babies." *Atlantic Monthly*, July 20. https://www.theatlantic.com/business/archive/2017/07/japan-mystery-low-birth-rate/534291/.

Sen, Gita. 1994. "Reproduction: The feminist challenge to social policy." In G. Sen and R. Snow, eds., *Power and Decision: The Social Control of Reproduction*. Harvard University Press, pp. 5–18.

Sexton, Sarah, and Sumati Nair. 2010. "A decade and more after Cairo: Women's health in a free market economy." In M. Rao and S. Sexton, eds., *Markets and Malthus: Population, Gender, and Health in Neo-liberal Times*. Sage, pp. 31–52.

Shah, Bina. 2018. *Before She Sleeps*. Delphinium.

Shah, Bina. 2021. "Patriarchy is the world's largest religion." January 29. https://www.goethe.de/en/kul/ges/eu2/grf/21095798.html.

Shih, Gerry. 2021. "In India, a debate over population control turns explosive." *Washington Post*, August 29. https://www.washingtonpost.com/world/2021/08/29/india-population-hindus-muslims/.

Shreffler, Karina, et al. 2015. "Surgical sterilization, regret and race: Contemporary patterns." *Social Science Research* 50: 31–45.

Simon-Kumar, Rachel. 2010. "Neo-liberal development and reproductive health in India: The making of the personal and the political." In M. Rao and S. Sexton, eds., *Markets and Malthus: Population, Gender, and Health in Neo-liberal Times*. Sage, pp. 127–155.

Singh, Holly D. 2014. "'The world's back womb?': Commercial surrogacy and infertility inequalities in India." *American Anthropologist* 116 (4): 824–828.

Singh, Holly D. 2018. "Surrogacy and gendered contexts of infertility management in India." In N.E. Riley and J. Brunson, eds., *International Handbook on Gender and Demographic Processes*. Springer, pp. 105–117.

Sistersong Collective. "Reproductive Justice." https://www.sistersong.net/reproductive-justice/.

SLaW (Something Like a War). 1993. Deepa Dhanraj (dir.). *Women Make Movies*.

Soare, Florin. 2013. "Ceausescu's population policy: A moral or an economic choice between compulsory and voluntary incentivised motherhood?" *European Journal of Government and Economics* 2 (1): 59–78.

Solinger, Rickie. 1992. *Wake Up Little Susie: Single Pregnancy and Race before Roe v. Wade*. Routledge.

Solinger, Rickie. 2019. *Pregnancy and Power: A History of Reproductive Politics in the United States*, rev. ed. New York University Press.

Solinger, Rickie. 2001. *Beggars and Choosers: How the Politics of Choice Shapes Adoption, Abortion, and Welfare*. Hill and Wang.

Spar, Deborah. 2006. *The Baby Business: How Money, Science, and*

Commerce Drive the Commerce of Conception. Harvard Business Review Press.

Stacey, Judith. 1983. *Patriarchy and Socialist Revolution in China*. University of California Press.

Steinfeld, Rebecca. 2015. "Wars of the Wombs: Struggles over abortion policies in Israel." *Israel Studies* 20 (2): 1–26.

Stern, Alexandra Minna. 2020. "Forced sterilization policies in the US targeted minorities and those with disabilities – and lasted into the 21st century." *The Conversation*, August 26. https://theconversation.com/forced-sterilization-policies-in-the-us-targeted-minorities-and-those-with-disabilities-and-lasted-into-the-21st-century-143144.

Stith Butler, Adrienne, and Clayton Wright, eds. 2009. *A Review of the HHS Family Planning Program: Mission, Management, and Measurement of Results*. National Academies Press, Ch. 3.

Stokes, Bruce. 2017. "What it takes to be truly one of us." Pew Research Center. https://www.pewresearch.org/global/2017/02/01/faith-few-strong-links-to-national-identity/.

Sussman, Anna L. 2019. "When the government seizes your embryos." *The New Yorker*, October 22.

Tanyag, Maria. 2017. "Invisible labor, invisible bodies: How the global political economy affects reproductive freedom in the Philippines." *International Feminist Journal of Politics* 19 (1): 39–54.

Taylor, Jamila K. 2020. "Structural racism and maternal health among Black women." *Journal of Law, Medicine and Ethics* 48 (3): 506–517.

Tepper, Sheri. 1988. *The Gate to Women's Country*. Doubleday.

Theobald, Brianna. 2019. *Reproduction on the Reservation*. University of North Carolina Press.

Tracey, Janey. 2017. "Rape and the ravages of colonialism in Octavia Butler's Dawn." *Ploughshares*, September 29. https://blog.pshares.org/rape-and-the-ravages-of-colonialism-in-octavia-spencers-dawn/.

Tsuya, Noriko. 2017. "Low fertility in Japan: No end in sight," *Asia-Pacific Issues*. Honolulu: East-West Center Publications, no. 131.

UNFPA. 2014 [1994]. Programme of Action, ICPD Cairo, 20th Anniversary Edition. https://www.unfpa.org/publications/international-conference-population-and-development-programme-action.

UNFPA Egypt. "Family Planning." https://egypt.unfpa.org/en/node/22543.

UNICEF. 2022. Resources Data Explorer: Chile. https://data.unicef.org/resources/data_explorer/unicef_f/?ag=UNICEF&df=GLOBAL_DATAFLOW&ver=1.0&dq=CHL.MNCH_MMR.&startPeriod=1970&endPeriod=2022.

UN Women. 1995. Beijing Declaration. Adopted at the United Nations Fourth Conference on Women, Huairou, China. https://www.icsspe.org/system/files/Beijing%20Declaration%20and%20Platform%20for%20Action.pdf

USAID. 2021. "Strengthening Egypt's family planning program." https://

www.usaid.gov/egypt/global-health/strengthening-egypts-family-planning-program.

US Census Bureau. 1973. *1970 Census of Population: American Indians.* Bureau of the Census. Subject Reports, PC(2)-1F.

Ushie, Boniface, Sara Casey, and Terry McGovern. 2020. "Insights into how the US abortion gag rule affects health services in Kenya." *The Conversation*, September 30. https://theconversation.com/insights-into-how-the-us-abortion-gag-rule-affects-health-services-in-kenya-145777.

Varley, Emma. 2012. "Islamic logics, reproductive rationalities: Family planning in northern Pakistan." *Anthropology and Medicine*, 19 (2), 189–206.

Vogel, Lise. 1993. *Mothers on the Job: Maternity Policy in the US Workplace.* Rutgers University Press.

Vintage Books. 2018. Interview: "Margaret Atwood: *The Handmaid's Tale* is being read very differently now." https://www.youtube.com/watch?v=7a8LnKCzsBw.

Volscho, Thomas. 2010. "Sterilization racism and pan-ethnic disparities of the past decade: The continued encroachment on reproductive rights." *Wicazo Sa Review* 25 (1): 17–31.

Waylen, Georgina. 1998. "Gender, feminism and the state: An overview." In V. Randall and G. Waylen, eds., *Gender, Politics, and the State.* Routledge, pp. 1–17.

Weigel, Moira. 2017. "We live in the reproductive dystopia of *The Handmaid's Tale.*" *New Yorker Magazine*, April 26. https://www.newyorker.com/books/page-turner/we-live-in-the-reproductive-dystopia-of-the-handmaids-tale.

West, Candance, and Don Zimmerman. 1987. "Doing gender." *Gender and Society* 1 (2): 125–151.

WGNRR (Women's Global Network for Reproductive Rights). 2004. "A decade after Cairo: Women's health in a free market economy." *The Corner House Briefing* 31.

White, Tyrene. 2006. *China's Longest Campaign: Birth Planning in the People's Republic of China, 1949–2005.* Cornell University Press.

White, Tyrene. 2010. "Domination, resistance, and accommodation in China's one child campaign." In E. Perry and M. Selden, eds., *Chinese Society: Change, Conflict, and Resistance.* Routledge, pp. 171–196.

Williams, Zoe. 2011. "End of communism hasn't helped Polish women." *Guardian*, April 8. https://www.theguardian.com/world/2011/apr/08/polish-women-communism-better-equality.

Wilson, Kalpana. 2015. "The 'new' global population control policies: Fuelling India's sterilization atrocities." *DifferenTakes* 87 (Population and Development Program, Hampshire College).

Wilson, Kalpana. 2018. "For reproductive justice in an era of Gates and Modi: The violence of India's reproductive policies." *Feminist Review* 119: 89–105.

Wolf, Margery. 1972. *Women and the Family in Rural Taiwan*. Stanford University Press.

World Bank. 2007. *Global Monitoring Report: Millennium Development Goals, Confronting the Challenges of Gender Equality and Fragile States*. https://openknowledge.worldbank.org/handle/10986/6637.

Yeung, Jessie, and Nectar Gan. 2021. "China says its restricting abortions to promote gender equality; experts are skeptical." CNN, October 1. https://www.cnn.com/2021/10/01/china/non-medical-abortions-mic-intl-hnk/index.html\.

Yip, Waiyee. 2021. "China: The men who are single and the women who don't want kids." *BBC News*, May 25. https://www.bbc.com/news/world-asia-china-57154574.

Yirgu, Robel, Shannon N. Wood, Celia Karp, et al. 2020. "'You better use the safer one … leave this one': The role of health providers in women's pursuit of their preferred family planning methods." *BMC Women's Health* 20: 170–179.

Young, Neil J. 2018. "'Family values' conservatism is over." *Slate Magazine*, June 20. https://slate.com/human-interest/2018/06/family-values-conservatism-is-finally-dead.html.

Yuan, Li. 2022. "'The last generation': The disillusionment of young Chinese." *New York Times*, May 24. https://www.nytimes.com/2022/05/24/business/china-covid-zero.html?searchResultPosition=1.

Yuval-Davis, Nira. 1987. "The Jewish collectivity and national reproduction in Israel." *Khamsin*, 10 July. https://matzpen.org/english/1987-07-10/the-jewish-collectivity-and-national-reproduction-in-israel-nira-yuval-davis/.

Yuval-Davis, Nira. 1993. "Gender and nation." *Ethnic and Racial Studies* 16 (4): 621–632.

Yuval-Davis, Nira. 1996. "Women and the biological reproduction of 'the nation'." *Women's Studies International Forum* 19 (1/2): 17–24.

Zelizer, Viviana. 1995. *Pricing the Priceless Child: The Changing Social Value of Children*. Basic Books.

Zelizer, Viviana. 2005. *The Purchase of Intimacy*. Princeton University Press.

Zumas, Leni. 2018. *Red Clocks*. Little, Brown and Company.

Index

Page numbers in *italics* refer to figures